Backroom Politics

BACKROOM POLITICS

How Your Local Politicians Work, Why Your Government Doesn't And What You Can Do About It

by Bill and Nancy Boyarsky

PUBLISHED BY J. P. TARCHER, INC., LOS ANGELES

Distributed by Hawthorn Books, Inc., New York

Copyright © 1974 by Bill and Nancy Boyarsky
All rights reserved
Library of Congress Catalog Card Number: 73-92097
ISBN: 0-87477-024-6
Manufactured in the United States of America
Published by J. P. Tarcher, Inc.
9110 Sunset Blvd., Los Angeles, Calif. 90069
Published simultaneously in Canada by
Prentice-Hall of Canada, Ltd.
1870 Birchmount Road, Scarborough, Ontario
1 2 3 4 5 6 7 8 9 0

Contents

1 Introduction—The People Who Can Make Life
  Miserable for Us All   1
2 The System That Runs the Cities   18
3 How It Works in the Suburbs   49
4 Corporations Above the Law   71
5 Cocktails and Campaign Contributions   97
6 Rx from the Legislature   126
7 The Politics of Sewers and Garbage   152
8 The Great Stadium Hoax   178
9 Waiting for the Transit Revolution   204
10 Too Many Agencies, Too Much Smog   228
11 Why You Don't Read about It in the Papers   255
12 A Few Who Have Succeeded   287
   Bibliography   323
   Index   325

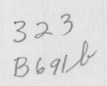

Authors' Note

The material in this book has been gathered from around the country to show a nationwide pattern of secret politics. We found our examples in such diverse places as Seattle, Chicago, New Jersey, and the suburbs around Washington, D.C. Our goal was to find illustrations that could apply to the rest of the country, to examine in human terms a few such cases, and—above all—to avoid the detached general-survey approach of the few books which have been written about state and local government in the past.

Much of our material comes from California. One reason is that we live there, work there, and report about its affairs. Another reason is that, as many writers have commented, California is a miniature America because of its size, its relative geographic isolation, and its diverse population of immigrants from other places.

Whatever state we visited, we found citizen activists eager to talk to us, to tell us about their experiences, to listen to ours. If this book is dedicated to anyone, it is to these reformers around the country.

1

Introduction

The People

Who Can Make Life

Miserable for Us All

This book is about how politicians, businessmen and labor leaders work behind the scenes to shape our lives, without our knowledge or consent. We are not dealing with the well-publicized officials who run the federal government. Instead, our cast of characters involves those who control the lesser-known governments of the 50 states and, within them, the more than 3,000 counties, the 17,000 cities, the 40,000 plus school districts, the almost 10,000 park, sanitary, fire·protection and sewer districts—all the obscure agencies and jurisdictions that are supposed to plan our neighborhoods, provide us with police and fire protection, run our buses and trains, operate our schools and universities, protect us from dishonest doctors, mechanics and barbers, get rid of smog, provide for our parks and collect our garbage. In short, it is about all those elected officials and bureaucrats—and the unseen forces that control them—who can make life pleasant, bearable or miserable for us all.

We wrote this book because—like other Americans—we found

ourselves helpless when we tried to contend with the officials who regulate the services necessary to life in our city. We investigated how state and local governments operate across the United States. In a few rare cases, we found citizens who were able to make officials responsive to them. But, for the most part, our worst suspicions were confirmed: State and local governments are run with almost total disregard for the average voter. We found countless examples showing how the system of backroom politics works. There is a good reason that "You can't fight city hall" is an accepted American slogan.

When we began writing, Richard Nixon returned to office in a historic landslide, was proposing to dismantle some of the power of the federal government and give it to the state and local agencies we knew were unprepared and unqualified to accept it. Within a year, the President no longer had the power to do that. Scandal gripped Washington, and it threatened our political structure at home and our security overseas. Watergate finally brought home the price this nation pays for tolerance of secret politics.

Practices that had not been visible to the American public during the election had surfaced, and they destroyed much of the power of the Nixon administration. Some of the same practices existed on the federal level that we were writing about on the local level—secret business campaign contributions, private deals made between politicians and special interest groups. Under the influence of hidden economic interests, public officials behaved as if they were adversaries of the public rather than its servants.

By the time the book was finished, Vice-President Agnew was gone after pleading no contest to charges that he had not paid income taxes on money given him by contractors hungry to deal with the state of Maryland, which he had served as governor. It provided an illuminating look at the same level of government we were exploring. A sordid local scandal was all that it was; it happened to be of national importance because it touched a high federal office. These are practices that Agnew correctly said are commonplace, business as usual in state and county politics. He was, he complained, merely a victim of "post-Watergate morality."

Of course, there is no such thing as a post-Watergate morality. For a guiding ethic, we need only Jefferson's words in the Declaration of Independence: "Governments are instituted among men deriving their just power from the consent of the governed. . . ." Political scandals, local and national, result when we, and those who govern us, forget this. Our purpose has been to show how we have lost control of the levels of government closest to us and to demonstrate how we can reclaim control. The Watergate scandal, the resulting public revulsion at political wrongdoing and the demand for reform gave us more reasons for writing this book.

A further reason, predating Watergate, was the nature of the times. In an earlier era, official indifference or immorality could be tolerated, for once it made life unbearable in one place, there was always somewhere else to go; there was another frontier waiting. In the nineteenth century, it had been the gold fields of California, the forests and farms of the Northwest, the fertile prairies of the Midwest. In the twentieth century, it had been a new frontier, the suburbs. Another subdivision was always opening, another town forming. But in the 1970s, the suburbs that looked so promising as little as a decade ago are nearly as troubled as the cities. There is no longer anywhere left to hide in metropolitan America. We have run out of space. It is this fact of contemporary life that makes it crucial that government be responsive to our needs.

But state and local officials rarely consider our welfare. Instead, the pursuit of happiness is made even more difficult in urban and suburban America because those who make the decisions are controlled not by the public interest but by special interests groups, primarily representing business, construction and labor. These politicians and their friends are the leaders who will directly determine our comfort, security and future by their management of the great emerging political issue of the 70s. This issue is growth—the conflict between the need to manage our limited natural resources and the need to have enough jobs.

Business and labor—always thought to be enemies—have actually been allies for years on the state and local levels. The 1970s will see their emergence as a combined national political force. Together they will shape policy on the basic issue we are discussing in this book—the inability of Americans to shape and control their political institutions, lives and comfort amid the shrinking resources of crowded metropolitan America. Privacy, quiet, clean air and space are in short supply, but their allocation is quietly decided by powerful influences. As with the energy shortage, decisions on these issues result in great economic benefits to a few and cause great hardship to many—the poor and middle classes who pay higher prices and higher taxes, while getting less in return.

POLITICS AT THE LOWEST LEVEL

Little has been written about the workings of state and local governments, yet their decisions have much more effect on daily living than the well-known policies and programs of the federal government. It is in the cities and their surrounding suburbs that the pursuit of happiness is most easily frustrated. Today, members of President Nixon's silent majority may live up to all of his preachings—ambitions, thrift and hard work—and then find their peaceful neighborhood destroyed by the decisions of an obscure local planning commission or their cherished home put beyond their means by an unfair tax law quietly approved in the state legislature.

We set out to show who really controlled these lower levels of government. As reporters, homeowners and parents of children in the public schools, we knew it was rarely the people we voted for. Instead, it was the people known in the political world as the Big Boys, the Heavy Hitters, the Fat Cats. In the pages that follow, you will meet them: the rich businessmen and influential labor bosses who cooperate in support of the man who represents both groups in Chicago, Mayor Richard J. Daley; the downtown magnates and union leaders who support Mayor Joseph Alioto's growing inventory of tax-supported convention facilities; the hotel men and other businessmen who persuaded Mayor John Lindsay of New York to spend tax dollars to renovate a private baseball park, Yankee Stadium; the land developers who shaped Los Angeles and its suburbs.

You will also meet the politicians who represent them in public. Their contempt and indifference toward most citizens make it easy to understand the current cynicism toward government and politics. Even before Watergate, public opinion polls showed people believed their elected representatives were corrupt. The evidence was in front of them—a highrise apartment in a neighborhood once reserved for single family homes; a freeway cutting through quiet residential blocks; a tax-supported public transit system with poor service; a shopping center where, only a few years before, real estate officials and city officials had promised a park.

The proof is overwhelming. It shows that our democratic ideals are betrayed daily by the men and women we elect to public office. Ironically, reliance on these ideals may account for our inability to influence government. Our misconceptions about the political process have led us to believe in an idealized system that does not exist. For too long, we have mistakenly believed:

That we can understand what is going on in government by reading what officials say, by relying on newspaper or television accounts of government meetings, or attending such meetings ourselves. Most of what we see is what politicians want us to see.

That the best way to retaliate against official neglect of our best interests is to write a letter to or vote against the responsible politician at the next election. Compared to the tools available to those who have money to buy the respect of politicians, a letter or a vote is wasted effort.

That elected officials are experts at running government, that they know best how to run a city, county or state, and that their main consideration is our welfare. We tell ourselves, for example, that the city planning commission allowed a shopping center to be built in the middle of nowhere because it would serve the community best there. In reality, many decisions that are important to our lives are determined by secret pressure from a special interest.

That our system of checks and balances between different government agencies, the press and the voters most often counteracts abuse by those who govern us. Sometimes, as with the Watergate scandal, this is true. There, an unrelenting press and judiciary exposed political corruption. But too often these normal checks and balances are absent in state and local government. At these levels press coverage is weak, and the laws governing the conduct of elected officeholders are so loose or so poorly enforced that politicians can betray the people they represent without being challenged.

That we actually are governed by the people we elected to office. All of the fond beliefs listed above are frustrated by one more fact of political life: that there is a government structure that is virtually invisible to the uninformed citizen. Powerful special interests control the people we elect—and thereby actually govern us. Public officials hide this process by erecting a complex series of boards, commissions and agencies to provide fundamental community services. These outwardly anonymous agencies are run by the few who actually shape neighborhoods and the lives of the people who live in them.

THE BATTLE OF MANASSAS, 1973

Our investigations turned up one example that best illustrates how wrong we are in our traditional notions about government. It is the story of County Supervisor C. Scott Winfield and the Manassas Battlefield.

Winfield sat in the front room of the comfortable house he had built himself, a friendly man in his middle age who had grown up in the woods and fields of Virginia. Dressed in Bermuda shorts, wearing a plain shirt, he gave the impression of being a modest country squire, not a rich man. He had retired from the service a few years before and settled with his wife in the country where he was born.

Winfield, chairman of the Prince William County Board of Supervisors in Virginia, lives near historic ground where the opposing armies met in the first great battle of the Civil War. The town of Manassas and the small stream called Bull Run are not far from his home. On July 21, 1861, the Union Army of General Irwin McDowell was sent retreating from Bull Run to Washington, only a few miles away, by General P. G. T. Beauregard's Confederates. It was this battle that made Americans realize the Civil War would be long and hard.

To the south were places where the nation was born and nearly destroyed—Williamsburg, the colonial Virginia capital; Mount Vernon, Washington's home; the Civil War battlegrounds of Wilderness, Petersburg and finally Appomattox, where Lee surrendered his southerners to Grant. They are all in Virginia, a treasury of the past. Americans come here from California, Illinois, Texas and all the other states to follow the paths of the bloodied old armies and look at the notes Patrick Henry used in his speech that ended with "Give me liberty or give me death."

"Well, history is fine," Supervisor Winfield told us. "But I think history should be put down in books."

So little respect did Supervisor Winfield and his colleagues have for the land around them that, without telling the public, they invited the Marriott Corporation to build a $35 million miniature Disneyland called "Great America" adjacent to the site of the Manassas National Battlefield Park. Early negotiations between the supervisors and Marriott executives regarding location, needed county services and permissions were held in private.

The Marriott Corporation is well known to America for the services it provides—hotels, quick-meal Hot Shoppes, the lasagna, steak and chicken served on trays to airline travelers. But history is not one of the firm's accomplishments. In its Great America park, Marriott proposed its own version of the American story, as unrelated to history as its airplane meals are unrelated to good food. Within shouting distance of where General Thomas Jonathan Jackson stood against the Yankees—and was forevermore called Stonewall—Marriott planned to entertain people in a sanitized America that never existed.

There would be a miniature New Orleans without sin, a county fair without drunks, a New England village without the fierce morality of the puritans or the rebelliousness of the founding fathers. An artificial lagoon would be the Atlantic Ocean. The Southwest, settled in the heat and blood of wars between frontiersmen, Mexicans and Indians, would be remembered by a cavalry fort that serves quick meals. And to crown it all, the county gave Marriott permission to build a tower 350 feet tall, overlooking the park, its walls and the neighboring historical battlefield.

A nearby county had earlier rejected Marriott's plan. When

Winfield and the other Prince William supervisors read about it in the newspapers, they quietly invited Marriott to their county. They later said their motive was the economic well-being of the community. Great America—and a factory-filled industrial park Marriott planned to build next to it—was portrayed as a magnet for tax dollars to the Prince William County treasury and for jobs for the area's residents.

Supervisor Winfield favored growth. Land development was good for business, and what was good for business was, in his eyes, good for Prince William County. He believed the county's population would double and be 260,000 by 1980, and he thought that would be a good thing. But Winfield wanted to dictate the kind of development the county would have—more people like himself, respectable, fairly prosperous homeowners who lived and worked in the county. He disliked the low-cost condominiums and apartments being built in the area because many of the people who lived in them were transients, working in the District of Columbia. The small living quarters repelled him. "You ought to be able to walk out of your back door and have a little yard that you can take care of," he said. "A few trees and a place for supplies. I think everyone should have that. Maybe I'm on the wrong side of the fence. Maybe I'm too old for this modern generation. All the land we have in this country. It's just a damn shame that they've crowded people like they were rats in a cage."

Winfield saw the proposed Marriott park and adjoining industrial development as a method of creating jobs for the kind of people he wanted to live in the county. With the jobs and the property tax revenue from the park and plants, Prince William County could do more for homeowners like himself, while reducing taxes. But Winfield was wrong. In actual practice, the development would do more harm than good to the county, changing it in a way that the supervisor could not—or would not—foresee.

It was the Marriott Corporation who would benefit most, not Prince William County. And because decisions were made at private, "informal" sessions between supervisors and Marriott executives, the reality was never debated by Prince William County residents until it was too late to stop the project. By the time the plans were made public, Marriott had obtained options on a proposed site and had gotten tentative approval for an unspecified number of buildings. Their number, design, size and purpose would not be revealed to the public until Marriott received final approval to begin building.

Aside from commercializing a national monument, Great America would overcrowd the nearby streets, and take police and traffic protection away from the surrounding community. And by overloading a sewage treatment plant that empties into the already polluted Potomac River, Great America would actually determine the shape of Prince William County for years to come. One supervisor said that with some "maneuvering," sewage capacity could be found for the park. The maneuvering would mean a curtailment of other kinds of buildings in the county, since they all depend on the same sewage system.

We had first read the developing story of Manassas in the Washington *Post*, mailed to our home in Los Angeles, 3,000 miles from the battlefield. Los Angeles is famous for its irreverence for the past. Historic homes and landmark theaters are ripped down without thought. A twenty-year-old office building is considered antique and is torn apart and rebuilt into something more modern. As we read the *Post* each day, we were surprised to learn that those whose roots were deeper in the American past had such little regard for it.

The Manassas battlefield was an important destination when we went East to research our book. The offices of the Prince William County Planning Department are located in a place called Woodbridge, not far from Supervisor Winfield's home. Woodbridge illustrates the process at work in this county and others across the nation. Located on U.S. 1 about two miles from the Potomac River, it once must have been a pleasant, green, rural place. Now Woodbridge is a clutter of apartments and condominiums. These are modern versions of the old townhouse, each sharing a common wall with the next, cheaper to build in the 1970s than a ranch-style tract home. Bulldozers have ripped away the forest and the new neighborhoods sit exposed in painful contrast to the green woods nearby. A shopping center dominates the scene, surrounded by an outsized asphalt parking lot. Even to us, used to the barren shopping centers of Southern California, it was an unpleasant sight.

The county offices were in a plain, two-story brick building, dominated by another asphalt parking lot. We were an hour late, after getting lost, and when we arrived in the planning offices, we were informed that the official we were scheduled to interview could not see us. He was in a meeting that would last the rest of the morning, and then would go out to a luncheon appointment.

We had the impression—later confirmed—that there was no meeting and no lunch, that the official had used our tardiness as an excuse to avoid talking to us about the controversial Marriott project. We asked the receptionist if we could see the planning file on the Great America project. It was a public record and, without checking with her superiors, she brought it to us—a thick, heavy file full of documents. We were taken into a small office and began to study it.

Suddenly, the official who had been too busy to see us appeared at the doorway. The meeting, he said, had ended early. He could see us now. We had found some interesting things in the file and were more intent on reading this material than interviewing a bureaucrat we knew would be reluctant to talk. We said that one of us would remain in the room, copying the files, while the other would conduct the interview. He hesitated a moment, and said no—both of us would have to come for the interview. But we could bring the file with us. He did not want to leave anyone alone with it.

As we had anticipated, the interview shed little light on the project. The file told much more.

Sewage was the main problem at Manassas. One report in the planning file was from the Virginia State Water Board which said the county had no spare sewage capacity for the park. The board did not know how to provide such capacity by the projected completion date of 1976, the national bicentennial. The county police commented on traffic congestion. Thousands more motor vehicles would crowd the new four-lane Interstate 66 Freeway— already inadequate for heavy weekend traffic—and the narrow two-lane roads around the park. The police told the planning department that "traffic, with its related problems such as accidents, traffic jams, hitchhikers, disabled vehicles, will be a major problem. . . . At our present level with the workload we are carrying, we would be unable to cope with these additional problems." The police also said that "crime, in and around the amusement park, will be a problem," and the only way the department could handle all the difficulties would be to employ additional officers. Thus a project that was supposed to relieve the county tax burden would add to it, with the salaries and fringe benefits of more county employees, plus the expensive equipment they would need.

Still another report in the file told of other dangers—physical blight to a countryside of unparalleled beauty. Michael A. Samordic, an assistant director of the Economic Development Administration, wrote a critique of the park in response to a request from county residents, who began opposing the plan once it was made public. This report also ended up in the planning department file. Samordic warned of "peripheral eyesores" such as gas stations, hamburger stands and quick food takeouts that could be expected near the park.

But none of these drawbacks were subjects of public debate until it was too late. Preliminary negotiations between Marriott and the county took place behind closed doors, according to the Washington *Post,* until "leaks to the press forced them to announce their plans at a public meeting." After the park was announced, private meetings continued. Late in February 1973, Marriott representatives and the supervisors discussed plans among themselves, before a public meeting was held, despite the Virginia Freedom of Information Act providing for public meetings of public bodies. The law specifically requires a public vote of a majority of the board, before a private meeting can be held, but no such vote was taken.

"Well, they weren't really secret," said Supervisor Winfield, when we asked him about the meetings. "When you're inviting an industry in, you don't do it in public session," he told us. "You lay the groundwork first. It's like you and I sitting here right now. We're not having a secret meeting, but they could classify it as a secret meeting." He said that the supervisors were afraid property prices would skyrocket if it were known that Marriott was interested in buying land for the Great America park. Thus county officials violated the spirit of the Freedom of Information Act and met privately, to help Marriott obtain the land at a more favorable price, a questionable use of government power. There was so much at stake for the county's residents that supervisors had a duty to make their invitation public, even though higher land prices might have made Prince William County less attractive to the Marriott Corporation.

By the time the Manassas Great America plan was unveiled, there were protests from citizens, but the supervisors had already approved the park. The only hope for the few residents who had begun to fight it was the possibility that the lack of sewage capacity would cause the state water quality control board to stop the project.

In working out details in the backrooms, Marriott, Winfield and the other Prince William County supervisors were following the practices common in local government around the country. Elected officials were giving tax-funded aid to developers to attract a project of doubtful value, on the promise of jobs and more tax dollars that might never materialize. In the process—by ignoring the public's right to debate the plan—the county was totally disregarding those who had moved into the community beforehand, settling into what they thought would be peaceful suburbia. Promised woods, they were getting industry. Attracted by quiet, they would end up with the smog and pollution of heavy traffic. As we show in later chapters, developers and other influential individuals are able to work with supervisors and with much more obscure government officials, to obtain government help for their developments—expediting complicated paper work, getting favorable rulings from regulatory agencies, even providing improvements to development sites.

To us the story of Manassas reveals that citizens are wrong in believing all politicians are crooks. The situation is considerably more complex. The laws governing the behavior of public officials are so loose that officials do not have to be corrupt in the eyes of the law to profit from their decisions. Often, in fact, politicians do not even gain materially from decisions that are contrary to the interests of people who elect them. Officials are often prisoners of past bureaucratic practices, or they may be persuaded to co-operate simply by the atmosphere of flattery and exclusiveness that prevails in the backrooms of political dealings. They succumb to the feeling of power that comes in belonging to the same elite club with rich and influential individuals.

What emerged from our reporting was the belief that even working strictly within the limits of the law and carrying out what is regarded as normal government work, many officials are so insensitive to the welfare of the public that they might as well be corrupt.

THE CAST OF CHARACTERS

When elected officials such as Winfield use their power in secretive, devious ways, it is easy for three pressure groups to dominate public policy-making. These are businesses like the Marriott Corporation, parts of organized labor and civil service bureaucrats.

Big Business—
From Outright Corruption to Campaign Contributions

Business control of government is not new. Men with money to invest in America's growth have always managed to get a special break in our Democracy. In the late nineteenth century, reporters such as Lincoln Steffens began exposing business' corruption of government in the new mass circulation magazines and news-papers. Muckraking journalism uncovered government scandals, but after several years working in it and a discouraging attempt to reform the city of Boston, Steffens came to believe that business control of government was an evil that could not be changed. He concluded it was built into the capitalist system. "What Boston suggested to me was the idea business and politics must be one; that it was natural, inevitable, and—possibly—right that business should—by bribery, corruption, or somehow—get and be the govern-ment," he wrote.

Steffens' theory was right, and his writing still has application to current problems. Business and politics are one. But the form of business influence has changed since Steffens' day. Despite his pessimism, the muckrakers were able to stop much of the open corruption in which politicians commonly took illegal bribes. Muckraking resulted in reform laws controlling the conduct of elected officials, as well as better enforcement of those laws. And, stories by later muckrakers produced tighter laws. Today, ruled by stricter conflict-of-interest laws, laws prohibiting secret meetings and requiring disclosure of campaign contributions, it is much more difficult for politicians to freely accept bribes, as they did in the late nineteenth century.

But businessmen have found other ways to manipulate the democratic process. Much of their leverage comes from the perfectly legal mechanism of campaign contributions, which will be examined in a later chapter. Since business will always try to manipulate the government that regulates it, it's important to understand how the contributions are given, what they buy, and how citizens can use campaign contribution information to counteract this form of influence.

Big Labor—
From the Picket Line to the Political Backroom

Labor is a smaller influence in the behind-the-scenes manipulation of the state and local political process. In national politics, labor's traditionally Democratic stance is in direct contrast to the views of conservative business groups. But at the local and state level, it is a different story, for on most locally decided issues, business and labor have common interests. Labor unions, especially the building trades that dominate the AFL-CIO, are just as interested as business in promoting the tall buildings, new housing and apartment complexes, the transit lines and other big developments. For example, in California in 1972, business and labor combined in their opposition to a proposal before the voters that would limit land development along the coastline to preserve its beauty. Jobs for labor and profits for business put the two old foes on the same side. The chapters to come will tell how labor often supports conservative or Republican candidates at the local level because of a similarity of economic interests.

A new twist to labor's role has come in recent years as municipal, county and some state employees have been enrolled in unions. These employees are not the traditional union members. Most are civil servants protected by job guarantees not extended to those who work for private enterprise. The majority do not have the right to strike, although an increasing number of public employees are insisting on that right. Rather than working out their differences with their employers in traditional labor-management confrontations, these unions tend to negotiate privately with elected officials. Rather than strike, they—like business—focus their efforts on influencing officials by making campaign contributions.

The Bureaucrats—
The Motive of Self-Protection

A third pressure group with great influence on elected officials is the government department managers, either civil servants or political appointees. Their role is more complex, but—like the other groups—their main interest is in perpetuating their own careers and increasing their own power. Often they follow policies based on political decisions of elected officeholders. But a bureaucrat—often by using technical jargon—is able to disguise the nature of such a decision by saying it is a technical problem with no alternatives. Elected officeholders, who set policy in general terms according to the wishes of their supporters, can usually rely on a department manager to take the blame for an unpopular decision or to advance complex arguments to confuse the public.

The need to manage huge agencies, such as those in charge of highway programs, creates bureaucratic dynasties. A new type of dynasty builder emerging in the seventies is the transit manager, in charge of urban transit now being built with government funds around the United States. He must steer the project through many difficult phases—from blueprints, bond elections to construction and operation. His primary attribute must be aggressive salesmanship, and he sells the concept of the biggest, most modern system as a prestige symbol—as well as a necessity—to the community. And while transit routes are represented as scientifically determined, they all have the same function—serving the needs of big businesses for employees and customers. Once the system is built, the manager becomes a powerful person, in charge of thousands of employees, millions of commuters and billions of dollars' worth of equipment.

The Forgotten Voter

But what about the one who is supposedly the foundation of our democratic society? This is the person to whom our book is directed, the forgotten voter, neglected because he has no special influence with officeholders.

The voter is ineffective alone. Effectiveness comes only in affiliation with groups strong enough to compete on the battleground of influence. Not all citizens are unaffiliated, but their membership may not be helpful in fighting for the needs peculiar to residents of metropolitan America. A plumbers' union member, for example, might agree with his union's stand on higher wages, but oppose its opposition to a law banning highrise buildings near the public beach he visits on weekends. A scientist for Standard Oil, unhappy with his family's dependence on two cars, might well object when his firm donates money to a campaign against using highway tax dollars for rapid transit.

Alone, frustrated, seeing his welfare consistently neglected, the voter takes out his anger in the one area of government spending where he is given a choice—taxpayer support of education. That is one reason money for schools is dwindling and the quality of education—especially in the cities—is declining in direct proportion to taxpayers' rage over their own helplessness.

The electorate is actually a collection of potentially powerful interest groups, each with its own cause: fighting a freeway; integrating a school or opposing integration; preventing highrises from ruining a residential neighborhood; getting public facilities for crippled people. Today there are more tools available for these people to make themselves heard than ever before. Campaign fund disclosure laws, public interest law suits, ballot initiatives are among these. By using the system skillfully, people can force it to meet their needs—or at least consider them. If they can recognize the issues that deal with their comfort and security, they can unite in groups to influence the government on these issues.

To us, reporting for this book was a fascinating journey through official indifference and a reassuring occasion to meet people who convinced us that the spirit of ingenuity and rebellion against injustice is not dead. But the subjects we covered are mundane—how a new sewer line can destroy a peaceful neighborhood, how a maze of agencies can quietly subvert a smog-control law.

The average citizen does not believe these are the great issues of the seventies. He would rather debate problems of war, inflation, and national scandals. But these better-known, better-reported and more openly discussed issues are not important to the tight band who profit from the decisions of state and local government. Their interest lies in the day-to-day decisions in the fields of taxation, development, growth and pollution. These special interests do not care whether children ride to school in a bus or whether the Justice Department brings conspiracy charges against Father Philip Berrigan.

The villains of this book are obscure people: a county supervisor, a local prosecuting attorney, a city planning commissioner. So are the heroes: a woman who went to court to fight Marriott's Great America in Manassas; a private investigator in Chicago's Better Government Association, uncovering corruption in city government; a citizen activist who led grass-roots workers to Sacramento to force the legislature to save San Francisco Bay from the developers.

These are the kind of battles that will determine how America lives in the future. They show that the villains are not unbeatable after all.

2

The System

That Runs the Cities

To residents and visitors, no two American cities could be more different than Chicago and San Francisco. No city has the inner vitality and economic resilience of Chicago—nor the brute political power and the vigorous debate that surrounds it. Chicago, the great marketplace of mid-America, is controlled by old boss rule, dead or dying in many places, but here surprisingly alive. The city's politics have not changed from earlier decades; with the power in the hands of the same group, the machine, and remaining there.

No other city in America has the combination of sophistication, seacoast beauty and cosmopolitan variety found in San Francisco. Unlike Chicago, the structure of city government has been changed by reformers. They have eliminated the nineteenth-century machine bosses, political parties and the patronage army that had kept California's local governments in the hands of one group.

In each city across the country, the formal political structure differs on the surface. For most, it falls somewhere between boss rule and progressive separation of power. But these outward differences are superficial. In San Francisco and Chicago—just as in other cities—things are run the same way. Government in all of our cities is really operated by the same hidden system—determining the shape of neighborhoods, the location of freeways and transit lines, the quality of schools, the smell of the air, almost everything that affects the quality of life.

Although he is only dimly aware of it, the city dweller's day is shaped by decisions of city officials. The city, through its building code, regulates how well his house is built. Through zoning laws, it decides the size of his yard, how close his neighbor's house is, how many people live on the street and what shops are nearby. The flow of traffic on his street, the number of businesses and industries to offer him jobs—all are within the realm of city government. It makes sure he isn't cheated by a store. It gives him the necessities of police and fire protection as well as the amenities of urban life—libraries, museums, parks, auditoriums. It can give low-cost housing to the old and poor, or replace slums with expensive condominiums for the rich. It provides or regulates water, sewage, schools, transportation, and garbage collection.

Whether or not a city works well for the average citizen depends on who is running it—and who it is being run for. As things stand today, the real force that runs each city doesn't simply come from the people through their elected officials who, in turn, use their power to serve the public, the way it is outlined in charts in the back of our high-school civics books. As voters we are too easily confused by diagrams showing the relationship between the mayor, the councilmen and the commissioners or how some cities give the real power to a city manager appointed by the city council, while the mayor is a public relations figurehead. The charts are meaningless. What they don't show is how three special interest groups actually control policy for their own benefit.

In all cities—whether they be Chicago, San Francisco, Detroit, or New York—the groups who know how to secretly influence city government are the same: One is the organized public employees, large numbers of people whose wages and fringe benefits use up much of a city's budget. Another is organized labor, a political force in electing each city's public officials. But the most powerful are the few men who run the banks, the retail stores, the real estate firms, the insurance companies, the industrial plants, the construction firms and all the other businesses that pour billions of dollars in taxes and payrolls into each city.

These businessmen shape each city to their own needs for new downtowns, for large office buildings, for thriving retail zones, for new hotels and restaurants, and for apartments and condominiums to provide living space for workers and customers for their businesses. City government helps them do this with a tremendous number of city-provided services. These services affect everyone who lives in the city, not just the special interest groups. That is why, in most metropolitan areas, poor and middle-class neighborhoods have been neglected or ripped down for freeways or huge business developments; why low-cost housing is seldom built; and why parks have low priority. In each city the middle class is moving to the suburbs.

Because of the similarity in the real forces that influence local government, American cities like Chicago and San Francisco are beginning to have the same look. New buildings are springing up haphazardly according to the dictates of real estate profits. In each place, downtown is booming, and people pour in and out of the buildings during the daytime. At night, the streets are becoming more and more deserted. Rapid transit is in fashion. Realizing that the new buildings need people and that the parking capacity of any downtown is limited, the business leaders of each city are abandoning their old friend, the freeway, and are beginning to push for rail rapid transit. In contrast to the growing support of transportation is the decline of each city's public school system. Decaying schools are the rule—full of violent and rebellious youngsters, dull administrators and frustrated teachers. Money for public schools is far down on the priority list.

Finally, the pattern of city services being delivered—and what they mean to the people who get them—tells us much about living in America in the seventies. Each city has been shaped in secret, in business clubs or chamber of commerce meetings, over lunch in expensive restaurants. By the time the plans are made public, it is too late to object—if anyone could find the place where objections are filed.

A look at Chicago and San Francisco tells how the powerful groups get special consideration, no matter what the external form of government. Each city illustrates this point in its own way. A clue to how it works can be found in the personality and style of the mayor.

MAYOR DALEY'S CHICAGO

From 1955 on, Richard Daley has been the mayor of Chicago, better known and stronger than any other mayor in the United States. He rules his midwestern empire with force and intelligence, supported by intellectuals and gangsters, blacks, Irish and Slavs, poor people, and—more important—the lawyers, bankers, manufacturers and retailers on La Salle Street, the financial center of the city.

He is part of the Irish immigrant culture, and grew up in the Bridgeport neighborhood where he still lives as mayor. He looks like power, with a big round face, a thick lower lip that curls downward when he is angry, and a large solid belly like politicians had before television, when they were not afraid to eat. He is defiant, resentful and contemptuous when he is criticized, convinced that he is right, conscious of the unique power he holds as both the head of the city government and the leader of the Cook County political machine.

One time an alderman, who was a university professor, criticized him for giving a city job to Tommy Keane. Young Keane was the son of Tom Keane, a friend of Daley's and chairman of the city council finance committee.

The professor-alderman believed the appointment of Keane's son was nepotism, and voted against it at the city council meeting. In a scene familiar to Chicagoans, the mayor flew into a rage. Shouting so loudly he could hardly be understood, Daley answered his critic: "I made this appointment because I knew Tommy Keane, the boy I appointed, since he's been a baby. And I know his mother Adeline Keane, one of the greatest women I know, not only in this city but in any city in the United States. A fine Polish-American woman, who raised a fine boy. And should that boy be told by any professor or faker that he shouldn't hold office because his name is Keane and she's his mother?

". . . and if this is the society in which we live, that we're afraid to appoint our sons, or our nephews or our relatives or are afraid to appoint any one member of our family because of what? Of fear of what might be said? Not the truth. But the fear. Who creates the fear? Who creates these phony issues? The very people we're talking about. Let me say to you very frankly, if you're a teacher, God help the students that are in your class, if this is what is being taught."

Ungrammatical, illogical, embarrassingly maudlin, the speech is typical of Daley. In his crude vitality and strength is the assurance that the aldermen who support him are vital and strong too—not effete intellectuals. Because of speeches like this, the Irish, Poles and other white ethnic groups vote for him; Daley is one of them, a son of working people, still living in the old neighborhood.

As Daley's speech ended, there was applause for almost a minute, roaring up to the ceiling, thirty feet above the city council chamber. The mayor, sitting on a chair like those of the fifty aldermen, was elevated by the stage at the front of the chamber. He listened in satisfaction. He should not have been surprised at the applause, for he controlled most of the aldermen. Only a few, like the professor, were independent.

The Machine Endures

The city has changed over the years. What endures is control of Chicago by the political machine, and control of the machine by Daley. When Alderman Tom Keane rose to defend his son's appointment to the city job, he eloquently told about the continuing flow of Chicago's political power: "I'd like to go back to 1896, when my grandfather was the Democratic leader in the community that I now lead," said Keane. "And in 1905 . . . he was succeeded by my uncle, and in 1910, my uncle was succeeded by my dad. In 1945, I succeeded my dad . . . I have never lived more than two blocks from where I have been born. I think I know and have seen the changes in the community in which I have lived. From German to Irish to Jewish to Polish to Spanish speaking. Whatever the changes were, and no matter how they came about, there was always a Keane representing the area. . . . Whether it be nepotism or not, the people of our community by their votes . . . have approved the kind of public service the Keane family has given them."

It's not just tradition that keeps families like Keane in office for three quarters of a century. More important is the machine, which dominates the city and shapes it according to the wishes of the businessmen who are the mayor's allies. It is run by the mayor, sitting on top of a political organization that looks like a pyramid—the Democratic organization of Cook County, most of which is occupied by Chicago.

As head of this county Democratic machine and head of city government, Daley has power unequaled by any mayor in the country. Although his political strength has declined in recent years, he still dictates the appointment of policy-setting boards, such as the school board, the library and housing authority boards, the transit authority and the park board, as well as other officials that run city departments. He is still the most significant factor in the nomination and victory of most elected officials. The price they pay him is their loyalty and obedience. This means that the aldermen on city council, who are supposed to serve as a check and balance on the mayor, are completely in his command.

Whether victory at the polls always means voter approval in Chicago, is hard to say. For votes are not always counted the same there as in other places. "Unadulterated vote stealing is [an] underpinning of the Democratic machine; in any given election, by reliable estimates, between 50,000 and 150,000 unlawful votes are registered for the straight Democratic ticket," said Neal Peirce in his book *The Megastates of America.* "Nowhere in America is vote theft practiced on so grandiose a scale." The city's Better Government Association, a private investigative group watching out for government corruption, has found that in Chicago elections, fictitious people have been registered to vote, votes have been stolen by the Democratic machine, derelicts were paid $2 to register, and dead people have been carried on the voter rolls.

But the machine does not rely solely on vote fraud as its means of staying in power. What holds it together is a perfectly legal practice built into city government—patronage, government jobs handed out to party workers and to those they designate. Virtually every resident in the city of Chicago knows or is related to someone who is in debt to Daley, directly or indirectly, for his job. Businesses allow the Daley machine to hand out some jobs in private industry, too, and some estimate that these bring the number of patronage jobs in Chicago to over 70,000.

At the bottom of the machine structure are those described by Mike Royko, the Chicago *Daily News* columnist, in his book, *Boss,* as the ones "who swing mops in public buildings, dump bedpans in the County Hospital, dig ditches, and perform other menial work. They don't work precincts regularly, although they help out at election time, but they do have to vote themselves and make sure their families vote, buy the usual tickets to political dinners, and, in many wards, contribute about two percent of their salaries to the ward organization."

Above this group is the precinct captain, who distributes favors and services to registered Democrats in his precinct, and in return for those favors, gets votes for the machine's candidates on election day. He receives a little better pay, a more pleasant job, and he knows that election victory for machine politicians means job security for himself.

Higher up in the machine structure are its officers, the ward committeemen and the city's legislators, the aldermen. The Democratic Central Committee gives these officials a number of patronage jobs to give away, depending on their power and prestige within the party.

Another part of the machine is the judiciary. Many judges come up through city and county government as lawyers friendly to the machine, and they were appointed by Daley or people who owed favors to Daley. As Royko pointed out, "This doesn't mean cases are always rigged, but one cannot underestimate the power of sentimentality." Machine lawyers are hired by business to deal with the city in "zoning disputes, big real estate ventures, and anything else that brings a company into contact with city agencies."

Daley the Builder

What Daley has done with all the power of the machine is to grant favors to those who have supported it. And what he has done to show the voter the productivity of his administration is to undertake enormous building projects. When he first took office,

Daley had to find building money that was not available from the federal government. So he used local government funds, stripping the city council of its power to make up the city budget. That way, he could take credit as the builder of the new Chicago. The aldermen, in debt to the machine for their office and their supply of patronage jobs, rubberstamped whatever he wanted.

Reminders of the mayor—and his prowess as a builder—are everywhere. The most used entryway to Chicago is no longer the railroad, but O'Hare Airport. A sign says Daley built it, and another sign tells visitors Mayor Daley welcomes them to Chicago.

Coming in from the airport on the freeway Daley built, a visitor is struck by the fact that Chicago is an old city with gloomy dark brick buildings, many of them put up after the Chicago fire in 1871. In the city, there are still a few old, middle-class white ethnic neighborhoods. Some have been ravaged by the freeway, evidence of the damage done by Daley's huge projects to once strong residential sections. But there are still many bars and small grocery stores, reminders of a time in this country when city life centered on such neighborhood conveniences. There are a large number of big Roman Catholic churches and parochial schools. The people on the streets in these areas are white; blacks live in dismal ghettos scattered elsewhere in the city. There the neighborhoods have a devastated look, with empty buildings, burned wreckage and crowded conditions as devoid of hope as anywhere in the country.

In the main downtown area, the Loop, is Mayor Daley's new Chicago. There are landmarks—the old, elevated train tracks, Lake Michigan, the Chicago River. But many of the architectural treasures of the past have been ripped down to make way for look-alike highrises.

Before Daley became mayor, there had been little new construction downtown since the early 1930s. But his administration nurtured the rebirth of the central business district with government-supplied services, including property tax breaks, improved transit, snow removal, police patrols, and street cleaning. Today it looks like downtowns all around the country—steel buildings rising high, sheathed in glass or aluminum.

Who Benefits and Who Doesn't

The machine has articulate defenders who say it produces more efficient government and better services than other big cities. When Don Bruckner, a vice president of the University of Chicago, came to the city as a reporter for the *Sun Times* in the sixties, he decided to test the organization of the machine he had read so much about. There was a hole in the street in front of his apartment, and he telephoned his Democratic committeeman, who assured him the hole would be filled. When Bruckner returned from work in the evening, the hole had been filled. The committeeman appeared at his door, introduced himself and handed Bruckner, a Democrat, a sheaf of voter registration papers. Then he took Bruckner down the street, introducing him to the neighbors and even pointing out the location of the bookie at the corner. He cautioned him to stay out of one bar on Saturday nights because of the fights there, and showed him a safer one.

"Bricks and stone" is the phrase Bruckner continually used when we talked to him about Daley and the machine—bricks and stone that were used to start building again in the decaying Loop, to convert poor neighborhoods into sanctuaries for the upper class, to save a rapid transit system when other cities were abandoning theirs.

But it is bricks and stone for some, and unending poverty and neglect for others. As one of the few Daley critics on the council, liberal alderman Leon Despres, wrote, "Chicago's most pampered neighborhood is the central business area, comprising downtown and the near North Side along Lake Michigan. When visitors speak of Chicago's 'dynamic, modern progress,' they usually refer to the central business area. There you see bold new buildings, daytime vigor, and excellent city maintenance. New projects are always in the works. Speedy public transit converges on the area. Hundreds of millions of dollars in expressways pour people into the area by day and back to the suburbs at night. Get off the subway anywhere in the central business area and you won't find a broken city sidewalk. Get off the subway almost anywhere else, and you will. Between the central business area and the outskirts lie large, almost uninterrupted gray areas of urban dry rot. This is where most Chicagoans live."

Several miles from the Loop, in the well-known black ghetto of Woodlawn, there are not enough garbage collections and not enough policemen for its crowded living arrangements. The only bricks and stones evident lie in heaps near abandoned buildings that no one bothers to demolish despite the danger to children, passersby and neighboring buildings. Owners are required by law to tear them down, but many don't bother, and officials let them get away with it.

"Walking on 63rd Street, it seems that Woodlawn has been the scene of some fierce warfare," wrote Bryce Nelson, correspondent for the *Los Angeles Times*. "Why else would it look like all those buildings had been bombed out and burned out? If not by war, at least by a major riot. . . . The destruction of Woodlawn was not a one-shot dramatic event; it was and is a process, the culmination of decades of physical and social neglect and decay." Fires are set by vandals over and over again in the same deserted buildings. Despite widespread arson, law enforcement in this part of Chicago is so poor that no one has been arrested for setting fires in Woodlawn in a decade.

There has been some money spent on poor neighborhoods, and it is loudly publicized by the Daley regime. But it is little in comparison to what is being spent downtown. According to Royko, Daley's "urban renewal program amounted to a stack full of charts and blueprints. Rats gnawed on black infants' feet, while money was used to build new police stations around the corner. The Daley years were underway with the values that would never change: things, concrete, glass, steel, downtown, business profit. Then if there's anything left, maybe something for the human being."

The Squeaky Wheel

"Part of the success of the machine is that it delivers the services to those who know how to ask for them," said Abner Mikva, who once represented Hyde Park and Woodlawn in Congress. "The squeaky wheel gets the oil," he told us. "Those who do the opinion shaping are the influence people in town. The machine delivers the services to the people who make the opinions, who then say, 'The machine isn't so bad after all; it works.'

"It's not surprising so many opinion makers say, 'For all its faults, Chicago is a much better city than New York.' For State Street, yes, it is. The Loop is better off than parts of Manhattan. The near north side is a neighborhood that is unparalleled in Manhattan. If you're a Rubloff [a big real estate operator], you think Daley's the greatest thing on wheels. And if you're Rubloff, he is. When Rubloff wants to get a decision, it isn't like New York, where you don't know who to go to to get a decision that will stick. . . . Here you just persuade Mayor Daley to do something and it will get done.

"But," Mikva added, "you drive through stretches of the West Side and you'll find slums unparalleled in any part of the country. For them, the machine does not deliver."

Mobsters, Hardhats and Businessmen

The machine delivers to several elements besides big business and the patronage army. The mob has always been an ally. "There is," wrote Neal Peirce, "a seemingly endless web of interconnection between the Chicago mob and Chicago politicians." From the early part of the century, through Al Capone in the twenties down to the seventies, the crime syndicate has had influence in Chicago politics. It is so ingrained a part of the city that it is tolerated by city government and its political leaders. It continues to buy policemen and politicians.

Another part of the machine consists of the traditionally Democratic labor unions. They support Daley not only because he is a Democrat, but because he is a builder.

But business is by far the most interesting partner in the alliance. It provides campaign contributions for Mayor Daley and his machine. It works with him on city projects, providing his plans with prestige as well as capital for privately built elements of his new Chicago. And the same conservative businessmen openly support Daley and the machine in election year. For example, one of Daley's political supporters has been Republican David J. Kennedy, chairman of the board of the Continental Illinois Bank and Trust Company, who once was President Nixon's secretary of the treasury.

Why would businessmen—well-dressed, polite members of good clubs, loyal supporters of the GOP—share in a partnership with the rough Irish Democratic mayor and business' supposed enemies, the trade unions and mobsters?

It is because all in the alliance benefit economically from Mayor Daley's administration—no one more than business. It has always been so in American politics. The investor who wants to build a subdivision on the edge of town, or knock down an old building to put up a highrise, needs permission from city hall. The owner of a large, downtown department store doesn't care if a mayor is a Republican or a Democrat, just so city hall keeps running to bring customers downtown and sends the police out when he gets robbed.

Practicality, not ideology, is what is important at city hall, no matter what the city. That is the way it is in Chicago's city hall—a fact that may surprise dedicated Republicans in other parts of the country who hold up Mayor Daley as the prime example of the evil, big city Democratic boss. It is the money of Republican businessmen, as much as anyone else, that helps keep Democrat Daley and his machine in power.

What City Hall Delivers

The rewards for such support come from a city hall that looks as crude as the city's politics. Built in 1906, the Chicago City Hall takes up an entire city block, with half of it housing Cook County officials. Greek temples influenced the architect, and there are columns around the building. But it is not an inspiring temple—just a massive, unfriendly building, well-guarded by uniformed policemen. The lobby has a high ceiling and is richly decorated in ponderous style. More noticeable than the decorations are the people in the corridors—many red-faced, pudgy men with short haircuts like Mayor Daley's and short, pudgy sausage-like fingers. There seems to be something about city hall that rumples clothes. Not the mayor's clothes. He is always impeccably dressed. It is the hangers-on who show that in city hall, pants sag and bag at the knees. Coats do not quite fit around the shoulders. The more style conscious wear no-wrinkle double knits, and they set the hallways ablaze with plum-colored sportscoats and light blue slacks.

Like city halls everywhere, the long corridors seem a perfect setting for angles, deals, whispered conversations and the fix, which in Chicago is called "clout."

Surprisingly enough, modern plans keep coming from this old building. One such project was the new 31-story civic center which has been built nearby. It is a huge complex, connected by underground walkways that are lined with restaurants and shops. Outside the civic center is the sculpture Picasso did for Chicago, big and bewildering to tourists, but increasingly beloved by the city. And the mayor built McCormick Place, a convention center along Lake Michigan. It wrecked the view, but provided exhibition space for the conventioners who stayed in downtown hotels. When it burned down, Daley built another one in its place.

Daley's latest and biggest plan to rebuild central Chicago was described by Dennis Byrne of the Chicago *Daily News* as a scheme arranged between "Daley and his powerful friends who occupy the corner offices in the city's banks and businesses."

The plan was called "Chicago 21" to symbolize the launching of the city into the twenty-first century a few decades early. Old railroad yards would be turned into high-priced residential areas, and eventually 120,000 more people would be able to live in the central city—well-to-do customers for the stores, banks, hotels, and restaurants. Rapid transit would be taken off the old-fashioned elevated tracks and buried underground. Aerial walkways would connect the new buildings. Government would build a new library and other facilities. Business, assured of cooperation from the city, would build theaters, restaurants, stores, a hotel and new apartments.

Chicago 21 was first unveiled to the public at a Daley press conference in mid '73. It was the result of months of planning between the Chicago Central Area Committee, a nongovernmental organization of downtown business interests, and the city. The

planners were confident they could succeed in this massive redevelopment where other big cities had failed. They had already
ironed out sticky details that might be sources of trouble. A
private organization would build the new downtown; a limited-
profit corporation would handle the money, and revenue bonds
would pay for the city's share by borrowing from future property
taxes the new buildings were expected to pay.

The whole thing would cost between $17 and $20 billion to
build over the next seventeen years, and the price tag would be
split by both the city and downtown business. The city would get
its share of building costs from the revenue bonds. In most cities,
such bonds are approved by voters. But in Chicago, they need only
approval from the Daley-controlled city council.

Daley's and business' scheme could have some merit; it might
greatly improve the central city if it were built. But, typical of
such plans, it was conceived in private by the people who will gain
most from it, and then announced to the public. Its main motive
was profit. Rather than trying to revive the city as a whole, Daley
and his backers are building an enclave for the merchants and the
affluent.

What the Machine Can't Deliver

Former Congressman Mikva saw the implications of such policies. "Life in the city can be very comfortable if you pick the right
area to live in," he said. "If you have influence to get to know the
power structure and can afford to send your children to private
schools. That's an absolute must in most parts of the big
cities. . . ."

For others, life in the city is not working out. Mikva said that
"Public schools in—almost without exception—all of the big cities,
stink. . . . They are poorly run, poorly financed, poorly admin-
istered, and nobody willingly will send their kids there. That
means that all of the people who would be influence makers will
either move away or send their children to private schools. . . .

"When the machine really ran as a machine, even the poor
people had representation to their precinct captain. He was a local
godfather who would take care of his block. Today, the local

precinct captains can't really do much. They're afraid to go out in the streets. And the kinds of things black people living in the city need are not the kinds of things that a black precinct captain can deliver. He can't deliver a better school system for the kids. He can't deliver better housing for the elderly, or even cleaner air."

The reason Daley can't deliver good schools, safe streets and clean air is that they are not thought to be a necessary part of the plan for a new Chicago. They are not essential services for the businessmen in the Loop, the political types in city hall, the mob, labor or downtown employees who commute from the suburbs or live in the new highrise apartments that have private guards and maintenance crews.

A MILLIONAIRE MAYOR FOR A BUSINESSMAN'S CITY

Mayor Joseph Alioto is a man of overwhelming force, charm and persuasiveness. He is as sophisticated as his city—an entirely different sort of man than Mayor Daley. Alioto plays the violin, which he learned when he was 11, and has more than a booster's pride that San Francisco is the only city on the Coast with a major opera company. He knows opera, loves it and is surprised when others do not share his enthusiasm. His wife, Angelina, has an antique store on Jackson Street, where rich San Franciscans shop for furniture, and sometimes the Aliotos search Europe for merchandise, skillfully combing Venice, Genoa or Paris for treasures.

In person, the mayor dominates a roomful of people. He's a salesman, raconteur, concerned friend, sophisticated name dropper, a fearsome adversary in a debate. In conversation, he focuses the full force of his hypnotic personality on the person he is talking to. Little of this is apparent on television, a medium that waters down his forceful speaking style.

Alioto first ran for public office in the mayoral election of 1967; his entrance into politics came unexpectedly when the man whose campaign he was managing died. Alioto had the support of old San Francisco business and labor from the beginning. *Examiner* columnist Dick Nolan wrote that insiders had predicted he could never win. They said, "He'll never make it. The day has passed in this city when [hotelman] Ben Swig, [former mayor] Elmer Robinson and that mob can get together in the back room in the Fairmont Hotel and decide who's going to be Mayor of San Francisco."

The predictions were wrong. Alioto got more campaign funds from big business and big labor than had ever been raised by a candidate in the city—$400,000. And he beat his own spending record when he ran for reelection in 1971, with a campaign that cost $550,000. The biggest contributors were himself; businessmen Cyril Magnin, Walter Shorenstein, and Ben Swig; and the Plumbers and Teamsters unions, each giving $10,000.

Before he ran for mayor, Alioto had been an attorney, heading the largest antitrust law firm in the country. Trained by five years in the United States Department of Justice's antitrust division, Alioto was able to attract many clients suing for restraint of trade, price fixing and other monopolistic practices. He had also represented many of the nation's large cities in antitrust suits, and from 1964 through 1967, won more than $61 million in damages for them. He had served as general manager and president of the Rice Growers Association, representing Northern California rice growers. He quickly expanded its annual sales from $25 million to $70 million, and modernized methods of transporting goods by sending rice to the Orient in ships designed as seagoing silos, able to handle huge amounts of bulk rice.

Like Daley, Alioto was from immigrant culture, an American upward striver. His father, a fisherman from Sicily, met his mother on a fishing boat on San Francisco Bay, where their families had taken refuge after the 1906 earthquake and fire. Being Sicilian might have hurt the mayor anywhere but in San Francisco, where the Italians and Irish for years were the dominant ethnic groups. In 1969, Look magazine accused him of close association with the Mafia. Alioto denied it and sued the magazine and the authors of the article. A federal judge ruled that the article was not accurate, but Alioto was unable to collect damages because he couldn't prove it had been written in malice. The article destroyed his campaign that year for governor of California.

Alioto is bald, and he dresses in dark suits that seem to emphasize his pale scalp and skin. In his city hall office he receives visitors in a high-backed chair, as if he deliberately wants to look like a powerful mafioso rather than a member of a rich San Francisco businessmen's society. He is proud of his ancestry, aware of the prejudice against it and determined to meet the prejudice directly. While he was preparing to run for the 1974 governor's race, one of his opponents was Assembly Speaker Bob Moretti, an Italian with a dark complexion and a tough, aggressive manner. Asked if the *Look* article would still hurt him, Alioto, thinking of his opponent, said, "Well, I suppose we'll have to let the voters decide which one of us looks more like a gangster."

Legal Troubles Multiply

Nationally, Alioto is perhaps more famous for his legal troubles than for his political career. While he was suing *Look* magazine for libel, the U.S. Justice Department brought criminal charges against him on another matter, accusing him of illegally splitting $2.3 million in legal fees with the attorney general of the state of Washington. It had grown out of antitrust cases Alioto handled for public utilities in Washington, in which he had won $16.2 million in settlements for the utilities.

His personality dominated the courtroom during the trial. Daryl Lembke of the *Los Angeles Times* described his behavior during his five and a half day appearance on the witness stand in his own defense. He lectured the jury on antitrust law, and paced and roamed about the court room. Said Lembke, "He even called a woman jurist by her name, as though he were still campaigning, and excused himself for turning his back to her as he stood at the easel" [explaining a diagram].

Alioto said that he had not violated the law, but had merely given the attorney general part of his fee in return for work he had done. It was not illegal for the Washington attorney general to engage in private practice at that time. The case went on for months, and Alioto's political career was thought to be finished. But before the trial was over, he ran for a second term as may.or, and won. Alioto maintained that the Justice Department's suit against him was a Nixon administration attempt to end his political career. "It was a tough election," he said after he won. "Let's face it. It isn't every day we have a national administration that tried to knock out a mayor." Finally, in June 1972, a federal judge ordered Alioto acquitted of the charges, and he was soon in the middle of his preparations to run for governor again.

He is the perfect mayor for the new San Francisco going up by the Golden Gate—a millionaire businessman for a businessman's city. He is the most articulate of the group of men shaping the city into a place for offices, expensive apartments and condominiums. Meanwhile, as in Chicago and other cities, middle-class and poor neighborhoods, whose protection is low priority, deteriorate or are torn down for more profitable buildings.

Housed in "San Francisco Renaissance"

Alioto's city hall is different from Daley's in appearance and style. The old city hall crumbled in the earthquake and fire of 1906, its lack of strength another sign of the dishonesty of its mayor, Eugene Schmitz, and the political boss of old San Francisco-style politics, Abe Reuf, who had it built with poor materials. San Francisco wanted its new city hall to be sturdy enough to withstand earthquakes, and it may be, with 8,000 tons of structural steel holding it together. It is French Renaissance in design, an ornate building faced in grey Sierra granite. Its dome is not the modest dome of most capitols, but an enormous copper one, now darkened with a rich blue-green patina. The building dominates the civic center square.

Old San Francisco politicians surround the mayor at city hall, Italian friends from the old days and people who know the neighborhoods. Some are from the Richmond and the Sunset, in the western part of the city where there are still neighborhoods of homes and small shops. Others are from the Mission District, which the Irish used to dominate; now it is the home of Irish, blacks, and "Latinos," the catchall phrase that describes a Latin American population containing such varied elements as Mexican Americans, Central Americans and Cubans.

But the politicians in San Francisco's city hall are not like their counterparts in Chicago—the willing prisoners of Mayor Daley's patronage. Unlike Chicago, there is no machine in San Francisco or anywhere else in California. That is not because Californians are particularly upright or civic-minded. It is because their laws are unlike those in most other states.

A Little History

To understand how this came about, it is necessary to look back to the early twentieth century in California, the culmination of a politically sinful era. The Southern Pacific Railroad—called "the Octopus" at the time—firmly controlled state and local government. Californians rebelled against this in 1910, as part of a national revulsion against corruption in municipal and state government. Called the Progressive Era, it was prompted by the economic abuses of business and the revelations of investigative reporters, the "muckrakers." In California, the reformers had a remarkable leader, Hiram Johnson, who was elected governor in 1910. They made changes that gave the state its own brand of politics.

The reformers were reacting to Southern Pacific's corruption of elected officials, as well as political parties and their nominating conventions. When Johnson and his Progressives took over the state government, they passed a law that destroyed the traditional role of political parties in local elections. The law eliminated parties from elections by making them nonpartisan. Statewide offices remained partisan, but a primary election was held to nominate candidates instead of the old party-run nominating convention. These changes also abolished the traditional structure of political parties. State and county party organizations were deliberately weakened by changes in the law. Primary elections were substituted for party conventions in choosing nominees.

And most important, statewide parties were devastated in the state by the institution of a practice called cross-filing. This permitted a candidate of one party to also enter the primary of the other party. As a result, officeholders were elected because of personal popularity, rather than party power.

The reforms made it impossible for a machine to guarantee continuing power to the crowd in any California city hall. Another element essential to a machine is missing in California—patronage.

All but a few jobs are covered by civil service laws. In Daley's regime, such laws exist, but are ignored. In San Francisco, they are strictly enforced. Applicants must pass examinations for jobs ranging from file clerk to high police officials, and once hired, they are protected from being fired unless their superiors can prove they are guilty of dishonesty or extreme incompetence. Such firings can be appealed by the worker, in long legal proceedings that make supervisors wary of dismissing anyone. The mayor cannot pass out jobs to loyal supporters, as Mayor Daley does. The glue that holds together the Chicago machine is missing in California.

How the Backroom Still Operates

As a result, the game in San Francisco City Hall has different rules than the one in Chicago. But it is the same game, with the same players.

In Chicago, Daley and the Cook County Democratic Party dictate who gets the Democratic nominations for city council and other offices. This endorsement almost always assures victory. Things are simplified for special interests. They can give one donation to Daley's Democratic machine. But in San Francisco, there is no machine to guarantee that the mayor's supporters will be elected to the legislative branch, the board of supervisors. Consequently, special interests have to work harder to be sure their friends occupy the eleven supervisor's seats as well as the mayor's office. In the city-county charter, the supervisors are independent of the mayor, and many of his decisions—making up the budget, appointing officials—are subject to their approval. He can veto their legislation. And theoretically, they can override his veto with eight votes, but this has never happened to Alioto, nor have they ever turned down a single one of his appointments.

One reason for Alioto's success with the board is also built into the city-county charter. When a supervisor's seat is vacant—and it often is, since the office is a stepping stone to higher office—the mayor appoints the new supervisor. Alioto usually has three appointees on the board. This makes him a strong administrator, and it is as close as any California mayor comes to being a boss.

The Pricetag of a Supervisor's Seat

Another way special interests can influence San Francisco city government is by helping candidates meet the high cost of running for the $9,600-a-year supervisor's jobs. Since the supervisors run at large and not by district, success calls for spending $50,000 on a citywide campaign. Candidates get this money from the usual source of substantial contributions, the big business and labor interests that want to build huge projects and stimulate business for downtown. They give to the supervisors' campaigns through faceless organizations: the Association for Good Government, Community Citizens Committee, Hotel Employers Association, Concerned Businessmen, Committee for Effective Government, and so on.

Why do they form these organizations? One supervisor, Clinton Copp—who, like the rest, gets some of these funds—speculated that this made it easier for groups to raise money, and that it is "primarily a camouflage." They want to avoid criticism from the public, and perhaps they don't want to let the voters know that the same groups are keeping their choices in office year after year. In addition, many big business and labor leaders give in their own names.

Campaign contributions will be dealt with in a later chapter. But it is important to understand city politicians' great need for this money to stay in power. Without a machine to get out the vote and provide the campaign funds, the San Francisco candidate must find his own supporters. Without party structure, California politics has become based on the idea of voting for the man, not the party. No one's endorsement can ensure a city candidate victory, and he is faced with the need to project a winning personality. The cost of doing this is enormous because of California's tradition of expensive political advertising techniques. It has resulted in a multitude of individual fund-raising drives, by candidates for local government, for the state legislature and for the major statewide offices.

And while candidates like to say their support comes from the little people, such a laudable accomplishment is usually true only in the case of losers. The winners get their money from the fat cats, the big business and labor men who inevitably want something in return.

All of this means that politicians come and go in California politics—unlike those in the Chicago machine who seem to stay in office forever. For example, Alioto, a relative newcomer to politics, is already nearly finished as mayor. San Francisco law limits him to two terms, and his second one will be up in 1975. As a result of the turnover and the mad scramble for political funds, the superficial impression of California politics is one of confusion. Nobody seems to be able to predict which candidate will win or where the power is. But understanding California politics is simply a matter of knowing where to look. Just as in Chicago, political power comes from the special interests that support the candidates. So instead of looking at an officeholder's party registration, the student of California politics should look at the public report of campaign contributions, on file with the secretary of state or the county clerk.

This does not mean that every officeholder strictly follows the wishes of his big campaign contributors. Business prefers to discreetly support someone who generally agrees with its aims, rather than to actually buy a candidate with outright illegal bribes. Major businesses, for example, bet on Governor Reagan because they knew his policies would give private enterprise more freedom. In other California races, business sometimes gives to both candidates—if it looks like a close race. They were glad to give to Mayor Alioto because he was a willing ally in their plan to build a new downtown.

Prophecy from Nob Hill

In 1955, a rich and worldly prophet spoke from a hilltop in San Francisco. His name was Ben Swig, and the hilltop was Nob Hill, where the California Street and Powell Street cable car lines intersect near Swig's Fairmont Hotel, one of the city's best.

"The whole San Francisco skyline is going to change, though not at once," he said. "We're going to have a great building wave. Money is going to ease up. We're going to become a second New York."

By the early seventies, with the help of Alioto and other politicians backed by men like Swig, many tall new buildings had gone up. They rose from the lowlands around Montgomery Street, within walking distance of the bay, to Nob Hill, which, not many years before, had been dominated only by the Mark Hopkins Hotel.

The best place to see the new San Francisco is from the bay, on one of the ferryboats that take commuters to Marin County. San Francisco is a city of amenities, culture, beauty and convenience. When traffic got too congested on the narrow Golden Gate Bridge, the bridge district board didn't build a new bridge or doubledeck the old one. The Golden Gate was the city's symbol, and any move to change it was unacceptable to residents. The board resumed the ferryboat service that had been abandoned when the bridge was finished, and now commuters to the prosperous suburbs in Marin County relax on deck, sipping martinis purchased at the busy bar inside.

From the boats today, the Top of the Mark, the bar on top of the Mark Hopkins Hotel, is hardly noticeable. It is overwhelmed by the tower Ben Swig built for his Fairmont Hotel and by other buildings that are obscuring the shape of Nob Hill and of nearby Russian Hill. Down below, Montgomery Street, the financial center which has always called itself the Wall Street of the West, looks like a small Manhattan. The Bank of America building juts fifty-two stories into the air. Crocker Bank, Wells Fargo Bank, the St. Francis Hotel, and the Hilton Hotel have all built highrise buildings that were not imagined a few years ago except by Ben Swig and a few other real estate developers.

Superhuman Structures

Dominating everything is the 835-foot-tall Transamerica building, huge at the bottom and narrowing at the top into a spire; it is a malformed pyramid that looks as if it were designed for a 1930s Flash Gordon serial. Transamerica is a holding company, controlling Occidental Life Insurance Company, land development corporations, United Artists films, Lyon Moving and Storage Company, and many other enterprises. Unhappy with the anonymity of the parent company, the directors decided to give Transamerica an identity with a new home office. They succeeded. Every painting and photograph of the San Francisco skyline is now dominated by the pyramid.

Some San Franciscans object to the strange shape of Transamerica's tower, but that is not the main problem. It is that San Francisco's business area is too small to hold the enormous structure and many more like it. The *Architectural Record* summed up this problem by concluding that San Francisco's location, surrounded by water, its hilly terrain and its small size "make it the most visible of cities, and the most vulnerable. . . . One pyramid may be assimilable; but what if there are others? At street level, and on the street, however, it is the scale of human experience in man-created space that is now different from what it used to be."

From a distance, the Transamerica Tower is not oppressive. But from the sidewalk next to it, it is. San Francisco has a downtown where people often travel on foot. It is a place for walking, for discovering small shops, poking into small bars, watching other people. The crowded streets had been lined with buildings that neither overwhelmed pedestrians nor cut out the sunlight and view. But the new highrises have changed that. Where the Transamerica building went up, there were once prosperous shops, restaurants and bars, all reflecting the city's distinctive culture and personality on the fringe of both Chinatown and Italian North Beach. The area was leveled for the tower, and its base now occupies two entire city blocks.

San Franciscans have long shown their desire to preserve what is unique about the city and have always had an aversion to cold, inhuman structures. They began the first freeway revolt in the 50s. Public protest had stopped highway builders from completing the Embarcadero Freeway, an elevated interchange that blocked the view of the bay. But despite the public's interest in preserving what they believed was a delicate city environment, the supervisors from the early sixties on approved nearly every request of private builders for a total of forty-five highrises that will be completed before 1975. For example, Transamerica Tower didn't just spring up, the product of Transamerica's builders on Transamerica's land. It needed the permission of the city for street closures. Transamerica officials gave to city officials' campaigns, and it is not surprising that the corporation got its street closures. The approval for the building was made in the early sixties, but the general public was unaware of the building and its design until construction began in the late sixties.

The highrises are basically daytime buildings. At night they are closed, and the streets are becoming empty of the people who once made the city a lively place after dark. As a result, much that was good about the city is disappearing. But to the men responsible for the creation of this cold and expensive downtown, the new San Francisco is not a disaster. They believed the old San Francisco was stagnating, and now it has been saved by thousands of construction jobs needed to build the highrises, and by the tax dollars and office jobs from the corporate headquarters that will be housed there.

There is some truth to that, but the gain to San Francisco is debatable. Many jobs on and in the new buildings do not directly benefit the city, since most workers in the downtown core commute from outlying suburbs and pay little or no taxes to San Francisco. As for Transamerica's property tax, there was the question of who really benefited from it. The corporation paid San Francisco over a million a year on the $40 million tower, but there was a catch. In 1966, the California voters had passed a ballot initiative that was advertised as a measure to eliminate tax breaks to insurance companies. Instead of doing this, however, the new law provided an even bigger loophole by allowing insurance companies to deduct local property tax paid on home offices from their state tax payments. The largest beneficiary of this tax break was Occidental Life Insurance Company, a division of Transamerica, saving more than $5.9 million over a 10-year period. Since most state money goes back into metropolitan areas for services that help the average citizen—schools, welfare, prisons—it is logical to conclude that when Transamerica used this loophole, it hurt government services to the average city dweller. Meanwhile, according to one estimate, the city is spending the $1 million Transamerica pays—and more—in services required by the huge building. The fortnightly *Bay Guardian,* a tabloid-sized muckraking paper, calculated the amount of tax paid by the highrises against what they get in city services—police, fire protection, engineering and administration, streets, sanitation, and transit. According to its figures, the city is paying $11 in services to highrises for every $10 it gets from them in property tax and other revenues.

On his part, Alioto has vigorously encouraged the construction of highrises, supporting the zoning changes needed for their construction. He joined the business community and labor unions in successfully opposing the ballot measure that would have limited new buildings' height. He backed a proposal by U.S. Steel—later killed by strong public opposition—to build a 550-foot-tall office building and commercial structure on public land at the waterfront.

The mayor likes buildings like the Transamerica Tower, and defends them as providing both jobs and beauty. "If we can get enough jobs for our people, that's the best guarantee against criminal activity," he said in response to startled public reaction to the finished tower. "If we get jobs for our people, we won't have to worry about federally subsidized housing. Employment is the most important thing we are addressing ourselves to. This is why we have taken the view, that within the framework of protecting the environmental qualities that are so important to all of us, that cities simply must progress, they cannot stand still. If they stand still, they tend to deteriorate. If they stand still they don't get the job opportunities that are so important.

"There are 6,000 permanent office jobs in the Transamerica building," he said. "This is better than some of those great big automobile factories we talk about where there might be 2,000 people in jobs. . . . We think it is a very beautiful building, with its redwood grove that is about to be placed alongside it. So there's an example of how you can actually combine jobs, aesthetic beauty and the sense of moving forward while you preserve." But Alioto was talking about preserving the city's prosperous economic climate, not the uniqueness of San Francisco and the blocks of small businesses torn out to make way for the new, huge buildings.

The outlines of future political debate were contained in Alioto's statement. With environmentalists demanding policies that limit growth, it would strengthen the coalition made up of politicians like Alioto, union-backed men who advocate policies that create jobs, and the businessmen who need growth as badly as their workers do. In the 1967 and 1971 municipal elections, Alioto's philosophy brought him good financial support to fight his opponents. As he planned for the 1974 election for governor, the mayor wondered about doing the same thing on a statewide basis.

What About the Neighborhoods?

Away from the central business district, Alioto's policies mean that neighborhoods once occupied by the poor are being torn down and replaced with costly apartments and condominiums. Even the middle class cannot afford to live in them.

But supporters of the mayor argue that there is much he has done for people other than the business-labor combine downtown. The prime example they use is the black ghetto of Hunter's Point and the Western Addition. These neighborhoods are undergoing a $100 million urban redevelopment, replacing World War II housing projects—some pronounced unlivable as long ago as 1948—with handsome low-cost housing for several thousand families. The project was the result of city and federal concern after riots in 1966 revealed the residents' despair and anger.

Early in 1973, when the federal government said it would cut off funds to finish the project, Alioto flew to Washington to fight for it. He won. The building was resumed, much to Alioto's credit in the black community. The project was a good one, with community support and participation in the planning. It had taken considerable city effort to get federal redevelopment funds for it.

But, as Donald Canter, San Francisco *Examiner* urban affairs writer, pointed out, the city wasn't going to spend a dime on it. The federal government required local government to pay a third of the cost, but the law allowed San Francisco to deduct the cost of any public improvements in the renewal area from their share. Canter wrote, "To make sure that the first Western Addition renewal area wouldn't cost the city a penny in cash, it was literally wrapped both physically and financially around the Geary Expressway project." The expressway was planned long before the ghetto riots. "Together with a few other odds and ends, San Francisco was able to amass $9.5 million in credits for the Western Addition project, $3.5 million more than it needed to pay for its one-third share of the overall redevelopment costs." The surplus was allowed by the federal government to be used as a credit toward other redevelopment projects. In other words, the number one showcase project for the poor is one that isn't coming out of the city's treasury. There is serious question whether the project would be pursued if San Francisco had to pay for it.

But the city is not shy about spending tax money on enormous redevelopment projects that benefit downtown. Plans for a more recent civic project show a dogged adherence to the old formula of investing tax money for business profit. This kind of spending is justified as benefiting the city's economy. The Yerba Buena Center is a $385 million urban renewal project supported by Alioto and the supervisors. The plans were unveiled in 1969 by the new mayor and other officials at a luncheon of the San Francisco Convention and Visitors Bureau, a semiofficial group of downtown business and hotel owners. The center will include a convention center, a 330,000-square-foot exhibition hall and a sports arena for 14,000 spectators. Downtown business leaders say they must have it for San Francisco's economic well-being. This ignores the fact that a number of civic facilities already exist for the same purpose, including Brooks Hall, an enormous undergound exposition facility at the civic center, as well as the civic auditorium, which has been modernized at taxpayer expense.

Construction of the Yerba Buena Center has not begun. It was stalled in the courts by suits brought by the San Francisco Legal Assistance Foundation on behalf of the residents who will be displaced by it. The center is going into a poor neighborhood south of Market Street, where there are 43 small hotels, an important source of low-cost housing for the poor.

Housing is a critical issue in San Francisco. Low-cost apartments, renting for $125 a month or less, do not exist in the city. Figures show that as the seventies began, rental vacancies in the city had dropped to 2.4 percent, a rate that indicates an acute shortage.

Yerba Buena Center had proposed, in the beginning, to build a

276-unit low-rent apartment building. It was a mere token for the 3,500 poor people, most of them elderly, who would be displaced. Later, a portion of the law suit was dropped when government funds were found for more low-cost housing. But Sidney Wolinsky, an official of the San Francisco Neighborhood Legal Assistance Foundation, continued the battle in the courts on behalf of the San Francisco taxpayers, who hadn't been asked if they wanted the project. He said the financing was unconstitutional. It had been approved by the supervisors and the mayor, but had not been put to a vote of the people. He believed that the center would be a drain on tax money.

"No major sports or convention center in the United States makes money without a public subsidy," Wolinsky said. "The real beneficiaries of this enormously expensive civic monument are some hotels and a handful of other special interests." Meanwhile, in ten urban renewal projects undertaken by San Francisco in recent years, low-cost housing for the poor was only a tiny portion of the plans. Out of 14,000 homes, condominiums, and apartments added or planned in these projects, less than half were considered low-cost housing. Less than 700 were public housing for the very poor.

In Alioto's San Francisco, just as in Mayor Daley's Chicago, it was a matter of priorities. Even a casual examination of civic policies shows that the campaign contributor gets big returns for his investment. But for the average taxpayer, it is a sadly different story. The San Francisco he has chosen to live in is being actively neglected by policies he has no voice in choosing. And it is his money that is paying for much of the destruction.

A DOWNTOWN UNLOVED BY SPECIAL INTERESTS

If there are any lingering doubts that special interests shape a city—and spur downtown development—we have only to look at Washington, D.C. After touring the cities, we were struck by the fact that the nation's capital is the one big city where downtown is near death. Its decay shows what happens when there are no special interests to develop a vital metropolitan center. More important, it shows that their influence—when held in balance with other voices in the community—is not all bad.

Washington has no powerful business structure. It is not a great trading or commercial center. National companies do not make their headquarters there. It is not like Chicago, San Francisco, or other cities which grew up as centers for transportation or trade or as market places for a vast agricultural hinterland. There is only one industry in Washington, and that is the federal government. Without that, nobody would have started that city on the unhealthy swamps of the Potomac. There are no fat cats to fill city officials' campaign treasuries. The powerful men in Washington spend their time trying to influence the President and Congress.

Even if there were a business community interested in influencing local government, there would be no local government for it to influence. Washington is a colony, governed by senators and representatives who do not live there. The city has a mayor, Walter Washington, but he is appointed by the federal government. He is merely a colonial governor, administering the policies of the rulers, and he will continue to do so until Congress grants the district home rule—the power to elect officials to govern itself.

At present, the district is still ruled by a 1910 ordinance limiting buildings to a height of 130 feet. The law was enacted to encourage the construction of fireproof buildings, and the idea behind it is no longer technically valid. However, a height limit makes some sense on other grounds. A seventy-five-story building next to the White House would dwarf it and destroy its historic dignity. But the law has had a profoundly adverse effect on downtown Washington. The main shopping center, several miles from the federal buildings, could benefit from new commercial buildings, with restaurants, shops and theaters. Instead, downtown Washington is a depressing collection of old department stores, small discount shops, and partially abandoned loft buildings. It is still the downtown of the turn of the century, left to decay. It is a dull, unpleasant place, threatening at night because of street crime. The Metro rapid transit system being built is the only hope of saving it.

In most cities, pressure from business and labor would have forced city government to repeal the outmoded height limit. But in Washington that couldn't happen. It is a convincing argument that there is some value in the business-labor-bureaucrat coalition that has run Chicago, San Francisco and the other big cities.

But the question is how much of a voice should these special interests have? Their role shouldn't be a secret one that disregards the quality of life for a city's residents. A special interest should be one voice among many, and its requests of city government should be open to public debate. Then a powerful influence can assume its true rule—as a legitimate part of the debate, willing to openly advocate its views—and take the responsibility, criticism and risk of defeat that goes along with such advocacy.

3

How It Works

in the Suburbs

We have seen how urban government works. The mayor and the legislators hand out favors to special interests, at great cost to the average citizen in tax money and the quality of life in the city.

As a result, those people who could escape have moved to the suburbs. But because of the way suburban government works, things are no better there. The suburbanite is faced with many of the same problems he thought he had left behind in the city. Often his difficulties are intensified by his disappointment and frustration at the destruction of his dream. In addition, because of the way suburbs are governed, he is unable to understand the cause of the destruction or know who is to blame for it.

Los Angeles County has the ultimate suburbs—sprawling, ugly, badly planned, built without regard for those elements essential to life in a residential community. On the county's eastern perimeter, the San Gabriel Valley illustrates what's happened to suburbs around the country. The homes, factories and shopping complexes in this area are relatively new; most built after 1950. Yet it is one of the most blighted sections of the Los Angeles basin.

·Toward the end of the flight from the East to Los Angeles, the traveler looks down on the desert, barren, uninhabited and beautiful. Then the view dims. On some days, brown or yellow smog covers the ground, and the visitor sees nothing until the plane approaches Los Angeles International Airport. But there are days when the view is clearer. Then the historic route of the pioneers, the stage coaches and the railroads can be seen—through the desert to the hills, over a pass and into the long San Gabriel Valley.

This is the traveler's first view of Los Angeles County, and it seems to confirm everything bad he has ever heard—that the Los Angeles area consists of thrown-together subdivisions, bad air, and crowded freeways. On the ground, in the San Gabriel Valley, the view is worse. Along the edge of the San Bernardino Freeway, some of the inexpensive tract homes expose their backyards to the passerby, providing an unedited glimpse of suburban life—small backyards, aluminum patio covers, sliding glass doors, clotheslines and children's tricycles. It is difficult to understand why people would endure living here, continually inundated by the noise and fumes of the busy freeway.

Off ramps bring cars onto local roads, and the scene is just as discouraging. Streets are lined with taco stands, bars, auto sales lots and other businesses, all bidding for attention with neon advertising and big, twirling signs. In other areas, there are gravel pits or factories. Occasionally, there is a new regional shopping center, gigantic alongside the small tract homes. Instead of trees, grass and shrubs, the landscaping consists of acres of blacktop parking lots.

All development in the valley went on as if land and air were something that could be wasted. It is an inhospitable, inhuman, formless place—without character, identity or beauty.

THE RUIN OF THE DREAM

The San Gabriel Valley offers a sad lesson to suburbs across the nation that still have something left worth saving—and to all those Americans who have fled the city in hope of a more tranquil life. Families built pleasant homes in areas set aside for residences, then found the rules had been changed. Like invading armies, freeway builders ripped up neighborhoods. Residential tranquility was destroyed when 300-unit apartment complexes sprang up—their tenants creating traffic jams, crowding schools, and overworking sheriff's deputies when Saturday night activities got out of hand.

Residents saw their surroundings deteriorate, but they did not know why. They may know how the United States entered the Vietnam war, because volumes have been written about it. But little is written about the decision making of the local bodies of government that shape day-to-day living.

Because such matters are so poorly covered by newspapers, radio and television, people assume the destruction of their neighborhood is an isolated case. It is not. Across America the forms of suburban government may differ—from village boards with control over a small amount of land, to county supervisors or commissioners with broad power over great amounts of undeveloped acreage. Despite what external form suburban government takes, residents are victimized by the same special interest domination of the local level of government. The stories told by California suburbanites sound like the ones told by people living in Fairfax County, Virginia, a suburb of Washington, D.C.; in the suburban towns outside Chicago; or in the rural outreaches of Oklahoma' Wagoner County:

Traditionally, county supervisors in Fairfax, Virginia, had indiscriminately allowed anything influential developers wanted. Even when reformers were elected to the supervisors board, they found it almost impossible to reverse past decisions that were ruining suburban neighborhoods. Concluded one new supervisor, "We're rapidly reaching a point when people will start leaving the area for homes farther out."

In the Chicago suburb of Hoffman Estates, big new apartment complexes overlook streets of twenty-year-old single-family homes. Reform officials promising to end domination by developers were defeated by the courts and by the indifference of neighboring village officials. Said one longtime resident, "We came out here because we were isolationists. Now look at it. It's like the city."

In Wagoner County, Oklahoma, women with no political experience took action against unresponsive county commissioners. Their investigations triggered the indictment of three powerful county officials. Said one of the activists, "We've tried to play nice, but we've learned how to play dirty. We've had some good instructors. . . . A lot of people probably don't think the county government is as important as the state and federal, but if you can't get it right at the local level, there's no hope for the rest of it."

THE POLITICS OF LAND DEVELOPMENT

Business' desire to keep men who favor them in power is not surprising. The way the suburban system works is summed up in gold letters engraved on one wall of the hall where the Los Angeles County Supervisors sit during their meetings. It reads, "THIS COUNTY IS FOUNDED ON FREE ENTERPRISE. CHERISH AND PRESERVE IT." In areas with large amounts of undeveloped land—such as suburbia—free enterprise means the sale and development of land. County officials have traditionally encouraged and subsidized this business, even though it is often destructive to the suburbanite's way of life.

Nowhere in the nation has land and wealth been so intertwined as in Southern California. "Buy land in Los Angeles and wear diamonds," was an advertising slogan in the 1880s. The land-owning Southern Pacific Railroad dropped its cross-country fare to $1 during that time, to lure immigrants westward. After World War II, ex-war workers and veterans used their FHA and GI loans to buy houses in the subdivisions that gave the Los Angeles area its present look.

If land is the key to wealth in suburbia, business must control the men who regulate the use of land—the elected officials who run suburban government.

The official who ruled the east side of the Los Angeles basin during most of its growth was County Supervisor Frank Bonelli. He was helped lavishly throughout his career by campaign contributions from land developers who needed his cooperation. The arithmetic of his career illustrates the workings of this legitimate method of influencing the law. His large campaign chest was never really needed because he never had a serious challenger. But without money to finance a big campaign—should it have become necessary—he would have become vulnerable. Challengers would have arisen, and he might have lost his position of power. The money guaranteed his staying in office. Any serious contender for his job would have had to get hundreds of thousands of dollars from the only available source—big business—and Bonelli had a monopoly on its support.

Bonelli's big contributors were the land developers, and in his votes on the board of supervisors, he favored them. He argued that he did it because development was good for the county. Any improved land, he said, was assessed at a higher rate and brought in more property tax dollars to the county. That was, however, a dangerous oversimplification. While land with homes does bring in more property tax than vacant land, it requires the most costly form of government services. And there is a difference between residential development near needed services and suburbs that spring up in the middle of nowhere where new schools, sewers, water, fire and police protection will have to be set up. Some communities have begun to discourage farflung suburban developments because of the high cost of bringing services out to them.

The View from the Top

Whatever the reason for his votes, land developers had a friend in Bonelli. Things have not changed much since his death, and a look at the way the supervisors run their domain makes it easy to see how—in the shadows of local government—control of a single official is often all a businessman needs. That is particularly true in suburban government, where a supervisor is allowed to be a little dictator for his own district.

The Los Angeles County buildings where the supervisors meet look as though they were designed by Mussolini. The massive structures and huge barren plaza seem ready to receive regiments of marching Fascist youth. But nobody ever marches there, and few visit the place. The county government complex is a monument to unresponsive government, and the County Administration Building is a fit meeting place for public officials trying to hide from their constituents. It is located in downtown Los Angeles, a 45-minute freeway drive for someone living in the farthest reaches of the San Gabriel Valley. If he makes the long trip, he will probably not find a place to park when he arrives. Most of the parking lots in the area have been set aside for county employees. The few nearby public garages are small and high-priced; often they are full.

When he gets inside, the visitor is overwhelmed by the huge, rambling administration building—with its labyrinth of underground tunnels connecting it to other government buildings across the plaza. And the huge, rambling county government set-up is just as confusing. Its budget is $2.8 billion a year, bigger than that of most states. It employs 72,000 people. It is under the absolute control of the five county supervisors. They set the property tax rate and preside over the welfare system. They are in charge of the county hospitals and other health services, the jails, the courts and the elections. They direct a large force of sheriff's deputies and firemen.

Are you unhappy about the county's regulation of smog? There is the air pollution control board to complain to—but its members are the five supervisors. Are you unhappy about the planning board allowing an apartment complex on your quiet residential street? You can complain to the zoning board; it consists of members of the planning board who are appointed by the supervisors. If you are not satisfied, you can go to the final appeals board, which happens to be the supervisors. Unhappy with your property tax assessment? The supervisors are the final appeals board for that, too.

Theoretically, each supervisor's power is limited since it takes a majority of three of the supervisors to approve a decision. But under a policy of "You scratch my back and I'll scratch yours," each supervisor's proposals for his own district are generally approved by his colleagues. All services for unincorporated areas—land, such as suburbs, where residents have not gone through the formalities of forming a city with its own governing council—are provided by the county, or by special districts subscribing to county services. Each individual supervisor's power in providing services is absolute because of his colleagues' willingness to go along with him.

One man decides on street signs, speed limits, oil wells, roads, location of sewers, housing and business developments. So when a land developer wanted to build a subdivision in the San Gabriel Valley, he needed the cooperation of Frank Bonelli, who would have to bring county roads, sewers, water, and power to serve the new homes. Bonelli also was in charge of enforcing zoning regulations that would determine the size, population and quality of life in the subdivision.

Like most suburban governments, there is no executive branch in Los Angeles County government, no mayor to balance the power of the supervisors, no voice to speak for the good of the area as a whole. The system of checks and balances present in most levels of American government—ineffective as it sometimes is—is strangely absent here, and the result can be disastrous for people living in the suburbs.

Political Show Biz

To get a feeling of how the suburbs are ruled, we sat in on a number of supervisors' hearings—Tuesdays and Thursdays at 9 a.m. At a typical meeting, the supervisors—in ten minutes' time—passed 120 items of business without discussion, holding over only four or five for fuller consideration later. The matters were read to the public by a clerk, not by name but by number. Provided with a printed agenda given out to the public, we found it impossible to read quickly enough to understand each item as the supervisors moved from one page of the agenda to the next.

During this ten minutes, close to $600,000 of the taxpayers' money was spent. Libraries and new roads were approved, as were a courthouse addition, a fence for a swimming pool, and improvements to existing roads. Extra appropriations were approved for unexpectedly high costs for a sheriff's station and jail. An architect was given $3,000 for preliminary plans of a $600,000 park. Four unsafe buildings were ordered torn down. An air show was approved, and several cash awards were given for unspecified deeds. One item was approval of an unnamed amount of money for an indefinite number of projects. Finally, visiting dignitaries were awarded expensive hand-lettered scrolls.

Often the agenda is not followed at the meetings, and a major frustration of citizen protesters comes in waiting all day to testify on an item that never comes up. On this day, business was pushed aside. The five supervisors leaned back in their big chairs and began clowning. It was Girls' Leadership Day in county government, and over a hundred young women from Los Angeles County high schools were there to become honorary county officials for a day. Their duties were to watch, keep quiet and be decorative. An hour was devoted to introducing each of the girls, their school offices and extracurricular activities. They, too, received scrolls. A county photographer rushed about, snapping pictures of each girl with the supervisor of her district.

The supervisors' hearing room holds nearly a thousand, but— aside from the high-school girls—there were fewer than 50 spectators at this meeting, most of them county bureaucrats somehow involved in the day's business. In the relative solitude of this audience, matters of great importance to homeowners had been decided. But to the community, the supervisors liked to practice the politics of powerlessness. On many decisions, they listened to reports submitted by the county administrative officer, and then followed his recommendations, as if he were a man of power. But he has none. The supervisors appointed him; he knows what they want, and he follows their wishes.

On issues requiring a departure from past policies, such as improving transportation or controlling smog, the supervisors often refrain from action, declaring that the state or the city or the federal government has the real power to act. Or each supervisor makes a speech, proposing a plan drastically different from what the others suggest. Finally, they delay a decision until more studies are made. Nothing is decided; each supervisor is on record as proposing a new—and often impractical—solution to the problem. If a taxpayer complains later, each supervisor can blame the others for not following his foolproof solution.

What lesson can the American homeowner draw from the way

these men run Los Angeles County? It was in this haphazard, seemingly incompetent manner that the supervisors presided over the destruction of the San Gabriel Valley. Behind the public spectacle of government meetings, suburban supervisors and the men who support them run things the way they want—regardless of the consequences for the people government is supposed to serve.

THE BONELLI STORY

The late supervisor Frank Bonelli was an official who shaped land so business could profit. Typical of the board he served on, he was no worse than officials everywhere who rule suburban communities.

It took less than twenty years to destroy the San Gabriel Valley—and it did not have to happen. The valley was ruined because its residents were confused by the secrecy and technical mumbo jumbo in which local government envelops itself. Voters unknowingly allowed land developers, industrialists and other businessmen to control the decisions of the area's most powerful official.

If a producer were looking for someone to play the part of a local politician, he wouldn't have gone wrong choosing Frank Bonelli. He resembled Adolph Menjou, the actor, and his manner was reminiscent of those fast-talking characters Menjou used to play in the films. In the words of that era, he was a "snappy" or "sharp" dresser, and his clothes had a thirties or forties look about them—as Menjou's did. Like the other four supervisors, Bonelli sat in the supervisors' meeting room in kingly style, looking down on unfortunate petitioners from an impressively high-backed leather chair.

When a citizen protested too much, Bonelli replied in a manner designed to convince the person never to make that mistake again. Typical was his treatment of a Mexican-American protesting welfare regulations at one supervisors' meeting. "Aw, go sit down and shut your mouth," Bonelli told Bufino Lopez. "Who the hell do you think you are?" Lopez replied he was "a taxpayer, that's who." Doubtful that a Chicano could be much of a property owner, Bonelli commented sarcastically, "Yeah, I'll bet you are—a big one, too."

Bonelli followed the growth-minded tradition of the supervisor who came before him, Herbert Legg. During Legg's uneven public career, he was indicted on charges of accepting a $10,000 bribe in a garbage franchise scandal during the fifties. Legg was dramatically cleared by the deathbed affadavit of his campaign treasurer, who said it was he and not Legg who accepted the bribe. The jury chose to believe the affidavit rather than the man who paid the bribe and who testified that Legg himself had thanked him personally for the "package" in the corridor of the county administration building.

Although acquitted, Legg's public career soon ended. When he died, he was succeeded by Bonelli, who owned an auto supply store and who had been mayor of the small city of Huntington Park and a state assemblyman.

Bonelli appeared to be a man of the highest moral character, a devout Catholic who, when an assemblyman, introduced a bill making it illegal to sell or give crime comic books to minors. During the McCarthy era, he was frightened by the rise of communism, which he saw as a threat "not in the guise of one overwhelming disaster, but piecemeal over a period of time, following a declared schedule of the foes of liberty." He opposed the legalization of the old frontier game of draw poker. As a supervisor, he went on record favoring economy in government. Running for reelection, he called for an end to increased government spending, pay raises and new county jobs. He denounced the welfare system for condoning "love-ins and fostering illegitimate births."

During Bonelli's long career in public life, there was never any evidence of wrongdoing. In fact, so respected was he that only death could remove him from office. But when he died, the public and Bonelli's contributors learned a little more about him. The owner of a modest business, whose public salary had never been more than $35,000 a year, he left an estate of more than $1 million.

In addition, part of his family's inheritance was the sum of

$118,405.25. It was his political slush fund—money given him at fund-raisers for his political campaigns, although he had always been virtually unopposed. In his will, Bonelli described the money as "gifts to me" and passed them on to his wife and two daughters. His personal fortune and how he got it are unimportant. His real legacy was the condition in which he left the San Gabriel Valley.

As He Lay Dying

Bonelli's dying extended over several months—and during that time a battle was waged over his job and its power. Although most of the people in his district had no idea of his duties or their effect on the community, his illness was a significant event to the political and business communities. The job was so important that ambitious state-level politicians were fighting over it. And a glimpse of the struggle that went on for Bonelli's job provides a fascinating look at how power is kept within the same select group.

When it became apparent to insiders that he was ill, the business leaders of his district began to worry—not over his health, but over their future. They needed a supervisor in office who was friendly to business and who would continue to aid the construction boom in the district with all the tools at the county's disposal—public works, such as parks, sewers, and streets, and crime and fire protection. Businessmen met quietly over lunch at the California Country Club—a contributor to Bonelli's campaigns—to discuss his ill health and figure out what they could do to ensure a friendly successor.

The messy affair even thrust Governor Ronald Reagan into the mud of local politics, for he was expected to appoint a successor if Bonelli died in the middle of the term. Four months before Bonelli's death, several state assemblymen went to the governor asking for the job. Two of these petitioners had been such close friends in the past that they had shared an apartment. But the race for the office was so bitter that their friendship ended.

Everyone knew Bonelli was dying, except for the public. They were assured by Bonelli's staff that he was healthy enough, only suffering from a "blood anemia condition," and that he was actively running county affairs from his bed at home. Staff members withheld the truth because they were worried about their future, hoping for a successor who would keep them on the job.

Finally Bonelli died—of long-term cancer, as it turned out. Governor Reagan appointed one of the assemblymen to succeed him, Pete Schabarum, and the business-dominated dynasty that began with Herbert Legg was preserved. Schabarum was a humorless, abrupt-mannered man in his early forties. He had been a conservative legislator with a reputation for honesty and independence. But when he stepped into Bonelli's job, he continued the supervisor's practice of cooperation with powerful interests. He kept Bonelli's staff, including the man who had raised political funds for both Bonelli and Legg. And the same big land developers who had supported Bonelli, financed Schabarum's campaign when he ran for the office in the regular election, a few months later.

What about the voters in the San Gabriel Valley? Why did they continue to reelect Bonelli when under his reign they saw the lovely valley community deteriorate? He stayed in office because most people, only dimly aware of the county supervisor, had little idea of his power. And even those who were more sophisticated were confused by the smokescreen of helplessness, the maze of agencies and commissions through which Bonelli worked and was able to deny responsibility for his decisions.

The Diamond Bar Story

To trace how special interests worked through Bonelli—and how his power shaped the suburbs—we looked at one large development in his district, Diamond Bar. It is miles southeast of the county administration complex, out the San Bernardino and then the Pomona freeways. The community began its growth during Supervisor Bonelli's reign. Since it was not a city, it was completely under his control.

Diamond Bar's developer was the huge Transamerica Corporation, builder of San Francisco's Transamerica Tower. The corporation's executives gave to Bonelli's political campaigns. Bonelli aided the project with a county golf course and whatever else the county could provide. Furthermore, when profits were not as great as the developers had expected, county planners—under Bonelli's direction—lifted zoning restraints on builders. They did this to redeem the developer's profit, despite the protests of the people who lived there and had elected Bonelli. These zoning changes substantially lowered the quality of life in Diamond Bar.

The area has its roots deep in California history. In 1840, the land was given to José de la Luz Linares by the Mexican governor of California, Juan Alvarado. It was named Rancho Los Nogales, after the wild walnut trees that grew there. For years cattle and sheep roamed the hills. By the late nineteenth century, drought had wrecked the old Spanish ranchos, and the owners broke up Rancho Los Nogales, selling it as farmland to the midwesterners and New Englanders immigrating to California. In 1918, Frederick Lewis, a rich world traveler, bought much of the land, named it Diamond Bar, and built a U-shaped mansion that cost him $75,000. Movie stars played there during prohibition. In 1943, William Bartholomae bought the ranch, and raised cattle on it until he sold it in 1956 to the Transamerica Corporation for $10 million. Bartholomae had bought it for $850,000.

To those speeding by on the freeway, Diamond Bar looks like the beginning of the carefully planned model community that Transamerica had promised. "Diamond Bar is Freeway Country" is what the sign says, and it is. The San Bernardino and Pomona freeways have brought the land within driving distance of jobs, but allowed those who live here to enjoy the country. California ranch-style homes are scattered up hills and through canyons, well away from the freeways. They have three or four bedrooms, two or three bathrooms, and family rooms. Optional extras include wet bars and billiard rooms. Houses are low priced at $21,000 to $45,000.

But things are not as pleasant as they seem. Residents had been promised the largest completely masterplanned community in the Los Angeles Basin. They had bought homes expecting a well-devised layout of streets, schools, parks and shops. But once they moved in, they found the masterplan was changed. Homeowners' well-being was sacrificed for the sake of the developer's profits.

The Zoning Game

Before the developer acquired the property in 1956, there was no zoning plan for residential and commercial use of the land. Zoning laws determine what can and what cannot be built in a neighborhood. Factories, gas stations and dumps, for example, make poor neighbors in an area that is all homes. Zoning laws also determine how many residences or buildings can be built on the land, and, ultimately, how many people can live in an area.

In the case of Diamond Bar, the developer itself drew up the original community plan, mainly of single-family residences, with a few apartment houses along the limited commercial areas and the golf course. The county accepted this as the zoning scheme for Diamond Bar. It was customary at this time for local government to let large developers do the zoning themselves, although an individual builder would not be given this leeway.

But plans were changed when the population boom Transamerica had anticipated didn't materialize. By the late sixties, the corporation decided not to develop the whole planned community according to the original design. Diamond Bar is on rolling hills, with some very steep land. It is costly to build on such terrain, and the developers found that people were unwilling to pay high prices for homes in the San Gabriel Valley. So, at Transamerica's request, zoning was changed to allow the flat portions of the land to be developed at great concentration.

Through the Diamond Bar zoning changes, it is easy to see how the planning process works to benefit developers who, in return, enrich officials' campaign coffers. The evidence is buried deep in county archives, and some of it has been destroyed. Most levels of government keep campaign records indefinitely. But Los Angeles County keeps them only for four years after the term of office involved has expired. That means that the oldest of Bonelli's campaign records on file is from his 1966 campaign, although he served as supervisor from 1958. The lists show that the general manager of the Transamerica subsidiary developing Diamond Bar was a campaign contributor. No amounts are listed on this record. Campaign laws were looser then, and Bonelli's lists are grossly incomplete. He had many anonymous contributors. Also, each year he had a fund-raising dinner. But he reported only contributions that came in on election years. For example, in 1966, after an easy reelection campaign, his fund was left with a $24,131.55 balance. Four years later, with no list of where it came from, the fund had grown to $95,000. There is no record of where he got the extra $70,000, but it is reasonable to presume that Transamerica gave him some of it, along with his usual list of supporters—the land developers, contractors and real estate firms in his district. Later, Bonelli's successor—who inherited many of the same supporters—was to receive help from the Transamerica Development Company and another Transamerica subsidiary, the Diamond Bar Development Corporation, each giving him $1,000.

Such contributions are part of politics. Although they are open to criticism, there is almost no other way for candidates to get money for election campaigns. It is part of the system, and here is where the new corruption of local government is found. The campaign contribution is now paid for a favorable ruling on land use by a businessman, instead of the old practice of giving a cash bribe for a streetcar franchise or for free rein to operate the numbers in the slums.

Diamond Bar's zoning exceptions illustrate what business can buy from local government—in a perfectly legitimate way. They also show what officials can do without being held accountable to the public.

All the zoning changes for Diamond Bar were approved by the Regional Planning Commission. But this agency was merely another arm of the supervisors. Each supervisor appointed the commissioner for his district. The planning commissioner made the planning decisions for that district—but he had no real power. The board of supervisors had to approve each decision of the planning commission, and it was the supervisor of each district who had the final decision on this matter, just as he had on everything else in his own district.

The Regional Planning Commission holds public meetings and listens to testimony of citizens and experts, but this isn't really democracy at work. Meetings are held in central Los Angeles, far from the suburban areas where the commission has jurisdiction. They are held during normal working hours, making it virtually impossible for citizens to attend. The board actually operates on the same principle as the supervisors, with each commissioner having total responsibility for preliminary approval of rulings in his district; the others consistently approve his requests. In public, their votes are usually unanimous, said one planning expert, "so you can't tell what's going on. They've got a backroom where they talk stuff over."

Bonelli's appointee to the Regional Planning Commission was Owen Lewis, who was a mortgage investment broker in the San Gabriel Valley. In other words, he made decisions involving the control of real estate development in the area where his business depended on that development. It was a conflict of interest, but not illegal because such appointments were not forbidden by law. The law has since been somewhat tightened in California. But in most suburbs around the country, conflicts of interest on local government commissions are the rule rather than the exception.

Lewis also owned land in the same area, not too far from Diamond Bar. The planning commission hires and can fire planning staff, and on several occasions Lewis told staff members how he wanted his land zoned. They obeyed him, and he was able to build four times as many units on his land as was normally permitted. Once, when a newspaper reported his interference, Lewis went angrily down to the county planning office to make sure his zoning exception hadn't been taken away.

The Planned Community's Massive Plan Change

Bonelli appointed Lewis to the commission just as Diamond Bar was getting underway. What Lewis allowed—under Bonelli's direction—were zoning exceptions permitting Transamerica to renege on its original promises to homeowners. The corporation came to the county planning commission in 1968, disappointed in the public's reception of Diamond Bar. Homes were not selling. It asked for a large section of the planned community to be rezoned. Instead of single family homes, it wanted to put in highrise apartments, forty units to the acre, and a 340-acre commercial development, as well as other changes. By rezoning the land the developer knew it would be easier to find buyers.

The hearing was held in the planning hearing room, in the downtown county complex. Homeowners learned about the hearing only a few days in advance. Most of them heard about it through neighborhood gossip, since only those residents who lived within 500 feet of the zoning changes had been formally notified. A notice did appear in a small local paper, but it was of a highly technical nature, appearing in the fine print of the want ad section.

Some Diamond Bar residents wrote to the commission asking for the meeting to be held during an evening—or in the neighborhood affected, but their letters were ignored. They remain unanswered in an obscure zoning file under the name San Jose District 21, which has no relationship to anything in Diamond Bar. Those wanting information about the area's zoning must know the name of the file, as well as in which office to find it. It took us several trips downtown to locate the information.

Most homeowners who wanted to protest had to do it in letter form. Only six people were able to appear in person and oppose the plan at the meeting. As one unhappy homeowner wrote, the hearing time made it impossible for most to attend. It was on a Tuesday at 9 a.m., and it was the first day of school. That eliminated mothers of school children, as well as those who were employed during normal working hours. There was no public transportation to the county building from Diamond Bar, nor was there adequate parking for those who might have wanted to drive.

One letter protested another of Transamerica's requests—to rezone an area that had been set aside for Diamond Bar High School into highrise apartments. The homeowner wrote: "We understand rezoning abolishes a much needed school site and replaces it with multiple family, high density dwellings, thus increasing the need for schools and eliminating available land."

The developer's representative at the meeting said that a change in the freeway route had made the site undesirable for a school. But the school superintendent wrote to deny this and oppose the rezoning. He pointed out that the area had been "masterplanned and zoned for compatibility of residences, schools and commercial properties. Nothing has changed." The district was already building a junior high school across the street from the disputed rezoning. If the zoning change was granted, the school official said, it would make the present junior high school incompatible with the neighborhood. His protests were ignored, and the zoning change was made. This meant there would be no high school, and the junior high would be on what would eventually become one of the busiest intersections in the area.

Another homeowner attended the meeting and went home to write Planning Commissioner Lewis a letter meekly complimenting him "on the thorough way your committee handled the meeting." She went on to lament that her neighbors had not had a chance to attend the little-publicized meeting. And she talked about the kind of community she had expected to live in: "If I may take you back seven years, surrounding us were beautiful hills teeming with delightful wild life. It was a quiet and peaceful place, well worth the extra expense and extra travel hours to and from work. During this seven years, the hills have been hacked away. We were all shocked to discover the freeway is directed through some of the backyards and certainly not between the hills." She said she knew they would have to accept the freeway, but "we wonder why we must accept the other ugliness and noise the Transamerica Corporation wishes to impose upon us because they can make more money from that property with rezoning."

Another owner wrote of her horror at learning the changes in store for her street. "When we purchased our property six and a half years ago ... Capital-Transamerica showed us the existing planned city for 75,000 population. Nothing was mentioned about rezoning, or that we would be involved in an unlimited commercial area." They were promised a corner lot, but now there would be no street next to them. Instead, the zoning change turned the next lot into commercial property. "Now Mr. Wilson of Transamerica just recently told us that in all probability a service station or hamburger stand would be built in this location."

One telegram to Lewis from two families seemed to sum up homeowners' feelings: " 'Diamond Bar, masterplanned community?' An obvious misrepresentation to homeowners who invested and settled in the area. Witness the procession of vague misleading floating series of signs proclaiming the location of future facilities which continually succeed each other. This proposed neighborhood revision is another injustice to present owner residents, jeopardizes invested values and the open country non commercial character with which they were enticed.

"You have an obligation to present owners to maintain residential atmosphere.

"Before you destroy, schedule and publicize an open hearing in the area at the local club house and sample the reception."

Sketchy notes were kept during the hearing. When it ended, nothing was settled, but Transamerica's representative said they would "work with staff," presumably the county planning staff. Approximately ten months later, there was another zoning hearing on the changes. Again, a handful of homeowners showed up to protest. The few lines of handwritten minutes reported their objection—"that they had purchased property under a planned community concept believing they knew what development would be." Their argument still failed to impress Commissioner Lewis. Five months later, most of the zone changes were unanimously granted by the county supervisors, on the unanimous recommendation of the planning commission. A few commercial spots had been denied, but a large highrise apartment area was granted that had not been requested publicly.

The most interesting thing about the Diamond Bar zoning file was the attitude of the homeowners who wrote to protest what was happening. They were all angry at Transamerica for the betrayal. Some of them knew Lewis' name and politely addressed questions to him about the time and location of the hearing. But not one letter mentioned the man who was responsible for the final decision. The setup of county government had hidden the fact that, as supervisor, Bonelli could have prevented what was happening in Diamond Bar. He was aware of the residents' complaints. But he considered Transamerica's rights more important than those of the voters who elected him.

A Golf Course in the Bargain

While Bonelli kept a low profile on zoning, he did take credit for the county's fine recreation facilities in his district. One of his greatest contributions to the Transamerica development was to provide a golf course for the new planned community. When the first Diamond Bar model homes opened, salesmen were able to promise prospective homeowners a feature that no other tract in the area could match—an 18-hole golf course, designed to give the place a country club feeling, but at little cost to buyers. It was being built and would be maintained by the county.

Soon after he took office, in June of 1958, Bonelli proposed that the county, at taxpayers' expense, build the golf course. The Diamond Bar community was only in the planning stage at this point. But the developer had been working for months on planning the project and getting approval from the county. And the construction of the golf course amounted to an outright gift to the developer of an expensive attraction that would help sell homes.

Diamond Bar's course was one of three undertaken by the county that year. Spending money on park land was not a habit of local government. But golf courses are regarded as a special case, since they bring in fees from users. This philosophy ignores the fact that such facilities never bring in enough revenue to pay the cost of running them or to pay back the initial large investment for land, clubhouse and landscaping.

With his colleagues' consent, Bonelli pushed through a proposal for the county to lease 174 acres of hilly land from Transamerica for $36,500 a year. Nothing had been built in the subdivision yet, and there was a protest that the county was paying too much for land that was currently being used as grazing land by a rancher for $350-a-year rent. That objection was brushed aside. Eventually, the supervisors approved plans to pay for an elaborate golf course, a $500,000 clubhouse, complete with banquet rooms, a huge dining room, a lounge and a coffee shop. Within a few years, the county—under the direction of Bonelli—took up the option to buy the land from Transamerica for $700,000. It was no bargain, since it was right on the freeway, and unusable for the kind of housing Diamond Bar was advertising.

A Stab at a Check and Balance

The purchase and building of this expensive facility was approved by the supervisors despite the objections of the county grand jury, a citizens' group entrusted by the law with investigating crime and civic waste. On the very day Bonelli was proposing the Diamond Bar County Golf Course, he had received a letter from the grand jury requesting that the supervisors quit building golf courses at county expense.

The county, said the grand jury, was paying too much for the golf course land. The price was not determined by the actual value, but on what the value would be once the county built the course. That increased the price of the land by several hundred thousand dollars, which is what happened in the Diamond Bar purchase.

But that isn't all that was wrong. The jurors believed construction of more golf courses amounted to subsidizing the recreation of just a few of the county taxpayers, and concluded: "There is great need in the county of Los Angeles for many and large capital expenditures, such as new jails, added quarters for juveniles, nurses quarters, hospital facilities, and many others. It appears to us that the acquisition of additional golf courses in the face of these needs is unrealistic, to say the least, and completely ignores the mounting tax burden." The grand jury asked that the supervisors stop such projects. But Bonelli was not required to follow their advice. He didn't.

Most important, he was free to work the deal without the approval of the taxpayers. The supervisors avoided putting such projects to a vote by borrowing the money from the county employees retirement fund, money supplied by employee contributions and tax dollars. County building projects are usually financed in one of two ways. One is out of current revenues, on a pay-as-you-go basis. The other is for the county to borrow money, but voters must first give the county permission to sell bonds to investors. The purchase of the bonds is, in effect, a loan, and the investors are paid interest—which is attractive because it is tax free.

But the supervisors didn't want to subject the golf course proposal to a public vote. Voters were turning down bond issues for much more necessary projects. So the county used the retirement fund. It didn't require a vote, but it did cost the county more interest than the voter-approved bonds. And it still was the taxpayers' money that eventually paid off the loan and the interest, even though their permission was never asked.

Diamond Bar's zoning and its golf course are just a few examples of a suburban official's tremendous power to shape his district and the lives of the people who live there to the tastes of those who can profit from them. Yet, the public believed the myth of powerlessness that the Los Angeles County Board of Supervisors had cultivated over the years. On television and in the newspapers, citizens had heard the supervisors blaming the state for high welfare costs, the federal government for smog, and everyone for bad transportation. There was little that they admitted they could do about anything.

The developers knew better. They understood the supervisors' absolute control over the regulation of land. They knew the workings of a system that actually let a single man run a district, free of public scrutiny. That power allowed the developers of Diamond Bar to double-cross homeowners. As we will see in our final chapter, pressure by the residents might have forced the county to make developers keep their promises. However, it would have taken busloads of people, marching into the County Administration Building, confronting Supervisor Bonelli with their troubles, using television and newspapers to publicize their protest.

There were homeowner groups, but as a city planner said, "They're still pretty naive; they're not politically sophisticated. They'll get a few busloads out for a single issue meeting, and that's it. They don't stay focused. They assume the elected officeholder is basically a good guy." In Bonelli's case, they were wrong. If they had known the land developers were paying his political bills, they would have had a powerful weapon to use in a campaign against him. That kind of information would expose his power—and make it difficult for him to abuse it. In suburban government, the official prefers to work in secret, out of the glare of public inquiry.

But Diamond Bar residents and the rest of the people in the San Gabriel Valley were inadequate to the job. They had little to say about what was happening, for they did not understand how the system worked.

If there is a lesson in the ruin of the valley, it is that such things do not happen by chance. They come about when special interests and compliant officials are able to hide the real decision-making process of local government from the public.

4

Corporations
Above the Law

The hills outside San Fernando, a suburban city in the valley north of downtown Los Angeles, are dry and dusty. If they look familiar, it is because years ago cowboy movies were filmed there. Ken Maynard, Buck Jones and the rest of the Saturday heroes rode up and down the washes, their progress recorded by cameramen from Republic or Monogram pictures. Now it is suburbia. Simple homes have been built on terraces dug in the hills, and the only noise is from children playing on quiet streets. There are still horses farther back in the hills, but they are the property of the nearby homeowners who have found a place where even a family of modest income can own a horse.

In 1968, the Lockheed Shipbuilding and Construction Company, a subsidiary of the aerospace company, began building a tunnel underneath these hills to carry more water to Southern California. Before it was completed, workers encountered inflammable methane gas. In June of 1971, a small gas explosion occurred in the tunnel and four men were injured. But work continued, and the next day gas exploded again. This time seventeen men were killed.

Five months before the explosion, on February 9, 1971, the area had been hit by an earthquake. The city of San Fernando was badly damaged. A new county hospital collapsed; freeways were destroyed, and people were killed. It was the worst quake in Southern California in almost forty years.

Lockheed knew it was digging in dangerous ground. This is earthquake country, and the area is a geologist's laboratory, cut by four faults in the earth's crust. The earthquake aggravated a problem that geologists had foreseen when the tunnel was begun—"the possibility of encountering some oil and gas in the westernmost portion of the San Fernando Tunnel."

More than two years later, the Lockheed company was found guilty of gross negligence in the deaths of the seventeen men, after the longest municipal court trial in the history of the state of California. Loren Savage, Lockheed's tunnel project manager, was also convicted of gross negligence. Another Lockheed official, Otha G. Ree, the safety engineer, was found guilty of three violations of the state safety code. Concluded the judge, "I can't imagine any other case where so many warnings of impending doom could be so callously and coldly ignored."

The forces that led to this disaster are not unique to the powerful corporation building the tunnel, nor to the quake-prone state where it happened. Similarly preventable industrial tragedies have occurred in West Virginia, Kentucky, New York and other states. It is for this reason that the deaths of the seventeen men are important. This particular accident happened because:

> Getting the job done was more important than the safety of workers; lives were gambled for contract schedules.

> Employers could recklessly disregard their workers' safety because they had little to fear if men died on the job. The state's large corporations had carefully seen to it that state legislators had weakened industrial safety penalties.

> Big companies had so much power over lawmakers and enforcement agencies that they were all but immune to prosecution—even for flagrant violations of industrial safety laws.

In harshest terms, this meant that big companies could afford to occasionally lose workmen's lives in the course of a job. They couldn't be charged with manslaughter. Unlike ordinary citizens, powerful corporations can control the laws that are supposed to control them.

As for a worker in a dangerous job, he has one more strike against him. Too often his union, in its role as his protector, has made deals with management, sacrificing safety provisions for a few benefits. This chapter, and the one that follows, will explain how these things come about, how campaign contributors are able to water down industrial safety laws, how the unions allow them to do it, and how law enforcement officers hesitate to prosecute the corporate offenders in court.

The story of the San Fernando Tunnel disaster is not altogether gloomy. As in Watergate, a courageous judge insisted on justice, and the corporation and its officers were finally punished. Torn between conflicting special interests, state legislators finally wrote a stronger industrial safety law. What interested us was the process through which it happened. For by understanding it, citizens are better able to fight back when confronted by the same sort of outrageous twisting of the law.

A HISTORIC THIRST

The story really begins in the early part of this century with the need to bring water to Southern California. Speed and a sense of urgency have always been a part of Southern California water projects. The area has always been aware that it is far short of the water it needs. "Whoever brings the water brings the people," said William Mulholland, builder of the first of the great aqueducts that bring water from afar. Without these aqueducts, there would be no Disneyland, no great plants to produce rockets to the moon or surfboards. Without water the arid plains of Southern California would not grow. Water is more important than any other resource, and the victims of the San Fernando Tunnel explosion were not the first to die in its behalf.

The first aqueduct was completed in 1913 to carry the water of the Owens River, in the Sierra Nevada mountains, 223 miles over mountains and desert to the city. The technology was crude: picks and shovels, mule-driven wagons and courageous workmen driven on by tough engineers. But it worked, and one day water poured into the San Fernando Valley. Suddenly, the dusty, barren land was worth something. Fortunes were made in the boom that followed.

In the same sort of earthquake fault country that the Lockheed tunnel diggers encountered, Mulholland built a dam and a reservoir for the water agency he headed, the Los Angeles Department of Water and Power. But the walls of the place he had chosen, San Francisquito Canyon, were porous, and as they became soaked with water from the reservoir they swelled and pushed against the sides of the dam. In January 1928, two cracks developed in the dam and were repaired. By March, new leaks appeared, but on March 12, Mulholland and his chief assistant, H. A. Van Norman, inspected the dam, declared it safe and returned to Los Angeles. A few hours later, when almost all of the residents of the area were asleep, the dam burst. The water was 100 feet high when it roared down San Francisquito Canyon and into the channel of the Santa Clara River, heading toward the Pacific Ocean. It swept through the little communities of Piru, Fillmore and Santa Paula, past Saticoy and Montalvo, and finally to the sea. The flood killed 385 people, wrecked 12,240 homes and ruined 7,900 acres of farmland. Mulholland was forced into retirement. "I envy the dead," he said.

But more water was needed for the subdivisions and factories that the business leaders of Southern California wanted. In the 1930s, they formed the Metropolitan Water District (MWD) of Southern California to bring water from the Colorado River to Los Angeles, San Diego, Ventura and Orange counties and parts of two other counties, San Bernardino and Riverside. Five pumping plants, each with nine pumps powerful enough to push 91,500 gallons of water a minute, forced the water across the Mojave Desert and over the mountains from Parker Dam on the Colorado. Pasadena, the Rose Bowl city and a member of the Metropolitan Water District, received the first water on June 17, 1941, just before a spell of dry years.

That the water was of an inferior quality—laden with minerals, tepid—did not matter. It was precious. So precious that the MWD was given extraordinary power to direct the distribution of the water, to manage its purification, and to build new facilities. Water delivery was portrayed as a technical matter, and the engineers who were in charge of it were given full authority.

The Water Agency and How It Grew

The fact that the MWD was a political body, run by a board of directors presumably answerable to the public, was forgotten. The board of directors was committed to a policy of growth, reflecting the Southern California businessman's belief in achieving wealth through rising real estate values. The engineers who actually ran the water system were committed to growth of the system. It was their system; the bigger it got, the better their jobs. Generally, the board deferred to the engineers. What had begun as a public agency was actually run autonomously—in total dedication to increasing its own size and power.

The manner in which board members were selected contributed to the agency's arrogance. They were not elected. Instead, they were appointed either by the governor or by city or county governments or by small water districts. Each of the appointees was answerable to the person or agency that appointed him, but the board as a whole was responsible to no one. When the water provided by MWD tasted bad or there was an explosion in a tunnel, there was nobody for the public to complain to—nobody, that is, who was answerable to the public at the next election.

The district began planning the San Fernando Tunnel project with its traditional sense of urgency. A U.S. Supreme Court decision in the late 1960s threatened to deprive the district of some of its water from the Colorado River, and the San Fernando Tunnel was needed to bring water from another source. As it turned out, there was no urgency. Due to a slowdown in population growth, the need for water was not as great as anticipated. Yet, the district did not revise its schedules. With bureaucratic single-mindedness, it continued making public statements about expected water shortages and the need for quick action to prevent them. When the district signed a contract with the Lockheed Shipbuilding and Construction Company, it offered the company bonuses to finish the tunnel ahead of schedule. As later events demonstrate, those bonuses brought an additional sense of haste and recklessness to the tunnel job. Just•as it had for years, the Metropolitan Water District was living by its own rules.

Lockheed and Its Power

Another fact that becomes important later in the story is Lockheed's own well-entrenched power. The company had been building aircraft in Southern California since the 1930s, but it meant more than airplanes to the social and economic life of the state. Subdivisions were built around its Los Angeles plant for workers to live in, and stores for workers to shop in. In the late 1960s and early 1970s, Lockheed continued to be one of the foundations of the area's economy. It began producing a new jet transport, the L-1011, at another airport far out in the desert at Palmdale. Following the pattern of the San Fernando Valley, subdivisions were built around Palmdale for the workers, and the city of Los Angeles made plans to build a great international airport there. But the L-1011 foundered financially, and Lockheed, beset by a number of other troubles, headed toward bankruptcy. Men laid off by Lockheed moped disconsolately around their Palmdale homes until Congress and President Nixon rescued the firm by signing a bill guaranteeing a $250 million loan. Lockheed was as important as any firm in Southern California, important and well connected.

The fact that a subsidiary of this influential company was building the tunnel seemed to influence, or at least overly impress, law enforcement officials, prosecutors and, in one instance, even judges. The fact that Lockheed was digging the tunnel for a water importation project increased its influence even more. It had signed a contract for the tunnel with the Metropolitan Water District. In the complicated contract between the MWD and Lockheed, Lockheed was given full responsibility for digging the tunnel; and in the prosecutions that followed, no charge was brought against the public agency. But the agency did proceed with the project knowing oil and gas would be encountered. The agency, and Lockheed, accepted a report from three consulting geologists saying "all known geologic conditions indicate that driving the San Fernando Tunnel is feasible. The Santa Susana Faults could present some difficulties. More than half the tunnel length will be dry and should be easily excavated. . . . The possibility of encountering small quantities of oil and/or gas in the Pico Formation should be anticipated. The tunnel will be in an area of known minor seismicity, but the possibility of serious damage from earthquakes, either during construction or within its useful life, is remote."

The report was made on November 6, 1968. On February 9, 1971, the big earthquake occurred. Later, after the San Fernando Tunnel explosion, Loren Savage, the tunnel project manager, admitted that the faults along the tunnel route moved during the earthquake and provided conduits for gas. In light of what happened, the geologists' report was, at the very least, overly optimistic.

Lockheed made that point in a $10 million breach of contract suit against the Metropolitan Water District. It accused the district of failing to warn the company of possible damage from the February 9, 1971, earthquake or warning it of the real danger of the gas and oil.

IN THE TUNNEL

It is doubtful that the victims of the explosion were aware of all this as they worked in the tunnel. Certainly they knew they were working under a tight schedule imposed by the Metropolitan Water District and Lockheed, but they could only put their safety in the hands of their bosses, their union and the state inspectors. All of them failed.

As befitted an aerospace firm, Lockheed brought the latest technology to the tunnel job. Tunneling had advanced since the days when William Mulholland's workers used dynamite and wood beams to burrow under the hills. Lockheed had designed "the mole," a huge drilling-excavating machine. A round shield as big as the circumference of the tunnel supported the earth instead of the wood beams used in the past. Inside the shield was an excavator that worked like a human hand, scraping the earth away. As the earth was dug out, it was raked onto a conveyor belt and loaded into railroad cars to be taken out. As the machine advanced, the tunnel was lined with concrete to support it. Three shifts a day worked on the tunnel: the swing shift, between afternoon and midnight; the graveyard shift, between midnight and 8 a.m.; and the day shift. Loren Savage, a construction engineer, was a new boss, taking full charge of a tunnel job for the first time and determined to make good. Success would help him professionally and financially, for his speed would be rewarded with bonuses.

For months, the work went quietly and quickly. There was no reason to pay any attention to the men laboring under the hills. No one noticed them until after the explosion. Then, the whole story came out in an investigation by a special committee of the state Assembly, forcing the truth from reluctant state officials and officials of Lockheed and the Metropolitan Water District.

Inviting Disaster

Throughout the hearings and the trial, evidence was presented of the crude, almost perfunctory safety precautions taken. Lockheed supervisors had made three crucial errors. First, there was the matter of the gas that the tunnel builders knew they would encounter when they reached the area of the Santa Susana Fault. Workers had met gas while digging another tunnel in the area, the Newhall Tunnel about 5,000 feet away, and there had been some small fires. By the time Lockheed's workers were approaching the Santa Susana Fault, the whole area had been shaken by the February 9th earthquake.

"We knew the gas zone was there," Loren Savage later told the Assembly investigating committee. "We also know we are in an extensive fault zone, and we also know that ... these faults in many places are conduits for gas."

On June 23, 1971, workers going into the tunnel for the graveyard shift smelled gas. Robin Romeo, an electrician, remembered that "as soon as I reached the heading [the end of the tunnel where the digging machine was operating] there was a bad odor of gas present and it was real bad. Myself and a number of the men had trouble breathing and had irritation of the eyes. I couldn't work at my station where I normally do because it's on what they call the return air side, the right side, and the gas was real strong on that side."

From the recollections of the men, the Lockheed supervisors seemed unconcerned about the gas. Eugene Pedigo, in charge of the crew, said he had received no instructions on what to do if he encountered gas. "I had no idea we were going to hit any gas," he said.

The crew tested for it, but, according to testimony, measuring was done improperly and by untrained men. Testing was done by a simple device called a Vapotester. Air was pumped through the machine, and if there was any gas, it registered on a gauge. Methane gas will ignite if it constitutes more than 4½% of the available air. Safety standards are much stricter than that. Work was to be stopped if the gauge showed 1%.

But the Vapotester itself had to be tested frequently with gas vapors found in the tunnel and with pure air, to make sure the gauge was accurate. And this had not been done correctly. One of the testers, Arvid Rassmussen, a veteran miner, testified that he tested the Vapotester by putting it in a tank of motor vehicle gasoline, using the fumes to check the gauge. This fuel, however, contains lead, which damages the Vapotester.

On the swing shift of June 23, the smell of gas was strong. Foreman Pedigo picked Jerry Nichols, who normally greased the mining machine and had little experience with the Vapotester, to do the testing. Pedigo told Nichols: "That machine will have to run without grease tonight, partner, because you just test for gas at all times. If you get any reading at all, we'll get the hell out of here regardless if it's 1% or ½%." Jerry Nichols got only one low reading on the meter, and, after steps were taken to improve ventilation, the gauge showed no gas content in the air. Later testimony showed that Nichols didn't understand how to test and was not sure what the readings meant.

Worker Robin Romeo remembered the whole testing procedure as being confused. "No one seemed to know what they were doing. A half a dozen men around the gas meter, someone saying 'You better take it here'; 'Take it there'; 'No, over here.' And when they did get readings . . . someone said, 'Well, this reading isn't bad enough.' 'No, we should leave.' 'No, it's a strong enough reading.' Which gave me a very insecure feeling. . . . So, meanwhile they did continue mining operations that night."

The air was getting worse. Robin Romeo remembered that when the digging machine cut into the earth, gas vapor would come out. "This gas that they were getting from the face was obviously under pressure," he said. "As they dug the claw into the face, you would get a shot of gas bad enough to knock you over." Bill Snodgrass, one of the operators of the mining machine, told foreman Pedigo, "I'm getting a headache." Pedigo told him to sit in front of the ventilating fan for a while, and he would take over the machine.

Just as Pedigo started the mining machine, the gas exploded. The actual cause of the blast—possibly a spark or heat from the machine—was never discovered. It was not a huge explosion, but it served as a warning of the deadly one that was to occur twenty-four hours later. And it was serious enough to injure four men. "It blew me out of the cage, down in the bottom of the shield," said Pedigo. "It blew my hat off," said Romeo. "I looked to the front, and all I could see from halfway up the tunnel and halfway to the ground was nothing but fire. It was all fire."

Ignoring this minor explosion was the second oversight. It was inconceivable that work on the tunnel would be resumed the following day, and without major safety precautions. But it was, with the permission of the State Division of Industrial Safety and the labor union representing the men. Under the law, the state could have halted work until safety was improved, allowing state officials to investigate to see if the law was being broken. The union, Local 300 of the Laborer's Union, could have pulled its members off the job. But work was not stopped. For labor, management and the State Division of Industrial Safety all seemed to think they were on the same side.

At 6 a.m., about four hours after the first explosion, tunnel boss Loren Savage telephoned the local state inspector, Wallace Zavaterro, to report the incident. Zavaterro had had a previous experience with Lockheed, and it had not been pleasant. In 1968, he tried to shut down a Lockheed tunnel project in another part of Los Angeles County because of many safety violations that had resulted in several injuries. His superiors refused him permission to close the job. It was understandable that Zavaterro approached Lockheed with caution this time.

Zavaterro imposed a few restrictions on Lockheed, telling Savage to telephone him at home if the gauge showed a 1% gas reading. Zavaterro also told Lockheed to obtain self-contained breathing devices and place them near the workers. Then he left after he, union chief Bucky Micelli and Lockheed official Savage agreed work could resume that day.

The men returned to work. Gas intensity was increasing, but still the testing machine showed there was no gas. The men were cynical about its accuracy. Suggested one, "Stick that prod over here, under my nose, because it's pretty heavy right here, real heavy." Edward Butterfield, a miner, said the gas "appeared as the [mining] machine was digging the dirt; the gas would accumulate and start building up, so they would shut the machine down and the ventilation would take the gas out."

The Graveyard Shift

During the next shift, from 3:30 p.m. to midnight, some of the miners said they heard Lewis Richardson, a supervising engineer for the Metropolitan Water District, try to stop work, but Savage refused. Savage told Richardson he would have to get a written order from a Metropolitan Water District superior. Richardson said that by the time he could reach outside to call his boss "the damn thing will blow up anyway." He was right. Richardson died in the tunnel explosion. He had remained over, working on the graveyard shift because another MWD engineer had been injured the night before.

Savage pressed on with the work. At one stage, a blowtorch touched off a small fire that scorched his pants, but still he would not halt work. An hour into the graveyard shift, Savage left, telling two others to take charge. He said he told them to "follow through with the procedures I had established," climbed aboard a small railroad car used to remove dirt and rode toward the entrance. "This crew was following through with my instructions," he said. "Everything looked in order. On that basis, I got on the locomotive and left. And we got about 5,000 feet down the tunnel, and we heard the explosion."

Only one member of the crew in the work area survived, Ralph Brissette. He described what happened in the tunnel: "Prior to the explosion, when I just felt there was something wrong, there was pressure on my ears, and immediately I told the motorman to move the train so the fellows would have a chance to run. It's quite close in that area. He didn't have a chance to move the train at the time the explosion occurred and I was blind and I was moving to try . . . to move the train and drive it out myself, and I felt another workman there and wanted to take one workman. He identified himself. He was in great pain, and I tried not to panic myself because breathing was very difficult, so I went back to the area where I was. . . . That's all I know until . . . I was in the hospital."

The third oversight involved the rescue equipment. Outside, Casey Barthelemess and some other workers tried to rescue the trapped men. State engineer Zavaterro had ordered breathing devices placed near the men, but they had been left far from where they were needed, and nobody knew how to use them.

"We went down to the hill and wanted to start a rescue operation by grabbing these units. . . . Nobody had been checked out on them." Frustrated, knowing their companions were trapped, the men could do nothing. Finally, the fire department arrived, but the fire chief did not know how to use the rescue units either. More time was lost while he examined them. In the end, only Brissette was rescued.

The records of the chief Medical Examiner-Coroner of Los Angeles County indicate that some of the seventeen victims might have lived if the breathing units had been nearby. Most of those killed were burned and battered, but five died from acute carbon monoxide poisoning.

Going into the tunnel afterwards, investigators found telling evidence of insistence on haste. Markings were on the wall of the tunnel, recording the speedy progress and also the names of those whose mistakes occasionally slowed the work.

FROM A FELONY TO A MISDEMEANOR

There was evidence that the employer had been careless with the lives of the men. Yet Lockheed had little to fear from the law. Law enforcement in industrial safety matters was incredibly weak in the state—especially when it dealt with powerful, well-connected corporations. That is not all that stood in the way of justice for the seventeen deaths. Ten years before, the law had been rewritten so that even in cases when employers recklessly allowed workmen to die, no major crime had been committed.

How could this happen? It happened because the public did not realize, nor did the press report, a fundamental axiom governing the conduct of state legislatures—appearances and reality are never quite the same. Most laws are written in secret, negotiated between special interests while the real authors and their motives are hidden.

The offense involved in the San Fernando Tunnel is termed "negligence." Years before, it had been a more serious crime. Until 1963, when a negligent employer caused a worker's death, the employer could be charged with involuntary manslaughter. This is a felony, punishable by a term in the state prison. But about ten years ago that was changed, and to understand the climate of industrial safety law enforcement under which the men in the San Fernando Tunnel worked and died, it is necessary to understand the complex maneuvers by which the legislature decreased the penalty for careless employers.

In 1963, part of a wall collapsed on the site of a new building for the Playboy Club on Los Angeles' Sunset Strip. A workman was killed, and the district attorney of Los Angeles County appropriately charged the contractors with involuntary manslaughter. But shortly after the indictment on this serious charge, the legislature passed a law that effectively wiped out the severe penalty. Under the new law, a boss whose carelessness kills his employees could no longer be charged with a felony. He could only be found guilty of a misdemeanor, a much less serious crime. The new law was signed by the then governor of the state, Edmund G. Brown, known to be pro-labor. There was no public outcry and little publicity.

On the surface, the California Capitol at that time seemed to be full of the workingman's friends. Governor Brown was a Democrat who had been first elected in 1958 with labor's support in a campaign marked by a great dispute between labor and employers. The legislature also seemed friendly to labor. The Democrats controlled both houses, and the speaker of the assembly, powerful Jess Unruh, was a liberal known to be sympathetic to labor.

But the reality was far different. Unruh was also a friend of business and worked closely with business lobbyists in the legislature. It is true that many proposals backed by the AFL-CIO, the Teamsters union and other labor groups were approved, but they passed with the sufferance of the business lobbyists, and there was a limit beyond which labor could not go. For it was business, not labor, who was most generous in campaign contributions and the most skilled in lobbying. It is important to understand how business actually controlled the legislature, for the same process was at work in the assembly industrial relations committee in 1963 when the law was weakened.

Most of the actual work of a legislature is done in such committees. This is where people testify for and against bills and where the bills are actually written. Sometimes the writing is done in open meetings, attended by the press and public. More often, it is done in private. Wherever it is done, special interest lobbyists exert tremendous pressure on members of important committees, sometimes actually dictating the language of legislation. Democrats were in the majority on the industrial relations committee, and that would appear to be a plus for organized labor. But Unruh had placed on the committee a mixture of liberal and conservative Democrats. The conservative Democrats joined with Republicans in voting to favor business. As a result, the California Labor Federation of the AFL-CIO found it difficult to have the committee approve many of its legislative proposals.

The Trade

But labor went along. It did so because of something known as the "quid pro quo" or "the trade."

In a legislature like California's where more sophisticated, businesslike methods have replaced the old-fashioned bribe, the trade is one of the most important facts of life. A price is paid for every important bill that is passed. The price is not a bribe. It is support for another piece of legislation.

In the trading over the industrial safety bill, management received the benefits of a weaker law. In return, organized labor received some increases in benefits for unemployment, illness and disability. Management's price for these benefits, it turned out, was too high.

The bill that weakened the law was introduced on March 13, 1963, not long after felony charges were brought against the employers at the Playboy Club construction site. The author was Assemblyman John Francis Foran, a Democrat from San Francisco. He is a short, cigar-smoking man, neither conservative nor liberal. He blends unobtrusively into the legislature and plays the game well.

The bill's passage was favorably reported in the *Sacramento Bee*, the capital newspaper which carries more state government news than any other paper in the state. "Safety Bill Provides for Fines," said the headline. The story told how "Stiff penalties for employers convicted of gross negligence regarding safety would be provided by a bill, AB 1799, introduced in the legislature by Assemblyman John Francis Foran of San Francisco." The story reported that "the bill would call for imprisonment for up to a year and a fine of not less than $5,000 or more than $10,000 in the case of a death to an employee resulting from an employer's gross negligence. In serious injury cases, the maximum penalty would be not more than six months or a fine of not less than $500 or more than $2,000." The catch, not mentioned in that story or noticed by any of the reporters from the several news agencies covering state government, was that it reduced the seriousness of the crime to a misdemeanor. Previously, district attorneys could prosecute the offense as a felony—involuntary manslaughter—using the full investigative resources of their offices. Foran's bill left the prosecution to city attorneys, who handle misdemeanors and are not equipped to prosecute complicated criminal cases.

The Buck Stops Nowhere

Why did Foran—a Democrat from San Francisco, where organized labor is especially strong—introduce such a bill? If the reason is unclear, it is because of another basic truth about legislatures: responsibility is difficult to pinpoint and nobody will take the blame.

Although the bill was introduced after the Playboy Club death, Foran told us that he had never heard of the incident. When we talked to him several years afterward, he said he had introduced the bill for two unions representing most of the construction workers, the Operating Engineers and the Building Trades Construction Council. Although he was technically the author, all that meant was that his name was on the bill and that he was the one who handed it to the clerk of the assembly, the technical process required for introducing a bill. Foran said that he had not actually written the measure himself nor taken part in the negotiations for it. "I frankly was not that intimately involved in the legislation," he said.

Assemblyman Foran's explanation that he knew little about the bill is quite plausible. Many legislators do not pay close attention to the bills they introduce. The actual legislation is often written by the special interests that advocate it—a labor union, a group of locksmiths, an organization of parents of retarded children, even officials of a state agency like the highway patrol. It is then handed to the legislator who is sympathetic to the special interest group, either because of past favors, campaign contributions or—in some instances—because he actually believes in the cause. During the course of the bill's passage through the legislature, the author may have little to do with it. Amendments are written by special interest lobbyists, who often appear before committees on behalf of the bill, sparing the legislator the need to testify. The only time the lawmaker whose name is on the bill must speak for it is on the floor of the legislature, where he is likely to read uncomprehendingly from an analysis written by the special interest lobbyists.

Most of the time, the public does not know the origin of the bill. The public thinks the legislator listed as the author is responsible.

It does seem strange, nonetheless, that two labor unions would back such a proposal. Foran explained to us that he believed the unions were merely carrying out the recommendations of a 1963 Governor's Industrial Safety Conference which considered the problems of penalties for industrial safety violations. He gave us the report of that conference to back up his statement. But when we examined the report, we found the conference had recommended no such thing. The conference had proposed an increase in fines, but had not recommended that the crime be lessened from a felony to a misdemeanor. All it said was, "In view of the fact that fines which are presently defined in the State Labor Code for violation of the state safety laws are outdated, it is recommended that this conference go on record as urging legislation to correct this matter. It is further recommended that labor and management associations work together to accomplish this end."

That recommendation was certainly not a mandate for weakening the law.

As we looked into the matter, we met sources in the legislature who told us what they believed was the real reason, and we reached the conclusion that they were right. The actual reason labor supported the bill was that it was part of a big trade. Management, frightened by the seriousness of the Playboy Club indictments, wanted weaker industrial safety legislation. Labor wanted increases in the social insurance benefits given to workers for illnesses and injuries suffered on and off the job and for times when they are unemployed. And that was the trade.

What is the evidence of this trade? There is no physical evidence, no notes or written agreements. But we know the result, and we know the practices of the legislature over the years. It was, for example, a matter of record that the union leaders placed high priority on obtaining increased social insurance benefits, tangible gains to bring back to their members. We know that management placed high priority on weakening what it considered burdensome safety restrictions. We know that industrial safety did not become a matter of widespread concern until the San Fernando Tunnel explosion, almost a decade later.

A SPECIAL SYSTEM OF JUSTICE

In the months that followed the explosion, there were several attempts to bury the matter. And law enforcement officials seemed to be standing by, hoping it would blow away. But the seventeen deaths, occurring in a populous area, was a major news event. Too many had died for the tunnel explosion to be forgotten or ignored.

The story of how justice was finally served provides a rare look at a system which nearly allows powerful corporations to put themselves above the law. There were three areas in which this was at work. First, there was the hesitation to prosecute. Secondly, attempts were again made to further water down the state industrial laws. Finally, once the trial was under way, attempts were made to tamper with the judicial process.

The Reluctance to Prosecute

After the initial stories on the explosion, publicity ended for a time. In this quiet period, the State Division of Industrial Safety—following its long-standing policy—did nothing to bring charges of negligence against Lockheed. For years, state officials had not been prosecuting industrial safety offenders. They believed a friendly chat was enough. In their expressed view, industries needed only a reminder to do what was right for the worker. In a report several years before the tunnel disaster, George Sherman, chief of the Division of Industrial Safety under the pro-labor Brown administration, said that "With the multitude of built-in checks and balances, [the law] tends to almost assure that if speed is what you are looking for, it is almost impossible to obtain because of the restrictive aspects inherent in 'due process.' " He favored educational drives and inspections in specific industries to stop violations. Such drives, he said, "produced results which caused remarkable and quick change and almost always this was accomplished by a limited proportion of prosecutions." Thus the policing done by the Division of Industrial Safety was guided by the state's long-standing tradition of amiable labor-management trading.

Whenever inspectors found a violation of safety laws, they tried to correct it by negotiations—usually without punishing the offender. It was as if a policeman had released a bank robber on his promise that he would return the money and not do it again.

Later, when a legislative committee began to investigate the tunnel disaster, legislators learned of this curious attitude—an attitude that contributed to the fatal negligence in the tunnel.

"I would say that in very few cases do they prosecute because it serves no useful purpose of any kind," state safety engineer Gordon Bunker told the committee.

"Let me see if I understand that correctly," said a surprised assemblyman, Larry Townsend. "You mean that there are many times when men are killed when we do not prosecute because of safety violations?"

"That is very true, yes," replied Bunker.

Thus the industrial safety agency did not offer the workers in the San Fernando Tunnel much protection.

Nor did the city attorney of Los Angeles, who was responsible for prosecuting industrial safety violations. The city attorney at the time was Roger Arnebergh, a thin, austere man who, over the years, had managed to keep out of the public eye. He had made a good deal of money in real estate, and as an affluent member of the Los Angeles legal community, he liked to mix with the senior partners of the rich and prestigious law firms in downtown Los Angeles, eating lunch at the California Club. Some of his friends were members of the most influential of these firms, O'Melveny and Myers, attorneys for Lockheed in the San Fernando Tunnel case.

Arnebergh's office specialized in civil cases, lawsuits against the city for damages and the like. There was a criminal section of his office that handled misdemeanor cases like the tunnel disaster, but in the opinion of many of his deputies, the criminal section was of second-string status.

Arnebergh had learned one of the most important lessons of politics—to make his office sound unimportant. He had become invisible, never involved in controversy. For many years the voters, unaware of him, paid no attention to the office of city attorney on election day. As a result, he was one of those anonymous incumbents who is automatically returned to office every four years. He was reelected until his defeat in 1973, when a young opponent conducted a campaign that focused unwanted attention on Arnebergh and the way he conducted the office. But, while Arnebergh was city attorney, there appeared to be little chance that his office would prosecute Lockheed for its role in the catastrophe which caused seventeen deaths.

Other Politicians and Other Motives

Action finally came from another part of the government process, from a level more visible than the city attorney or the State Division of Industrial Safety.

The San Fernando Valley, site of the explosion, was the home of the speaker of the assembly, Bob Moretti, who was interested in finding out what happened. Many of his constituents were angry about the failure to do something about the explosion, and Moretti responded to their feelings. In addition, he was planning to run for the Democratic nomination for governor. In the weeks after the explosion, Moretti launched an intensive investigation of Republican Governor Reagan's administration of the Division of Industrial Safety. This would give Democrat Moretti a chance to score points against the Republicans. By fall, a special legislative committee conducted public hearings in Los Angeles on the matter.

Moretti also assigned two persistent investigators to the case, Jack Johnson and Jerry McFettridge. Johnson, who headed the inquiry, had been a newspaper reporter and had owned a small news service before going to work for the legislature. He was an unusually determined man. Afflicted with lung troubles, he had to use a bulky breathing device at times. But he did not let it interfere with his life. He lugged it on backpacking trips in the Sierra mountains so he would not miss fishing with his children. Both Johnson and McFettridge were at first looked on with disdain by the downtown Los Angeles lawyers representing Lockheed. The attorneys, however, underestimated their foes.

Johnson and McFettridge became convinced that Lockheed was attempting to tamper with an important piece of evidence, the testing device that was used in the tunnel to test for gas vapor. It was a crucial piece of evidence because, from all the testimony, Lockheed's greatest failure was in its refusal to adequately test for gas. Workers said that they didn't think the testing machine was accurate and that at least one of the testers did not know how to use it. In the tunnel, the machine had shown many readings below the danger point, and, citing these readings, tunnel boss Savage insisted that the work continue. If the machine were found to be defective, then the low gas readings it showed were incorrect, and the workers were right, the tunnel was filled with gas. But if the machine were found to be working properly, and its readings were correct, Savage might be able to justify his insistence that the digging continue. In that case, he might be able to defend himself with the argument that the explosion was a sudden and unpreventable accident, unforeseeable by him and the company.

The Missing Vapotester

State safety engineer Wallace Zavaterro had not been able to find the testing device in the tunnel after the explosion. But late one evening, two months later, Bob Ree, Lockheed safety engineer, called Lt. Lewis Biro, the acting commander of the Los Angeles Police Department's Foothill Division detectives. He asked Biro to accompany him into the tunnel. Ree told Biro that he and another Lockheed official were going to look for the body of one of the workmen. Sixteen had been recovered, but the seventeenth body was still missing. Significantly, Ree did not contact state engineer Zavaterro who, by this time, had forbidden anyone from entering the tunnel without state permission.

Lt. Biro accompanied Ree and another Lockheed employee into the tunnel. Inside they made a discovery. It was the long lost Vapotester, which seemed to be in perfect condition. There was not a burn or a dent on it, even though the man who was supposed to be using it at the time of the explosion, Bob Warner, had been so badly mutilated that only forty-seven pounds of his charred body had been recovered.

Neither Lockheed nor Lt. Biro reported the discovery to the

state. State inspector Zavaterro did not hear about it until months later, and then he had to force Lockheed to turn the machine over to him. The unusual circumstances of the belated discovery, the failure to report it to the state, and the good condition of the device made investigators suspicious that Lockheed might have substituted a new Vapotester for the one that had been in the explosion.

Re-enter Arnebergh

By this time, pressure from the investigating assemblymen had forced the city attorney, Arnebergh, to enter the case. He appointed a young assistant, George Bane, to prosecute. But Bane said later that his superiors did all they could to hamper him, denying him investigatory manpower, time and encouragement.

Bane wanted the arrest of safety engineer Ree on charges of illegally removing the Vapotester from the tunnel. Ree had left California, but assembly investigator Jack Johnson found him in Seattle, at the Lockheed Shipbuilding and Construction Company's home office. Bane asked a Los Angeles judge for a fugitive warrant with high bail, explaining he was afraid Ree would run away. The judge agreed and set bail at $100,000.

Bane said Arnebergh exploded when he heard about the bail. He called the offense "a stinking misdemeanor." Bane said Arnebergh ordered him into his office and, while attorneys for Lockheed watched, shouted his outrage at the young lawyer. Bane considered it graphic evidence of Lockheed's close ties with the city attorney, and said it was not the first time he had encountered such evidence. According to Bane, the Lockheed legal team repeatedly discussed the case with his superiors. Despite this, Bane prosecuted the case, and Lockheed was found guilty of concealing evidence as a result of its delay in producing the testing meter. Ree was found innocent.

After this trial, Bane put all of his complaints against Arnebergh in an office memorandum, and was fired. But by that time the case had become so well publicized that Arnebergh could no longer avoid filing negligence charges against Lockheed, Savage, Ree, and Pedigo. Bowing to public pressure, Arnebergh assigned one of his best assistants to the case, Roosevelt Dorn.

More from the Legislative Bag of Tricks

Dorn began the prosecution in the Los Angeles municipal court of Judge George Trammell. In the midst of the trial, Judge Trammell learned that a bill had been quietly passed by the legislature that made it impossible to prosecute Savage, Ree and Pedigo. Early in 1971, an unimportant bill had been introduced in the assembly designed to allow some state employees to take leaves of absences without pay. It was passed by the assembly without any debate and sent to the senate industrial relations committee for a routine hearing. It was ignored and lay dormant there from May until November 18, about five months after the tunnel explosion.

On that day, it was revived, providing us with another illuminating glimpse of how laws are actually made and unmade. This is not the trade, which we discussed earlier. This goes far beyond the trade. Here, we are dealing with outright deceit.

The legislative session was on its way to adjournment, and the attention of the press and most legislators was on a fight between the Democrats and Governor Reagan. But Senator William Coombs had something more important in mind. Coombs, known to represent the point of view of the construction industry, was, in the slang of the legislature, "a bill pirate." He took the unimportant bill and introduced amendments that completely changed its meaning. Since the bill was so routine, only Coombs and an assemblyman who was his ally, Paul Priolo, paid attention to these amendments although their content was highly significant. The amendments said that supervisory personnel such as Savage and Ree could not be held responsible for acts of negligence toward fellow employees. Only the corporation could be held responsible. The law passed both houses and was signed by Governor Reagan. In the confusion of the moment, only those most interested knew what was in it.

The law went into effect in April 1972. That meant that the prosecution of Savage, Ree and Pedigo was illegal. Only the non-human corporate entity could be prosecuted for negligence. Unlike a human defendant, a corporation cannot serve a jail term. The only penalty would be the fine—a small amount to a huge company like Lockheed.

Judge Trammell ruled that the law was unconstitutional. The effect of exempting individuals from prosecution, he explained, would be to repeal virtually the entire industrial safety act for negligent supervisors, who would no longer be liable for their errors. But the title, he noted, merely said that the bill gave leaves of absences to state workers. It thus violated a section of the state constitution designed to prevent misleading titles of bills. The judge ordered the trial to go on.

An Attempt to Tamper with the Judge

The trial was a long one. It began July 24, 1972. The transcript was 13,374 pages long by the time the jury began deliberations. On July 27, 1973, the jury found Lockheed guilty of sixteen counts of gross negligence and ten violations of the state industrial safety code. Savage was found guilty of sixteen counts of gross negligence and nine violations of the industrial safety code. Ree was convicted of three violations of the safety code, and found innocent of nine other counts. Foreman Pedigo was found innocent of all four safety code charges against him.

After the verdict, Judge Trammell revealed how two of his fellow judges tried to persuade him to agree to a settlement that would have allowed Savage, Ree and Pedigo to escape prosecution.

In August 1972, while the jury was being selected, the judge disclosed that city attorney prosecutors and Lockheed attorneys made a deal, or a "plea bargain," as it is called in the law. Under plea bargaining, a defendent bargains for a lower sentence in return for a guilty plea. In that way, the prosecution is spared the expense and trouble of a trial. In this bargain, Lockheed agreed to plead "no contest" to sixteen counts of gross negligence. Despite the fact that prosecutors had sufficient evidence to win their case, all charges would be dropped against the three Lockheed employees, Savage, Ree and Pedigo. The judge, while being allowed to fine Lockheed, would agree to a minimum financial penalty against Lockheed, even though the law allowed additional fines.

Judge Trammell rejected the plea bargaining. He said that it "would be a gross miscarriage of justice" to dismiss the charges against Savage, Ree and Pedigo. In October, a similar proposal was discussed. Trammell again refused it, reminding the prosecution that it had said it had enough evidence to "obtain and sustain a conviction."

In February, there was a third discussion of a modified deal. At this time, Trammell told prosecutors and defense attorneys that two fellow judges in the municipal court had approached him. He said the judges suggested that he "dump the case."

"I mean, what was done, in my opinion, was improper," Trammell told the attorneys. He told the prosecutors that "they should be screaming their heads off that someone was trying to influence the trial judge in their case to, quote, dump the case."

Defense attorney Douglas Dalton said he thought Trammell might have misinterpreted what the judges said. "Now apparently they [the two judges] were of the frame of mind that it is a case that should be disposed of, not as far as I know, from any improper motives. . . . [It] could be a completely well motivated thing by the people charged with the administration of the courts. But the thing that worries me is that you interpreted it, as infringing on your province as a trial judge."

"No question about it," replied Judge Trammell, ". . . there is only one reasonable way to interpret that, and that is trying to influence a judge on a decision he is going to make."

After the trial, the presiding judge of the municipal court transferred Trammell to the traffic court, which reporter William Farr wrote in the *Los Angeles Times,* is "generally regarded by court observers as a demotion." Trammell, meanwhile, turned over the names of his two colleagues to the State Commission on Judicial Qualifications, a judicial body that investigates charges against judges. He did not reveal their names to the public, nor did he provide more details of what happened.

The trial did not finish the story of the Lockheed Tunnel. It continued in appeal courts and, as related in our next chapter, with more intriguing maneuvers, in the legislature. What we have learned so far was how it took an extraordinary combination of a courageous judge and an unexpectedly aroused legislature to punish Lockheed and its supervisors for their disregard for human life.

Laws are usually written to provide prison sentences and fines to punish those who break them. In dealing with individual offenders, the police and the prosecuting attorneys are in business to arrest people, to gather evidence and pursue a case to conviction. Their success is measured in arrest and conviction rates. And although a police department cannot catch every criminal, it seeks to prevent crimes by arresting as many as possible and publicizing the cases. A citizen hesitates to drink when he drives or to cheat on his income tax because he has read of others who have been disgraced by harsh penalties.

In the case of the San Fernando Tunnel disaster, there was a double standard in the way laws were made and enforced, which gave large campaign contributors, corporations and politically influential labor unions an advantage that nearly amounted to immunity from justice.

It is difficult for the citizen to fight this double standard because it is carried out in secret. As the next chapter shows, pressures such as campaign contributions are often not clearly evident. Later in the book, ways to fight the secret influence of powerful pressure groups will be discussed. But for now, there is a lesson in the story of the San Fernando Tunnel explosion. The legislature did investigate—prompted by outrage at wrongdoing, concern for the feelings of San Fernando Valley constituents, and eagerness to attack the Republican administration. These are all good reasons, political reasons connected by the ballot box to the hopes and fears with which politicians confront election day. In the end, Lockheed and its supervisors could not evade the law. The San Fernando Tunnel explosion case showed that government, often immoral and devious, can be forced to correct itself.

5

Cocktails

and

Campaign Contributions

At mid-morning in the California Capitol, the lobbyists gather in a section of hallway on the third floor known as "lobbyists' row." There are alcoves in the wall with benches, and the lobbyists sit on them, a living mural of special interests, representing bankers, oil companies, manufacturers, unions and the rest. They smoke cigarettes and exchange gossip like good friends do, united in a common job of influencing the forty state senators and eighty assemblymen who make the laws for California.

Six hundred and fifty groups were represented by lobbyists in the 1973 session of the legislature, and most were business enterprises. They were as diverse as the economy of the rich and productive state, and all of the businesses were regulated, in some way, by the state. After examining the businesses' relationship with the legislature, Carey McWilliams, editor of *Nation* magazine and the best analyst of California politics, concluded, "California's legislature is really a corporate state in which commodities, not people, are represented."

Once business ruled alone. But with the rise of organized labor in the 1930s and 1940s, the unions sent their own lobbyists to Sacramento and created their own intricate web of influence. Like that of business, it was held together by friendships, steaks, liquor, favors and, in a few cases, genuine beliefs.

The friendships are important. At noon or at dinner time, the lobbyists and the legislators frequently meet at Frank Fats, the popular Chinese restaurant, or the more elegant Firehouse, or the new place, Ellis', run by a bartender who had become so popular he was able to start his own restaurant. The legislators and lobbyists, many dressed in white shoes and colorful doubleknit suits, sit at tables in the bar or the dining rooms, sharing stories, and talking over legislation.

The scene is the same in state capitals, city halls and county buildings, in all parts of the country. In every state capital, there are the restaurants and bars where lobbyists and legislators drink. A drink appears without asking; the bartender nods his head to the end of the bar where the lobbyist is sitting. The recipient raises his glass in a silent toast of thanks.

Gestures of friendship are not enough. The real glue is money— campaign contributions given to legislators by the business and labor groups the lobbyists represent. This chapter tells how the California legislature finally managed to improve the state's industrial safety laws, more than two years after the deaths of the seventeen men in the San Fernando Tunnel, the subject of the preceding chapter. The combination of money and friendship is at the heart of legislative maneuvers to strengthen the laws. It is a story of many failures and a final, unexpected success, providing an intriguing example of how laws are made. It also shows why good legislation is so hard to come by. In many cases it can be passed only if the power of the campaign dollar and legislative-lobbyist friendships can be neutralized or resisted.

THE GREATEST EVIL

Money is the greatest evil in American politics. At both the national and local levels, money can force elected men and women to actually break the law, but more often it sends them into a descending spiral of compromise. The first concessions are small, but eventually the politician becomes involved in deals so outrageous that not even the closest friends of the officeholders can recall the early high idealism that prompted them to run for office. Not all are guilty. The most honest decry a system that forces them to go humbly to those who hold the funds and ask for help. "I am always embarrassed and humiliated to have to do these things," said Senator John Pastore, a Democrat from Rhode Island. Joseph Cole, a Cleveland businessman who was the Democratic national finance chairman and a supporter of Senator Hubert Humphrey for many years, has watched candidates in all levels of government beg for money. "It is very disheartening," he said, "when I watch a presidential candidate demean himself and drive himself" to spend a few minutes with a big contributor.

In just twelve years, the cost of campaigning has gone up steeply. In 1960, John Kennedy and Richard Nixon reported spending just $24 million between them. From April 7 through December 31, 1972, the candidates for the presidency of the United States reported they spent about $79 million. It was just part of the huge amount of money expended in the campaign; it did not include the large amounts for earlier primary elections or for big campaign operations set up far in advance of election year. Nor did it include under-the-table contributions.

Presidential candidates are not the only ones caught in the trap. So are candidates for the Senate and the House of Representatives, for state legislatures, city councils and county boards of supervisors. In America's large cities and populous counties, the day has long past when a citizen can simply present himself for office to a community of friends and neighbors. Politics has become theater. Voters are now treated as audiences to be won over by expensive advertising and trickery. In every state of the union, the corrupting process has been the same—a decision to run, often made with the sincerest of motives, but debased in the last weeks of the campaign in a terrible scramble for money to buy time on television, to finance another public opinion poll, to hire spies, to finance fake counterdemonstrations, or to embarrass opponents.

Where the Money Goes

As usual, the narrow room where the California senate committee on industrial relations meets was crowded with the lobbyists from business and labor. In this room, just off lobbyists' row, the committee was preparing to hear testimony on the bill strengthening the industrial safety act.

There were some good men sitting on the industrial relations committee, but even the best of them would admit the pressure under which they labored. We pause at their meeting because their deliberations will provide us with a view of that pressure.

There is another reason for pausing at a committee of the California senate. The action that will unfold in this chapter will take place in conditions more conducive to good government than in most state capitals in the country. The California legislature is considered one of the most progressive, higher paid than the others, with a large and professional staff of advisers capable of providing elected officials with independent information to counter the self-serving arguments of lobbyists. An aggressive press corps covers legislative activities in an independent manner, publicizing such matters more than in most other states. Although much business is transacted in private, the great majority of committee meetings are open to the public. Legislative expense accounts are a matter of public record. Many of the steps urged by reformers were taken in Sacramento years ago. Yet even here, as we shall see, the road to just laws is a tortuous one.

The Surface Appearance—And the Undercurrent

The argument taking place in the senate industrial relations committee that day was so subtle that any casual observer sitting in for the afternoon would have missed it.

As we saw in Chapter 4, there had been a glaring weakness in the industrial safety law, making it impossible to charge employers or their supervisors with felonies if their negligence caused the deaths of workers. As a result, the accused in the Lockheed Tunnel explosion were only charged with misdemeanors. After the tunnel explosion, the trial, and the publicity that accompanied it, the climate in the legislature was favorable to passing a bill once again permitting felony prosecutions.

But, while this laudable step was being taken, business lobbyists, led by the California Manufacturers Association, a trade organization of all the major industries in the state, were maneuvering to make the law weaker than it had ever been. To do it, they worked in backrooms to wipe out the entire system of industrial safety inspection in the state. But they failed. The story ends with the governor signing a stronger bill.

The manner in which the business lobbyists were attempting to dismantle the industrial safety control system was an instructive example of how appearances can be completely deceiving in the workings of government.

Ironically, their opportunity to weaken the bill came from federal legislation. In 1970 Congress passed, and President Nixon signed, a law prompted in part by a series of accidents caused by employer negligence. It was the Occupational Safety and Health Act. It created a new federal agency, the Occupational Safety and Health Administration, to write and administer stronger industrial safety laws for the entire nation. Each of the fifty states was told to bring its laws up to the new federal standards or else Washington would take over industrial safety inspection within the state's boundaries.

It was a good plan, except that many of the new federal standards were not as strict as those already in existence in California. With all its weaknesses, the California industrial safety system—adopted in 1913 as part of the Progressive movement—had many provisions that were stronger than any in the nation. The California law was particularly strong in the latitude it gave the state in shutting down dangerous jobs, although it was a power that had been used sparingly in recent years.

But there were other parts of the California law that were weaker than federal standards. And there were many technical differences between the two that had to be resolved. Thus California had to submit to Washington a new occupational health and safety plan, one that would presumably answer the technical requirements of the federal law, tighten up weak provisions of the state law, and yet keep those sections that were stronger in California. If such a plan were not adopted by the legislature, signed by the governor, and submitted to Washington in time, the federal Occupational Safety and Health Administration would step in. If that happened, the strong points of the California law would be lost and that would be of great benefit to employers.

The San Fernando tunnel explosion occurred in the midst of all these developments, and it was a disaster of such magnitude that not even the most reactionary employer would dare come out openly against industrial safety. The senate committee's job was to draft the new California plan, and as discussion began, all sides spoke firmly in favor of safety. Some were sincere and others were not.

THE COMMITTEE

Assemblyman Jack Fenton, who had exposed the depths of safety neglect in his investigation of the tunnel explosion, wanted the new California plan to be even stricter than the previous law. For him, the preparation of a new plan provided an opportunity to eliminate all the weaknesses he found during the tunnel investigation. For employers, who were represented by influential lobbyists, the hearing offered an opportunity to weaken the law even more. As discussions over the new plan continued, the strategy of the employers' lobbyists was clear—delay action until the federal deadline passed, at which time Washington would begin administering industrial safety in California.

Once before, in 1972, Assemblyman Fenton had introduced a bill to strengthen the industrial safety law. It had passed the assembly, but was killed in the senate where business lobbyists made their last stand. Now, in 1973, it had again passed the assembly and was awaiting its first hearing in the senate committee on industrial relations. It was not a well-publicized meeting. Only three reporters watched on a day when most attention was on the legislature repealing an onerous and unnecessary sales tax increase. But the men who counted were there. On one side were the opponents of strict industrial safety standards, the California Manufacturers Association, the California Farm Bureau Federation, the California Chamber of Commerce, and the construction industry. In support of a strong law were Fenton's labor allies from the AFL-CIO and the Teamsters union.

There were four Democratic senators and three Republicans seated in the high-backed chairs behind the large half circle of a desk on the rostrum. The room, long, narrow and almost empty, could have seated about one hundred spectators.

Since the Democrats controlled the committee and they, at least in the public mind, represent the working man's point of view, it should have been easy to predict the fate of Assemblyman Fenton's bill. The four Democrats were openly pro-labor, the three Republicans pro-business. The result—approval assured. But nothing was assured. What would follow was a political play, acted on two levels. One was apparent to the casual spectator. But the other could only be understood by the lobbyists, the legislators and a few others in the room.

The Men and Their Motives

As always, each of the legislators was motivated by a variety of interests. Among them were his own ideologies, the needs of his constituents and the claims of his campaign contributors. As each listened to the testimony, he weighed these interests and made up his mind. We focus on three of the men, important actors in the drama: Senator Alan Short, Senator Craig Biddle, and Assemblyman Fenton himself.

Short, seated at the center of the rostrum, was the chairman of the committee. He is a Democrat from the small city of Stockton, a decaying transportation and farm market center in California's agricultural Central Valley. Following the current vogue at the Capitol, he wore brightly colored clothes including a yellow sport coat, yellow shirt and yellow tie. He ran his committee with the speed and efficiency that befits one who has been in the system for many years. He had done good things in that time. He was one of the men who had made the California legislature such a mysterious mixture of enlightenment and special interest. Often, from that citadel of selfishness would emerge programs so far ahead of what other state legislatures were proposing that observers could scarcely understand the significance of them.

For example, in the 1950s, Senator Short had made it his business to become interested in the state's mental health program and in the big warehouse-like hospitals where the mentally ill were kept. He was an author of the Short-Doyle Act, which created centers where the mentally ill could be treated in their own communities away from the huge and impersonal hospitals. Thousands of parents of retarded children found him to be a fighter against a state bureacracy that, even under the most liberal administrations, tended to ignore their complaints about state institutions. However, legislators were free to vote their consciences on good-works legislation because these were issues in which business and its lobbyists took little interest. Mental hospitals and retarded children were outside of the realm of private enterprise.

On the issues that counted to those who financed political campaigns, Senator Short was a stalwart of the legislator-lobbyist world, and he played the game well. He was, for many years, chairman of the senate committee on business and professions, which considers every piece of legislation regulating licensed businesses, ranging from the medical profession to racetracks and barber shops. Frequently there is no liberal or conservative side to that type of legislation. There are only the arguments of one special interest against another.

One of the best illustrations of this point occurred several years before in the legislature, on an issue unrelated to industrial safety. That year, there was a fight between competing segments of the oil industry for the right to develop a large off-shore oil field in Southern California. On one side was "big oil"—Standard, Shell, and the other well-known major companies. On the other side was "little oil," independent firms, little only in the sense that they were not as large as Standard or Shell. Big oil was allied with the government agency that controlled the field, the city of Long Beach. Defending that side in the legislature was the speaker of the assembly, Jess Unruh, who was a liberal Democrat but who had close ties with Long Beach business interests. Joining him was the leader of the senate, Hugh Burns, who worked closely with lobbyists for Standard and the other big oil firms. Speaking for little oil was the lieutenant governor of the state, Glenn Anderson, who had close political ties with Edwin Pauley, operator of the most important independent firm.

No ideology was at stake here, just which of the oil interests would benefit most. At one committee hearing the administrative assistant to the lieutenant governor got up and began to portray the issue in liberal-conservative terms, speaking of the wealthy and powerful Pauley as a fighter against monopoly. A young reporter watched the performance in disbelief. Unruh, who understood the system well, walked over to him and asked, "Tell me, what's the liberal side of this issue?"

Most of the bills that had come before Senator Short as head of the business and professions committee were of a similar non-ideological nature. This committee heard scores of bills every year affecting business. These bills usually concern only those involved in the business and apply to few other Californians. As a result, they are unpublicized, yet they can provide great profits to the businesses they affect. In many legislative sessions, for example, there are long discussions over the laws affecting beauty shops. The proposed laws would not affect the consumer, just the internal workings of the state-regulated beauty shops. Beauticians' trade organizations give campaign contributions in the hope they can ease the passage of such legislation.

Decoding the Contribution Lists

When Senator Short was reelected in 1970, he received campaign contributions of $79,651. He was no longer chairman of the business and professions committee, but he was still a member, and his report of contributions amounts to a survey of businesses with an interest in the committee's deliberations. Short's contributions ranged from Denny's Restaurants, a large chain, to racetracks; from the Independent Auto Dealers of California to the International Telephone and Telegraph Corporation. (While corporate donations are forbidden at the federal level, they are legal in state and local campaigns.) Twenty contributions were from the medical field, from nurses' groups, chiropractors, psychologists, pharmacists, and one organization with an intriguing name, the Public Vision League, the campaign contributing arm of the state's association of optometrists, whose licensing procedures are under the committee's jurisdiction.

Most legislators said there was nothing wrong with the system, that a campaign contributor had no more influence with them than a noncontributing citizen. But, if the system were so innocuous, then why did so many legislators insist on making it so difficult for the average citizen to identify campaign contributors? Under the law—made by the very people it regulates—campaign contribution reports are kept in only two places, the legislative district involved and in the state capitol. It is not easy to find them, and often the entries on candidate's reports are meaningless.

For example, many of Senator Short's contributors, as he had them listed, were impossible to connect with the interests they served. Take three names from Short's list: "H-P Trust," "Joseph Farber" and "Kenneth Ross." What and who are they? Some information can be found in an obscure publication of the legislature's joint committee on rules. It is the directory of lobbyists and is available for the asking if you know what you want and whom to ask. Other information is available from the reports of one or two more conscientious legislators who actually provided brief descriptions of such mysterious listings. In 1972, Secretary of State Edmund G. Brown, Jr., issued a two-page list describing some of these contributors.

From these sources, we were able to determine that the H-P Trust is the campaign contribution operation of Hollywood Park racetrack, with its funds distributed by the track's lobbyist, James Garibaldi. Garibaldi is also listed in the 1973-74 lobbyist directory as the representative of Blue Chip Stamps, the California Association of Highway Patrolmen, the California State Auto Club Association, the Pacific Outdoor Advertising Company, the Signal Companies (a conglomerate), and the Wine and Spirits Wholesalers of California. Joseph Farber turned out to be the lobbyist for the Delta Packaging Company, the Pacific Coast Coin Exchange, the Stockton Terminal Company, the Veterans of Foreign Wars, and the Native Sons of the Golden West (a lodge). Kenneth Ross is also a lobbyist, representing the American Cement Corporation, the Associated General Contractors, the California Portland Cement Company, Continental Airlines, the Flying Tiger Line, the Los Angeles Turf Club (operators of Santa Anita Race Track), the Monolith Portland Cement Company, Pacific Western Industries, Inc., and the Southwestern Portland Cement Company. The cement companies were part of the highway lobby; in 1970

Senator Short was chairman of the senate committee that ruled on state transportation policy.

The people in Short's district paid little attention to the seemingly unimportant work that occupied much of the industrial relations committee's time. But several of his campaign contributors were vitally interested. Among these were the building industry employers who gave through the California Council of Professional Engineers, the California Sheet Metal Contractors, the Association of Motion Picture and TV Producers, the Plumbing-Heating-Cooling Contractors, and the California Employment Agencies Association.

Labor gave big, too. The largest single contribution came from the AFL-CIO's Committee on Political Education. The Teamsters union donated $600. Contributing less than $500 were the California State Conference of Operating Engineers; the Laundry, Dry Cleaners and Dye House Workers; the Sacramento Typographical Union; the International Brotherhood of Electrical Workers; the Journeymen Barbers Association; the United Steelworkers Union; the Teamsters Packing House and Allied Workers Organizing Fund; the State Building Trades and Construction Council; the Brotherhood of Railroad and Airline Clerks; the Cannery Workers Political Education Welfare Fund; and the Sacramento Central Labor Council.

Senator Short had to balance the interests of his campaign contributors in considering the industrial safety bill, as well as his own personal beliefs. And since the interests of big business and labor contributors were conflicting in this case, Senator Short had a dilemma.

Ducking the Dilemma

The year before, Short had the same dilemma when the 1972 version of the same bill was before the industrial relations committee. Then, he solved it in an interesting manner, which angered Assemblyman Fenton and other supporters of the bill. Short had voted for the bill in the industrial relations committee. But when the bill came up for the last hearing in the senate finance committee, on which he also serves, he was not there. One of Assemblyman Fenton's assistants had sergeants of arms look everywhere: in Short's office, in other committee hearings. Finally, a secretary in Short's office said he was ill. He had, supporters of the bill believed, "taken a duck" and had not had the courage to vote at all. In the assembly, where voting is recorded by pressing a red button for "no" and a green button for "aye," Short had, in the language of the legislature, voted "the yellow button." And the bill failed without his vote.

This year, Short was again the deciding vote. There was no way to know how he would vote. Fenton knew the three Republicans would vote against his industrial safety bill and three Democrats would vote aye. Democrat Short was the swing vote.

Biddle's Easy Road

On the other side of the rostrum from Senator Short was Senator Craig Biddle, a Republican from Riverside, a city that used to be a pleasant place in the heart of farmland east of Los Angeles. But now it is trapped under the smog that backs up each day from Los Angeles.

Senator Biddle was opposed to the bill because of his beliefs— beliefs that fitted the needs of the conservative growers and businessmen in his district who paid for his political campaigns. As a conservative Republican, his backers could count on him to vote against the bill. He did not share the dilemma of Short, a Democrat consistently forced to balance the desires of campaign contributors with opposing interests.

Biddle's background deserves study as an example of the making of a conservative legislator. In addition to representing the city of Riverside, Biddle also represented the irrigated farmlands of the Coachella Valley, where desert has been turned into productive earth by Colorado River water stored behind the federal government's Hoover Dam. It is an agricultural empire, where grapes, melons, tomatoes, lettuce, dates and cotton grow, enriching the comparatively small number of growers who own the land. Without water from a government project, their land would be desert and so they accept help gratefully. But while accepting government's water, they reject its interference with the way they treat their employees.

These growers are not farmers in the conventional sense of the word, but are proprietors of large businesses that happen to be farms. Often, they are not individuals, but are absentee corporations. In the tradition of California agriculture, they have profited in the past from low-paid migrant labor, imported for the growing season, housed in miserable dwellings and sent on their way after the harvest. As employers, the farmer-businessmen in Biddle's district regarded strict industrial safety laws as an outrage, an unjust infringement on their rights.

His Contributors

Biddle's view of limited government was in accord with the view of the growers and of the business community. The Century Club, an organization of Republican businessmen in Riverside, donated $9,000 to his campaign. United for California, another conservative pro-business fund-raising group, also gave $9,000. He received $2,000 from a Republican congressman, Victor Veysey, who is a grower in Biddle's area, presumably from Veysey's leftover campaign contributions—a customary procedure among officeholders who share political views. Among the contributors were the California Railroad Association, $500; the California Medical Association's political action committee, $2,500; the Western Growers Political Committee, $400; Association of California Life Insurance Companies, $500; the California State Real Estate Association, $400; the California Medical Group of Sacramento, $1,500; Standard Oil, $400; and Sears Roebuck, $500.

Biddle's campaign contributions show the advantage of being a conservative in a legislature so heavily dominated by business. No compromise of his beliefs was necessary in order to keep obtaining their contributions. And he also benefited from the treasury of the state Republican party, which relied heavily on donations from conservative Republican businessmen. The Republican State Central Committee donated $15,000 to his campaign, and fellow Republican senators gave $6,600 from a fund financed by contributors. Not surprisingly, Biddle listed no contributions from organized labor, whose views he opposed.

But like many legislators, there was more depth to Biddle than a list of his contributors would reveal. He was not just an obedient servant to his financial backers. In many ways, he was an independent man, a lawyer who had been both a deputy district attorney and a public defender. While in the assembly, he had taken a thoughtful look at matters of criminal justice. He had served as chairman of the assembly criminal procedure committee, balancing the demands of Ronald Reagan conservatives against those of liberals. In 1967, he was the assembly floor manager for the bill which liberalized California's then strict law against abortion. He was, however, a dedicated Republican, and in times of crisis, Governor Reagan could count on his support.

He was a good senator, and on the imperfect scale of legislative performance, a harder working one than Senator Short. But, like Short, he was subject to pressures on every vote and had to balance them. On the matter of industrial safety, the pressures on him coincided with his beliefs. He was a fortunate man.

One Lawmaker's Freedom to Crusade

Standing before the committee was the third character in our drama, Assemblyman Jack Fenton, a Democrat and the author of the industrial safety bill. In the amiable atmosphere of Sacramento, Fenton was an exception, a surly, angry man who did not try to make himself liked. He was dressed like the others, maroon sport coat, blue slacks, white shoes. But his manner was abrasive, as if to say to his colleagues, "Accept me on my terms."

He was a lawyer who looked as though he had come up from the streets, a blunt brawler who would be uncomfortable in polite society. He was intelligent, with a good grasp of politics, and he was loyal to his good friend, the speaker of the assembly, Bob Moretti. When Moretti decided to investigate the San Fernando Tunnel explosion, he gave the assignment to Fenton's assembly industrial safety committee, knowing Fenton was smart and mean enough to stand up to the Lockheed officials and those law enforcement officials who were trying to ignore the corporation's negligence. Moretti had made the correct choice.

Although Fenton's list of campaign contributors was evidence that he belonged to the lobbyist-legislator club, it also showed why he felt free to take on the fight for increased industrial safety. Unlike Senator Short, Fenton received few contributions from firms employing large numbers of people. Kaiser Aluminum was an exception, but Kaiser was an enlightened employer and had tried to work out a settlement on the industrial safety bill.

One of the entries on his report of campaign contributions was "V. Dennis Kennedy, trustee," $1,000. A look in the roster of lobbyists showed that Kennedy was a lobbyist, representing the California Auctioneers Association, the California Mortgage Brokers, the Pest Control Operators of California, and the California Forest Protective Association, which was a deceptively named association of logging companies. A total of $750 came from what was described only as "CREPAC." This was the political fund of the California State Real Estate Association. Another $1,000 came from something listed as "ABC Burlingame." This was the political fund of the California Teachers Association. Other contributions were from the California Teamsters Legislative Council of San Francisco, $850; National General Corporation, an insurance conglomerate, $1,250; the Horsemen's Quarter Horse Racing Association, $1,000; the International Brotherhood of Electrical Workers; the California Medical Association; the Los Angeles County Employees Association; the steelworkers union; Los Alamitos racetrack; the California Chiropractic Association; Bullock's, a retail department store; and Kaiser Aluminum.

Fenton was popular in his district. As a result, he had no need to spend all of the $20,965 he had raised for his reelection in 1972. So he gave some of it away to other political candidates in a manner that increased his own political power. He reported giving $5,000 to the Assembly Democratic Caucus, the organization of lower house Democrats helping to finance the campaigns of Democratic assembly candidates. If the Democrats retained control of the assembly, Fenton's friend, Speaker Moretti, would stay in power. In addition, Fenton gave $1,000 each to six Democratic assembly candidates, some of whom won. Thus by giving $1,000 to Fenton, lobbyist V. Dennis Kennedy and the others were buying more than access to a single assemblyman. They were buying access to a leader to whom favors were owed.

A Semblance of Open Debate

Each of the three legislators—Short, Biddle and Fenton—found himself in a different situation. Short's difficulties were the greatest. Forced to raise a large amount of money for a difficult reelection campaign, he had accepted large amounts of money from both sides in the industrial safety dispute. Biddle was ideologically in tune with his campaign contributors, who opposed the industrial safety bill. Fenton, like Short, accepted help from both business and labor. But the financial requirements of his campaigns were not as severe as Short's, and he was not dependent on the support of large employers.

As the meeting got underway, Fenton opened with a brief explanation of what the bill would do. What he didn't mention was how the elements of the bill had been decided on. As has been pointed out before, much of what happens in legislative bodies is decided in the backrooms, before public meetings are held. In these private meetings, the complex relationships created by the lobbyist-legislator-campaign-contribution system are put to use to reach quiet agreements and avoid public fights, if possible. What it amounts to is old friends sitting around and trying to work out a deal.

The legislature, years before, had passed the Brown Act, forbidding government bodies to meet without allowing witnesses from the public and the press. But the legislators had exempted themselves from its provisions.

All of the members of the industrial relations committee knew of the private negotiations on Fenton's bill. They knew the content of the negotiations. They liked it that way. They would have found it hard to function under a different system. In this case, for months before the committee hearing, meetings had taken place in Senator Short's office to work out a compromise between those who opposed the bill and those who wanted it. Fenton's staff spoke for those who favored the bill, including labor unions whose interest in industrial safety had been intensified by the San Fernando Tunnel explosion. Business lobbyists were there, as well as Short's assistant. They had worked out what Fenton thought might be an agreeable compromise between opposing points of view, and there was not much more that could be said.

He was wrong. At the committee hearing, A. J. Libra, the lobbyist for the California Manufacturers Association and chief opponent of the bill, stepped to the witness table and offered an entirely new set of amendments. He had written them himself, as many lobbyists do. Everyone understood long negotiations meant death to the improved industrial safety bill in the waning days of the legislative session. And if the bill were delayed and allowed to die, the federal regulations would take effect. The tactic came as a surprise to Fenton, who protested that Libra had not presented these suggestions in the pre-hearing negotiations.

But when Fenton objected that Libra was, in effect, breaking the agreement reached in Senator Short's office, Biddle—opposed to the bill—protested. His protest was an example of a frequently played legislative game—the self-righteous double-cross.

"I wasn't party to those negotiations and I don't think any member of this committee was a member" [of the negotiating team], he said. It was an attempt to muddy the issue. Members of the committee had been told what was happening in the private talks. But his strategy enabled Biddle to attack the bill on entirely new, and irrelevant, grounds, that it was the product of mysterious secret meetings.

His statement surprised Senator Short, who had carefully followed the negotiations in which his assistant had tried to draft a bill that would satisfy both Short's labor union and employer campaign contributors. "We worked pretty hard on negotiations," Short told Biddle. He said each side had given, and there had been a "quid pro quo," something given in return for something received.

The new attack by Biddle and lobbyist Libra, viewed as a double-cross by Short, meant that Short might now feel free to vote aye. But supporters of the bill could not be sure until the end.

The Opponents Speak Up

After Libra spoke, other lobbyists opposing the bill appeared at the witness table. Each followed the legislative custom of starting out a speech against a bill by saying they favored such legislation, or at least the concept of it. To an outsider watching one of these meetings, it often appears there are no opponents to anything. "We want the present safety program to work for the benefit of California industry and California labor," said Ed Couch of the State Chamber of Commerce. But before he was done speaking, it was clear that the chamber opposed the bill.

The California Chamber of Commerce was typical of the opponents. While not a campaign contributor itself, the chamber is composed of the businesses that influence politics and government in California. The president of the chamber in 1973 was B. F. Biaggini, president of the Southern Pacific Company.

While not the power it had been in the early part of the century, the railroad was still deeply involved in California government. It contributed to legislative campaigns through the California Railroad Association and was involved in local as well as state government. In Los Angeles, for example, Southern Pacific wanted to build a $26 million real estate development, but a small parcel in the middle of SP's property was owned by a family who refused to sell. Unable to deal with the property owners, the railroad persuaded the county government to condemn the land, use part of it to widen the street and sell the rest to SP. The plan collapsed when a dissenting supervisor told the press about SP's campaign contribution to the official proposing the condemnation.

Another lobbyist who testified worked for the California Farm Bureau Federation, representing the large corporate farm businesses in the state. He also said he favored state regulation of industrial safety but insisted on amendments that would badly weaken the bill. Supporting the farm lobby and the chamber of commerce was the lobbyist for the state's contractors.

Short's Decision

But Short had made up his mind. As chairman of the committee, he cut off the discussion, called for a vote and voted "aye." The bill passed the committee 4-3 with the Democrats voting for it and the Republicans opposed.

Unlike his performance of the previous year, Short stuck to his decision this time. In the senate finance committee (where he had failed to appear for last year's vote) he voted "aye," although Fenton felt a momentary twinge of fright when Short left the room briefly. But he returned and he was available later on the senate floor when the bill came to a final vote in the last few days of the 1973 legislative session.

Short's decision to support the legislation and his ability to stick to it ended the lobbyists' attempt to delay the bill with a battle over a new set of amendments. Seventeen lives, and the resulting trial, had clearly shown the weakness in California's industrial safety enforcement. Employers who threw away lives to increase profits were able to get off with light penalties. But, as we have just seen, the bill that would strengthen the workers' protection, was almost defeated.

LUNCHES, DINNERS AND CHRISTMAS PRESENTS: THE CAPITOL LIFE STYLE

The maneuvers over this bill demonstrate how legislation is fought out in hidden arenas, in a complex way that makes it difficult to understand what is happening or to know how to influence the discussion. A major force in these discussions, we have pointed out, is the campaign contribution. But there are other factors, touching on the social relationships between elected officials and their financial supporters, and on the unique life style of the legislative community.

Life in Sacramento has changed from the years when legislators drew salaries of $100 a month and were happy to accept a free lunch or dinner. One old-time lobbyist even took care of lawmakers' funeral expenses. He knew, of course, he could expect no more favors from the departed, but the gesture made a strong impression on surviving colleagues.

Today, with a salary of $21,120 a year and expense accounts of about another $10,000 annually, legislators can buy their own meals. So, who picks up the dinner check is often not as important as the conviviality which extends to every level of Capitol society. There is, for example, the matter of the secretaries' lunches.

The Capitol secretaries guard legislators' offices with jealous vigilance, coolly grading visitors on a scale of importance. Those low on the scale might never get in to see an official. Others have to wait a long time for an appointment with a legislator or even an aide. The smarter lobbyists shamelessly court the secretaries with lunches, dinners, candy and Christmas presents.

A number of things hold this closed society together. Friendships between lawmakers and those who want something from them flower in the small town atmosphere, continuing a tradition that goes back to the earliest days of the state's history and is common to state capitals elsewhere. Years before, many California legislators were beery old hacks who would leave the boredom of their homes for short legislative sessions, ready to be entertained. In hotel rooms, lobbyists would accommodatingly lose to legislators at poker. Stories linger about the drunken trips with girls down the Sacramento River to San Francisco on the two steamers, Delta Queen and Delta King, and the St. Patrick's Day celebrations in the assembly when everyone put on funny hats, drank too much and made speeches in fake Irish brogues.

The style has changed, but the Capitol is still a fiercely competitive market place for influence. In 1967, the legislature went on a year-round status in what it said was an attempt to become more professional and less indebted to special interests. Salaries were raised, and senators and assemblymen began moving their families to Sacramento. With wives in town, bars emptied at night. A few years before, the downstairs bar at the El Mirador Hotel—called the "snakepit"—had been full of hookers, legislators and reporters. The guitar player at the bar was once arrested for pimping.

But no more. The legislators have taken on the manner of businessmen and now look like sales managers of prosperous middle-sized firms. They are younger than before. The beer bellies, red noses and almost senile doddering of another day would not sell in the television politics of the seventies. Businesses hired new lobbyists to match the new legislators. They were experts in taxes, state finance or water law, smart enough to negotiate with the well-educated consultants the legislature had employed to advise the senators and assemblymen. Instead of long evenings at the bar, lobbyists and legislators may well pass a word on a Sunday afternoon while their families play at the swimming and tennis club or on a skiing trip to the mountains.

Campaign contributions fit nicely into the social life, reinforcing friendships. Without the contributions it would all fall apart, for they are needed for what officeholders consider the most important part of their business—getting reelected.

"Select and Elect"

In the 1930s, a tall, fat man became powerful in Sacramento because he understood the way money, conviviality, favors and sometimes brute force are used in government. His name was Art Samish, and he represented nationwide liquor distillers and California breweries. This master lobbyist was a great power in the California legislature from the middle of the 1930s until he was convicted of income tax evasion twenty years later. When California's great governor, Earl Warren, was asked by Lester Velie of *Colliers* magazine who had more power in the legislature, he or Samish, the governor replied, "On matters that affect his clients, Artie unquestionably has more power than the governor."

Art Samish was called "The Secret Boss of California," a title he liked so much that he used it for his autobiography, published in 1971. He worked from a fourth-floor suite in the Senator Hotel, across from the Capitol, and he seldom appeared in the legislative halls. Instead, he listened to reports from Porky Flynn and other assistants who then relayed his orders to compliant assemblymen and senators. "One time," recalled Samish in his book, "Coors [a brewery] tried to come into California with a six ounce bottle." Samish represented California beer makers and Coors was out-of-state. "We didn't like the competition. Besides, those bottles could easily get into the hands of children. That wouldn't be right. So we managed to get through a law stating that the minimum size of the beer bottle in the state was eleven ounces. Goodbye Coors."

Artie Samish no longer entertains legislators at a table heavy with lobster, canapes and the best liquor in Sacramento. And the men who have succeeded him are not so crude as to send a Porky Flynn over to the assembly public morals committee to dictate the contents of a liquor bill. But the lobbyists are still called the Third House in testimony to their power. Though their style has changed, they still follow a formula devised by Samish many years ago.

"Bribery? Promise of Reward? Intimidation? That was for amateurs," Samish wrote. "It certainly wasn't for Art Samish. It was merely this: Select and Elect. That was all. I simply selected those men I thought would be friendly to my client's interests. Then I saw to it that those men got elected to the legislature. . . . Sometimes an assemblyman or senator might have disappointed me. Maybe he voted the wrong way on a bill I wanted. Too bad for him. I did my best to see that he didn't return to the legislature after the next election." In the new legislature, the lobbyists stuck to the same system, and, when they lost an election, they moved in quickly to make friends with the newcomer.

Initiating the Novice

Raymond Gonzales learned about the system when he was elected to the assembly in 1972. Gonzales was a professor of Latin American studies at Cal State Bakersfield, a small state university in an oil-producing and farming community at the southern end of the Central Valley. It is a conservative place, and only thirteen percent of the population share Gonzales' Mexican-American heritage. Despite the history of ethnic prejudice in the area, Gonzales won, helped greatly by the endorsement of the conservative local paper which considered the incumbent assemblyman a do-nothing. Immediately after his election, Gonzales told Kenneth Reich of the *Los Angeles Times* that corporations sent him checks to "erase my deficit." There was no deficit. Gonzales ran a low-budget campaign, and had even made a home movie commercial to be shown on television. The race had not cost him much.

Once in Sacramento, Gonzales asked some assembly leaders about serving on the important assembly education committee, for which the college professor thought himself qualified. He said he was told his prospects for such an appointment were not bright. The committee, he was informed, was a "juice" committee. Juice is money, and members of such a committee receive plenty of it from lobbyists for their election campaigns. One of the most generous contributors was the teacher lobby, through the California Teachers Association. He was too new at the legislature to qualify for such a position of advantage.

But unsolicited gifts began arriving at the Gonzales' modest home. He said he asked a member of the Assembly staff what to do about it. "If you can eat it or drink it, take it. Otherwise don't," the staff member told him. He said he was told about "gifts appearing in your office when you get there—a refrigerator one day, a case of mixed drinks the next."

Gonzales returned the money and worried about the rest. He said he liked the lobbyists as individuals, but was concerned about their clout. "What bothers me is that they feel they have to do what they do," he said. "The Third House is an important part of the legislature. I'm sorry that it is, but it is. For instance, we've got a case of wine delivered to the house and from people I'm not even familiar with. But I guess it's a standard procedure. They want to get off on the right foot with you. I'm not making any personal criticisms. It's the system. These people have a very big role to play and I'm not sure it's the best thing for the state."

Even this mild criticism is unusual, and was heard because Gonzales was a newcomer. Such relationships are less troubling to more experienced legislators. They say they cannot be bought for a gift or a campaign contribution. Nothing was asked by the donor, they say, and nothing was promised. That is largely true, for politics operates in an unspoken language. What the contributions buy is something called "access"—the ability to go directly to a legislator, or a mayor or a governor or a city councilman or a President of the United States, and make a presentation. The average citizen does not have such access. About the best he can do is write a letter.

ACCESS

The story of Al Alquist and the railroad grade crossing bill best illustrates the meaning of the word access. Most people who know the California legislature would readily volunteer to be character witnesses for Senator Alquist, a quiet, gray-haired man of the deepest liberal convictions. He worked in the Southern Pacific Railroad yards for sixteen years and then was elected to the legislature from a suburban city. In 1970, in a seemingly hopeless crusade, he ran for the Democratic nomination for lieutenant governor and actually won it, making his liberal speeches to tiny audiences in a plodding, sincere way. The fact that he was defeated with the rest of the ticket in November does not diminish his accomplishment.

Alquist did not consider it a matter of ethics when Donald Reisner, the lobbyist for the California Railroad Association, came to him with a bill to be introduced. The association, which had donated $300 to Alquist's campaign in 1972, when he faced little opposition for reelection, felt the old railroad man was a natural person to approach. "Alquist is familiar with our problems," said Reisner. "We felt he would understand." Alquist introduced the bill, a blatant giveaway that would save the railroads at least $500,000 a year by reducing from ten percent to five percent the share the railroads pay for construction of grade separations, which are street and highway railroad crossings over railroad tracks. The railroads' saving would come at taxpayers' expense because the other share of construction costs are paid for by state and local governments. Because of the tremendous volume of legislation, the bill got little publicity. It passed the senate public utilities and corporations committee, of which Alquist is chairman, by 6-0 and then passed the senate all but unnoticed.

That is what access means. It was not just a $300 contribution to an easy campaign that needed little money. The contribution was a major gesture of friendship, an important part of a relationship that gave Reisner access to an important legislator.

And what is noteworthy is that Alquist, the liberal, performed the favor for some of the nation's largest corporations. When the railroads went looking for friends, they paid no attention to ideology or political party. Like Artie Samish, they worked for the election of men who voted for their economic interests.

The System's Universality

The nationwide nature of this system was illustrated in a conversation with Joseph Alton, the county executive of Anne Arundel County, Maryland. In 1973, a federal grand jury in Baltimore began looking into the management of the county. It was the same grand jury that investigated the conduct of Vice President Spiro Agnew as governor of Maryland and county executive of Baltimore County. Alton was the son of a sheriff of Anne Arundel County, and he had been sheriff himself for twelve years. Later, he ran for state senator and then for county executive. He was the dominant political figure in the county, an area of rapid suburban development and of competition for profits between developers and contractors. The grand jury's investigation centered on the relationship between government officials and contractors doing business with government, and Alton had no hesitation in discussing his own relationship with businessmen. In an interview with Paul Edwards of the *Washington Post,* for example, Alton made these points about the power of money in local government and how political belief means little to those who play the game:

"If you don't like either party and you want to build your organization, it takes a lot of money. The money comes from special interests.

"I didn't stay in office for more than 20 years without playing the game. I've financed people in both parties. I've run for [county] executive every time with a coalition of Republican and Democratic candidates for council. We won every time and I attracted the financing.

"Anytime I've gone to a public affair, I've always come back with a pocketful of business cards of people who want to do work for the county. We gave some work to everyone who asked to do some work here. But we always got our money's worth."

Even reformers—or those who say they are reformers—find it difficult to escape the system.

In 1972, Dan Walker, a vice president of Sears Roebuck who had headed a famous presidential commission studying violence in America, decided to run for governor of Illinois. The public opinion polls showed not many people knew who he was. Paul Simon, the lieutenant governor, was favored to win the Democratic nomination and then face the incumbent Republican governor, Richard T. Ogilvie, in a year when Republican fortunes looked promising. It did not look like Walker had much of a chance. But he walked the length of Illinois in a successful stunt to win publicity. And on that walk he talked about how big business campaign contributors ran the state government. He was a tall, handsome man and the voters liked the way he walked across the state, wearing work clothes, a red bandanna around his neck. Most of all, they liked the way he attacked campaign contributors and Mayor Daley's Chicago machine. He beat Simon for the Democratic nomination and then defeated Governor Ogilvie.

But after the election, Walker owed a campaign debt of $1 million. To pay it off, the reform governor used the techniques he had so strongly criticized. The Chicago *Daily News,* after obtaining copies of Walker's fund-raising documents, reported he had obtained money from the traditional sources—firms doing business with the state, the labor unions, and companies licensed and regulated by the state. Scores of businesses contributed, even though Walker had criticized Governor Ogilvie for accepting contributions from corporations. The paper told how bankers and executives of other industries regulated by the state were asked to attend unpublicized fund-raising luncheons. And, despite his campaign promise to disclose the identity of big contributors, Walker had not released their names. In fact, the paper said, Angelo Geocaris, Walker's fund raiser, assured some executives of firms doing business with the state that Walker would not immediately issue an executive order—one he had promised the voters—that would have required disclosure of the firms' names.

That is how it has always been done, and Mike Royko wondered in his *Daily News* column, "Why pick on Dan Walker for doing nothing more than the rest of them have done?" He answered the question: "The thrust of Walker's campaign was that he was above the methods used by other politicians, that he wouldn't use the methods used by other politicians, that he wouldn't use the nasty tactics of a machine.

"Now he is doing exactly what he has condemned. Machine politics consists of using the leverage of government to strengthen a political organization.

"So when the Walker organization hustles contributions from companies who fear the loss of state business, they are using the same kind of muscle as a ward boss who makes a city employee work a precinct to keep his job."

AN ATTEMPT AT REFORM

Abuses have increased as the costs of political campaigning have gone up. The series of political scandals lumped together under the name of Watergate were caused, in part, by the wild scramble for campaign contributions by President Nixon's reelection committee. Scandal always breeds reform, and so after Watergate, state and local governments around the nation began enacting laws regulating campaign contributions and requiring disclosure both of contributors and of the financial status of public officials. Largely these laws were prompted by disclosures in the press, and when resulting public opinion forced the Alabama legislature to pass a financial disclosure law, it tried to punish the press by making reporters disclose their own finances before they were permitted to cover news events in the Capitol. In California, the legislature's fear of a tough voter initiative advocated by *Common Cause* prompted the lawmakers to pass a law requiring fuller disclosure of their campaign finances.

Another proposal for reform is public financing of political campaigns. It sounds good on the surface, but it is as potentially bad as financing by the traditional fat cats. Government—the elected officials who want to stay in power—would suddenly be able to decide who is a legitimate candidate entitled to government-distributed campaign funds. Instead of a meaningful reform, public financing could become another tool to stifle dissent.

The Matter of Enforcement

In the final analysis, the answer is stricter disclosure laws, plus intense enforcement, for the first time, of present laws. For no matter how tough the law, it still must be enforced by public officials. We found an example of how difficult this can be in California. In 1970, the highway lobby organized to fight a ballot measure that would have allowed the use of gas tax revenues for rapid transit. The campaign against it was an expensive and successful one, and although the law required public disclosure of who financed it, the organizers were reluctant to disclose the source of money. A report filed with the Secretary of State, Edmund G. Brown, Jr., listed a $90,000 contribution from an anonymous source. Brown doubted such a big contribution could come in without the organizers knowing the source of it. He asked law enforcement officials to investigate.

The case was under the jurisdiction of the district attorney of Sacramento County, where the state capital is located and where the report was filed. The Sacramento district attorney, John Price, was firm enough in prosecuting murder in his jurisdiction, but reluctant to step into the more controversial area of investigating political misbehavior. He, after all, was an elected official too. Questioning the anonymous contribution report, Brown had written Price, "I find it difficult to believe that every single person connected with the committee against Proposition 18 (the gas tax measure) is ignorant of these bashful contributors." Price refused to investigate, claiming he was powerless. "As district attorneys do not have the power of subpoena," he wrote Brown, "I have no way of determining at this time the identity of the contributors." He was correct in saying he had no subpoena power. But he ignored the fact that he could have turned the case over to the Sacramento County Grand Jury, which has that power.

Two days after Price refused to investigate, Brown's deputy, Tom Quinn, was able to track down the real source of the contributions—oil companies which did not want their identity revealed to the public. Brown believed there was evidence of conspiracy to commit election fraud, a felony. But Price never prosecuted. Such attitudes were almost universal among law enforcement officials. As a result, there has not been a conviction for election fraud in California since the 1920s.

Meaningful Enforcement

What would help? Stricter enforcement of existing laws requiring disclosure of campaign contributions, with an independent public agency given the job of auditing the candidates' reports to see if they are truthful.

The reports should contain the identity of every campaign contributor with the amount of his contribution; names listed in alphabetical order, with address, occupation and employer so there is no doubt about the identity of the contributor. Individual names should be cross-indexed with the names of corporations they represent. Contribution lists should be much more easily available to the public. In the case of state officials, information should be available around the state instead of just in the capital or in a state legislator's home county. For local officeholders, the information should be available in a number of government offices, not just city hall or the county archives.

Finally, a specific prosecutor—the state attorney general, perhaps—should be given the responsibility in law for conducting prosecutions, just as the U.S. Justice Department prosecutes violations of the federal election code.

But all the disclosure laws in the world will not do any good if nobody uses the information to evaluate officials' integrity and performance, or if the press does not publicize the reports.

As we will discuss in the final chapter, campaign contribution information makes effective ammunition for those fighting to influence government officials. It is a frightening experience for an officeholder to face a citizen armed with a list of contributors and the willingness to embarrass the official with the information at a public meeting. It is seldom possible to precisely pinpoint the reason for enactment of a law. But the campaign contribution is a major motive in what happens in backroom trading and deals. The Samish principle of "Select and Elect," and the campaign contribution, may well be a permanent part of our political system. But with meaningful campaign finance disclosure, voters can judge for themselves who is making the decisions and why.

6

Rx from

the Legislature

A doorbell rang in a slum neighborhood not far from the Pacific Ocean. It was one of those places in California where the poor seem to live better than they do in other states. The weather, usually temperate, covers everything in a deceptively pleasant cloak of sunshine and sea breezes. Frame bungalows instead of tenements house the poor. But the despair is just as severe as in other places. There is hunger, loneliness, and the people are easily victimized. It is a suitable setting for a story of deception.

An old man answered the front door. A man, wearing the white clothes of a physician, and a woman, dressed like a nurse, greeted him. From public records, the man and woman knew many people in this neighborhood were receiving assistance from Medi-Cal, a federal and state program to provide medical assistance to poor people. Medi-Cal had been intended to permit them to be treated at private physicians' offices at government expense and extend to them the same quality of care given everyone else. The old man was nearly deaf and blind, but he knew that in his wallet was a ticket to survival—his Medi-Cal card. Without it, he was condemned to wait in long lines in the halls of county hospital, on the other side of town.

The man and woman told the old man they had a better medical plan for him, operated by a Dr. Vincent De Paulo. "They said it was a better program than the Medi-Cal," the old man later wrote to the Los Angeles County Medical Society. "I am hard of hearing and almost blind. I didn't understand them, and I couldn't read what they wanted me to sign. I have my own heart specialist, and I don't want to go to Dr. De Paulo."

His visitors were not a doctor and a nurse. Wearing white uniforms that they later insisted were not disguises, they were paid commissions to sign up the poor for a new form of government-financed medical care. The professional enrollers were persuasive, and the old man signed up, turning his life over to Dr. De Paulo's medical clinic.

Dr. De Paulo is one of California's new medical entrepreneurs, proprietors of medical clinics franchised and paid by the state to give health care to all the poor people they can sign up in their area.

The clinics are called prepaid health plans or health maintenance organizations. They are run by private corporations that, in exchange for a flat monthly fee for each member, provide him with complete medical service. No matter how often a patient is treated, or how serious the illness, the fee is the same. State government, using fifty percent federal funds, pays the monthly charge. The organizations are able to provide treatment on this basis because a certain number of members require no care. On the average, the cost of care is less than the fees collected, leaving room for a profit.

In the tremendous expansion of the prepaid groups in the state since 1971, many clinics have been thrown together by investors new to the health plan field. California also has a number of better prepaid plans that have grown slowly, over the years, and have built up-private, working-class clientele, such as labor unions and employee groups. Altogether, 200,000 Medi-Cal recipients are enrolled in both the older and the newer prepaid plans, and the state is hoping to eventually include seventy-five percent of California's two million needy.

Previously, Medi-Cal recipients went to individual doctors, who charged the government for each service they performed. The prepaid concept is a break with traditional American medical practices and has been strongly opposed by most of organized medicine. So far, medical association criticism of the prepaid groups has generally been justified. In their rush to launch a program they hoped would reduce the cost of medical aid to the poor, state officials have imposed few controls on men like De Paulo. Since profits come in when the new business-run clinics keep costs low, the results can be disastrous for members. Patients complain of too few doctors, long waits for care, a shortage of prescription drugs, and a frightening lack of emergency care.

As we will see, despite many clinics' poor records, the legislature and the state administration have refused to demand better performance. In the previous chapters, the special interests were external groups working to defeat good legislation. In this chapter, the forces are internal, part of the legislature itself—officeholders' own ambition and, in some cases, their desire to profit from their outside business interests.

With the state's permission, suede-shoe operators prowled poor neighborhoods selling medical care like encyclopedias or vacuum cleaners. Law enforcement agencies were at a loss to end the types of deception being used to make the poor sign up with the prepaid plans. In the summer of 1973, a Los Angeles deputy district attorney, looking into enrollment frauds, explained that his office had the legal power to stop such practices. But, he said, "There is some question as to whether we want to do this; the agencies involved say they don't want to put these people out of business. . . . The governor is very anxious that these plans work and not be disturbed by lawsuits." Law enforcement that would have moved against an individual doctor who defrauded his patients was paralyzed by permissive administrative policies.

FROM POOR NEIGHBORHOODS TO
NATIONAL POLICY TO YOU

One day, if federal government plans are completed, much of the middle class, as well as the poor, could be receiving their health care from prepaid plans. Dr. De Paulo and his colleagues are, in effect, pioneers in this new style of medical care. Already a handful of other states—Hawaii, Maryland, Massachusetts, Michigan, New York, Oregon, Rhode Island, Utah and the District of

Columbia—have such health organizations, although on a much smaller scale than California's.

With the cost of medical care rising, President Nixon in 1973 signed the Health Maintenance Organization Act, a revolutionary plan to determine whether these organizations can provide an alternative for expensive fee-for-service care for Americans. The act provides $375 million over five years to subsidize more health maintenance organizations throughout the country. Employers with at least twenty-five workers will be required to let them have the option of joining a prepaid group. Eventually, one hundred million Americans could be covered.

Unfortunately, there is no guarantee that federally subsidized health organizations will be better than California's. A 1972 U.S. Senate committee report said that while federal legislation was intended to encourage good medical care, "it is clear that effective quality control mechanisms do not exist in the health care field. There are neither standards nor fully developed methods of assessing the quality of care." In other words, the federal program, like California's, would be started without quality standards.

Bright Hope of Medicaid

In the beginning government-funded medical aid had been intended to raise—not lower—the quality of care given the poor. How had it all come about?

In 1965, following years of effort by Presidents Kennedy and Johnson, Congress finally passed a plan giving the government the mechanism to provide private medical care to the poor. Washington and the states split the cost. Under pressure from the American Medical Association, which feared federally run socialized medicine, the government gave the main responsibility of administering the program to the states. Every state but Arizona took advantage of the program. It was called Medicaid, except in California, where it was called Medi-Cal. Eventually, Medicaid and Medi-Cal were to form a national system of assuring every American a high level of medical care.

After a few years of Medicaid's operation, it became apparent that the cost of providing private doctors to the poor would exceed the states' willingness to pay. Illinois, New York and the other large states were faced with runaway costs. In California, the most populous state—and one of the most generous in its benefits—it was costing $1.5 billion a year in state and federal money. The sum represented one-fifth of the $6 billion a year the program was costing nationally. Even the sparse population of New Mexico bankrupted its Medicaid program by 1971.

The afflicted states tried to find ways of reducing costs. Illinois used medical association review boards to determine the length of hospital stays, and a large number of the state's physicians took part in an effort to cut hospital costs. In New Mexico's program, physicians used computers to help evaluate hospital stays and treatment for common diseases.

Inflation Hits Medi-Cal

In California, the deficit was the largest—over $100 million in 1970—and the state's attempt to reduce the cost of the program was unique. The attempt was promoted by Governor Reagan, who had consistently attacked government aid to the poor. In his own words, his constituent was "the forgotten American, the man in the suburbs working sixty hours a week to support his family and being taxed heavily for the benefit of someone else." Consequently, the governor had never accepted the idea behind Medi-Cal—the use of tax money to raise the quality of medical care available to the needy. He had openly declared war on the program in 1967, soon after he became governor. In a televised "message to the people," he held a Medi-Cal card up to the camera and told his middle-class supporters, "You are actually being taxed to provide better medical care for these card holders than you can afford for yourself and your family."

When it became apparent that the Medi-Cal program was in financial trouble, he and his close adviser, Dr. Earl Brian, began searching for a way to make drastic cuts in health coverage and other benefits to the poor.

Brian, a politically ambitious doctor in his late twenties, headed Reagan's Department of Health Care Services and the Medi-Cal program. He is a tall, bulky young Texan, a graduate of Stanford

Medical School with little experience practicing medicine. He shares Reagan's view on the issue of aid to the poor, and he was able to suggest innovative ways to cut programs for the needy. He rose quickly in the administration.

Brian's attitudes were apparent at a legislative hearing, when a state assemblyman asked him how he could justify sending near-blind children with severely impaired vision to school after the Medi-Cal program had stopped providing eyeglasses to all but the legally blind. The assemblyman had said, "How can we talk about . . . associating this with whether we can afford it or not? And we're talking about people who are wards of the state."

Brian was unruffled by the question. "Well, Mr. Duffy, I don't see that we are condemning these children to going to school without having the necessary vision care. I would point out that there are many states that do not provide this service at all." He was right; there are states that do not give glasses even to the legally blind.

Reagan and Brian hit upon a formula they believed was bound to save the state money from Medi-Cal as well as from the welfare program—as much as $200 million a year. As it turned out, there were no substantial savings, but this was not apparent for a long time because the administration was so secretive with the records of its health program.

The feature that was promoted as the biggest money saver was a change in Medi-Cal benefits, limiting each recipient to two doctor's visits and two prescriptions a month. A private doctor would be paid for nothing else, not even emergency care, without prior authorization from the state.

Reagan called the reforms "the most comprehensive ever attempted any place in the United States." They had to be approved by the legislature, but were opposed by Democratic lawmakers who had traditionally supported increased aid to the poor. But Reagan was determined to crack down on those he believed were "welfare cheaters." This had been one of the main issues in his campaign for governor.

The bill was introduced in the legislature in 1971. By August, a battle developed that delayed adjournment of the legislature for two weeks. Once the compromise was worked out, the bill was passed and hurried down to the governor's office for signing. Almost unnoticed by reporters and lawmakers was the bill's most significant change—a clause enabling the widespread growth of prepaid health plans. Democrats didn't quarrel with this portion of the legislation, for they thought it was a step toward a national health insurance, which they favored. Later, as it turned out, many of them were to profit personally from passage of this legislation.

The details of the prepaid plans—how they would be set up and regulated, what standards they would have to meet—were left to the administration to work out. Unrealized by most, Medi-Cal's use of the prepaid plans was a tremendous victory for those who opposed social legislation, and an opportunity for Reagan and Brian to institute the kind of conservative reforms they believed would help them run for higher office.

The Hopeful Past of Prepaids

What form the prepaid plans would take was vague in the minds of legislators, who had settled their business and cheerfully left the Capitol on vacation trips. In the past there had been only a few prepaid health plans. The first was started in California by Henry Kaiser, an industrialist who was concerned with the medical care given to workers in his World War II shipyards, which were built hurriedly in the San Francisco Bay Area and brought in thousands of workers to an area where there were not enough doctors. Kaiser took over and improved an old hospital, and, for a nominal sum, his workers received everything from physical examinations to surgery at the Kaiser clinic. The economics were simple. Workers could budget their medical expenses and be spared catastrophic medical bills. The only requirement was that they use Kaiser facilities and Kaiser staff, limiting the freedom of choice they would have had with private doctors. Since many workers required little care, the medical plan took in more money than it spent, using the surplus for expansion; the whole operation was run on a nonprofit basis.

After World War II, the Kaiser plan was expanded around the state, and thousands of people who did not work for Henry Kaiser joined. As medical costs increased, the demand for similar plans grew, and medical societies—initially fearing the Kaiser plan as a form of socialized medicine—slowly began to change their view. In 1954, the longshoremen's union in the northern California city of Stockton began negotiating with Kaiser. Private physicians in Stockton made a counter offer, and by doing so they conceived another form of prepaid group. They would provide medical care for the longshoremen for a fixed fee. Union members would be able to see any private physician who belonged to the newly formed San Joaquin Foundation for Medical Care. As Kaiser members, they would have had to go to a clinic. The San Joaquin Foundation gave longshoremen more of a choice. Today, the foundation and the county medical society are virtually the same organization, and ninety-six percent of the physicians in the Stockton area belong.

In all of the prepaid plans, the economic rule is the same: the fewer sick, the more money that the plan has left over at the end of the month. That rule worked well with groups such as the San Joaquin Foundation, and the Group Health Cooperative of Puget Sound in Seattle, Washington, all of which grew slowly, in competition with private practice doctors. The competition forced them to offer good care. In the case of Kaiser, when its members were dissatisfied, they were free to quit. With the foundation, doctors knew if they didn't offer good service, the longshoremen could go back to negotiating with Kaiser. It would have been bad business for its members to profiteer.

GETTING REAGAN'S PLANS ROLLING

But none of the existing plans could accommodate the kind of rapid growth that Reagan envisioned for his program. He decided he would encourage private businessmen to set up new prepaid plans. That policy turned the system over to entrepreneurs—giving them what amounted to franchises in health care.

To get a contract with Medi-Cal, a private medical corporation is formed, usually by doctors, to offer the prepaid medical services. They open a clinic with examining rooms, laboratories, X-ray facilities, a pharmacy, eye and dental care, as well as a rest home, ambulances and 24-hour emergency service—a complete range of health care. Since most of the new clinics lacked complete facilities, many of them contracted outside business to provide services.

Under the original Medi-Cal system, a doctor is paid a set fee by the government every time he sees a patient. Under the prepaid program, the government pays the corporation of doctors a flat monthly fee per poor person enrolled in the plan—whether he needs care or not. It is done under a state contract. Aid recipients are classified as good and bad health risks. For each good health risk, the clinic receives about $20 a month. Much more is paid for bad health risks, such as the totally disabled, up to $111 a month. For that sum, the clinic is to provide complete medical care—if it is needed.

State officials said their main concern was to save money. Proprietors of the prepaid plan were paid for all the Medi-Cal recipients in the area they could persuade to sign up—up to 100,000 of them in one case. Clinic owners were supposed to give the state a ten percent discount below what it had cost to treat a given number of patients under the old system.

The discount was a clue to the Reagan administration's view of the way the poor used free programs. It felt that the poor were going to the doctor too much under the old system, and would be going less to clinics that had more control over their patients. For basic to the administration's faith in the concept of prepaid clinics was the belief that the poor liked to go to the doctor when it was not necessary and that physicians liked to treat and hospitalize people—even needlessly—to earn extra money.

In setting up contracts with private groups, the administration explained it was handing the risk for medical care back to the doctors. Reagan and his aides liked to think they were offering doctors an incentive to keep the poor well, rather than to over-treat. But Assemblyman Henry Waxman, a critic of the plans, put it differently: "Keeping a patient healthy is one way for a prepaid plan to make money—not treating if he is sick is another."

Outwardly, Medi-Cal recipients were given a choice. They could remain in the old system—with its benefits greatly limited by the administration—or they could sign up with one of the new clinics. If they chose a clinic, they would lose their Medi-Cal cards and their freedom to choose physicians.

Who Gets the Savings?

From all the evidence, the administration's plan was a success in cutting down the recipients' visits to doctors. But there was some question about how much Medi-Cal money was being saved. Since the contracts were not open to competitive bidding, the actual financial arrangement between the state and the prepaid contractor was confidential. At one point, officials predicted they could save ten percent of the $1.5 billion a year it cost to run the Medi-Cal program. Another time Brian felt it could save as much as twice that percentage—$300 million. But, he added, until the programs were fully enrolled and under way, "It is difficult to say what the savings will be."

But a number of critics contended the state was being secretive with its records because savings were not as great as had been anticipated. They didn't doubt that medical service to the poor had been cut. But they felt the savings were going into the pockets of the doctor-businessmen who were running the prepaid health plans. This hunch turned out to be correct. At the end of 1973, A. Alan Post, the legislature's financial adviser, released a study showing that two of the largest plans were charging the state more than the regular Medi-Cal program had cost. Contracts were negotiated in private and, said Post, "are determined by who can negotiate the best with the state."

What About Profits?

The matter of profits in the prepaid plans was crucial. Steve Thompson, a legislative consultant studying the program, said its major flaw was that the state was contracting "with groups whose primary objective is to make money off the prepaid contract and whose secondary objective is to provide care under a system whereby you're paid so much per recipient. These two objectives conflict with one another. Good care costs more money and reduces the profit."

The state supposedly would not contract with prepaid health plans that were profit-making. But there were innumerable ways to get around this—and most of the medical entrepreneurs did just that. Medi-Cal officials insisted that the amount of profit being made by the plans was none of the state's business, as long as they were providing good medical care. As we will see, Medi-Cal administrators made little serious effort to ensure the quality of this care. But if they had known the amount of profit made by a plan, they would have known how much was being spent on treatment—one indication of the quality of care.

In his series of stories about the new prepaid franchises, Robert Fairbanks of the *Los Angeles Times* described the prepaid plans as "another goldrush . . . under way at the Capitol, only this time the nuggets are a new form of franchise—state Medi-Cal contracts to provide health care for the poor."

Theoretically, the prepaid plans could not make a profit because they were nonprofit corporations. But they could overcome this handicap through an elaborate network of holding companies and subsidiaries. In the case of the plan with the largest state contract, Consolidated Medical Systems, it and a number of profit-making companies were all operated by the same profit-making parent corporation, HMO International. The president of HMO International was the same Dr. Donald Kelly who ran the state-franchised Consolidated Medical Systems. The parent corporation and all of its subsidiaries were profit-making, except for Consolidated. And all of them were health-related companies, including pharmacies, laboratories, hospital emergency rooms, medical real estate, insurance, X-rays and a medical equipment company.

The catch was that Consolidated, the non-profit corporation, brought in nearly $2 million a month from its state contracts. Consolidated used that money to buy all supplies, rent real estate, and subscribe to services from HMO International's other subsidiaries. Consolidated even paid the parent corporation a fee to manage it. HMO International and all its profit-making companies were making their profit from the nonprofit Consolidated.

With this setup, it is easy to see how Dr. Kelly and his associates could make a profit with a nonprofit corporation. Interestingly, Kelly, aside from being an osteopath, was an experienced stock-broker. Cashing in on all of this knowledge, he was able to put his HMO International on the stock market.

H. Bradley Jones, a member of the governor's Health Advisory Board, which advised the Medi-Cal program, knew about Kelly's profits and said he saw nothing wrong with the arrangement. "Indeed, I'm dedicated to the idea that you've got to be able to make a profit," said Jones, who is also a corporation lawyer. "In fact, as a lawyer who has been specializing in tax law and corpora-tion law, as I have, I can make the cynical statement that there is no such thing as a nonprofit corporation. This applies to their church, their school, any element they want. Somebody's in there for a buck. They have to be because they have to survive in a capitalist society. This being the case, it is the worst kind of hypocrisy to insist these groups be run by nonprofit corporations, the funds of which are being siphoned off for the profit of a number of people.

"The Kelly program, for example, is a publicly run company which is deriving most of the profit, ultimately, from the [non-profit Medi-Cal] operation, and as its earnings go up, Dr. Kelly is able to watch the stock go up.

"We've checked very carefully the records of Consolidated through our medical audit teams, including a physician, a dentist, a nurse, and a pharmacist, and they detect no underutilization [medical jargon for keeping costs down by not treating sick patients]. We just don't see it. Now, we don't want to see it, probably, because [we] like the idea of being able to have people cared for where a physician does not have a direct motive to have his patient hospitalized or an incentive to overtreat."

The Quality of Care

What kind of care did the plans offer Medi-Cal recipients? There were a few interested groups who were outraged at the state's treatment of the poor—and who saw the implications for the rest of society. The Los Angeles County Medical Society—a conservative group opposed to government intervention in medicine—gathered a binder of complaints documenting how prepaid plans were failing to provide needed care. Typical was the story of how an infant—critically ill with staph pneumonia—was brought to Pacoima Memorial Lutheran Hospital in the middle of the night because a prepaid clinic was closed when emergency care was needed.

This case and nearly a hundred medical emergencies like it were brought to Pacoima Memorial because the North Valley Medical Group was not fulfilling its legal obligation to provide 24-hour emergency service to plan members. The hospital administrator concluded: "The responsible medical community continually has to bail this group out to prevent tragedy."

Other failings of the prepaid plans came to light when the California Council for Health Plan Alternatives investigated the Consolidated Medical Service prepaid plan. The council is affiliated with the Teamsters union, and it helps union groups evaluate health plans. Specifically, it found there was not a single obstetrician at Consolidated's twenty-one clinics. Physicians joined the clinic and then left at a frantic rate. Seventy-five percent of the doctors on the staff in 1972 were new.

There were far fewer physicians to serve Consolidated's members than were available to the general California population. The group employed only one doctor for every 1,375 people enrolled. The statewide ratio for the general population was one doctor for every 554 people. In addition, Consolidated could not prove that it had made binding agreements with the outside specialists it listed in its brochures as being available for consultation. The council also learned Consolidated "provides less than half the amount of hospital care given by other health care plans in California, including group practice prepayment plans."

Tom Moore, director of the council, concluded that Consolidated "represents a new and rapidly growing form of profiteering medical care organization designed to exploit our members, the poor or anyone else who becomes a member. Responsible union leaders should not only protect their membership from this kind of organization, but should actively oppose the growth of these programs in the community at large."

Bending Over Backwards Not to See It

Critics maintained that overtreating was one matter, but neglecting patients to increase profits was another. In his articles for the *Los Angeles Times,* Fairbanks said that it was not difficult for the plans to make money by cutting corners on care because there were few state controls on quality. This could be seen in the case of one plan that was notorious for its lack of night emergency care. But a Medi-Cal inspector was willing to overlook the problem after a friendly chat with the plan's administrator. He explained the plan had neglected emergency care in the past, but assured the inspector that it wouldn't happen any more. The inspector was conducting one of the biannual medical audits required by the state. After talking to the administrator he found him "in agreement and [he] indicated that all necessary precautions would be taken." Despite the group's bad record the inspector concluded that it was "a satisfactorily operated medical clinic." Its contract with the state was renewed for another year.

The state's quality control was so lax that, early in 1973, complaints from interested groups forced the Department of Health Care Services to hold public hearings before renewing any more of the prepaid plans' first-year contracts. The hearing room was an auditorium in the state building in downtown Los Angeles. It was packed with welfare mothers and the testimony was punctuated with cries from infants as well as heckling from those dissatisfied with the plans. Many in the audience were from organized welfare rights groups who felt they were being short-changed by Medi-Cal. Representatives of newspapers were absent, and the hearings were not covered by television stations.

The operators of the health plans came well prepared, bussing supporters downtown and providing them with box lunches. The sincerity of some of the witnesses was questionable. One woman testified in favor of Marvin Health Systems one day and for Dr. Vincent De Paulo the next, although it was legally impossible for her to belong to both plans at once. She denied to the state examiner that she had appeared for both plans, although people in the audience recognized her. And she had committed no crime. The state took so little interest in the truth of the testimony that it did not require witnesses to take an oath.

Dr. De Paulo, whose recruiters we met earlier in this chapter, had a Medi-Cal contract to provide care for some 3,000 poor. Some who were dissatisfied with his clinics had tried to quit and transfer back to the old Medi-Cal plan. Originally such transfers were not permitted; once a Medi-Cal recipient signed up, he was committed to the plan for a year. But with increased complaints, the state had eased that rule, permitting people to quit a group if they were unhappy. De Paulo's group was aware the state currently permitted such transfers. But the office lost the disenrollment forms, and those trying to quit had to remain in the plan until, after several months, the state interceded in their behalf.

De Paulo said he was doing his best, and he was bitter that organized medicine had publicly attacked him. But he admitted he had problems. "We were losing charts," he said. "We had too many patients. . . . We have done less than perfectly. I am not a good businessman. I am not a good administrator. Some of our mistakes have been depending upon professional enrollers. We've cut that out."

After nearly a year of being the sole source of medical aid to a large group of people, Dr. De Paulo admitted that until the previous week, his group was not always answering the telephone at night. Nevertheless, a state inspector recommended, without qualification, that the contract be renewed.

Health Advisory Board member H. Bradley Jones defended the awarding of contracts to men like De Paulo, whose performance at running his clinic was not good. Jones pointed out that one problem with the prepaid plans was the long period of time it takes to set them up. A congressional report estimated it took three years before a prepaid plan became fully operational, even under the best circumstances. Said Jones, "It's been very rare in the history of the country that people have been expected to build up a business as big as this and show operational perfection. One problem is the speed of growth and the great need and the fact that there is so much money involved. We have in this year's budget, a $2.6 billion health budget in which $1.6 billion goes to Medi-Cal. Because of the tremendous amount of money, there's tremendous danger of waste. Also, there's an opportunity for greed, avarice and fraud. We have to exercise great stewardship over that much public money." This attitude was typical of the Reagan administration. It was willing to overlook the plans' flaws because they were expected of the infant program. Meanwhile, the governor's major interest was in watching the state's budget.

But Jones—and the administration—seemed little concerned with exercising careful stewardship over the health care of poor people. A federal health planning commission looked at the Medi-Cal franchises and concluded, "The motivation of the program appears to be economic. It appears the Department of Health Care Services found it necessary to offer the incentive of making more money from Medi-Cal recipients than heretofore, perhaps even more than from non-Medi-Cal clients." The group said more supervision of the plans would protect the rights of Medi-Cal recipients even though it may "dampen the enthusiasm for seeking such contracts."

As the program drew more criticism, the California secretary of state, Edmund G. Brown, Jr., began looking into the finances of Medi-Cal. But officials of the Medi-Cal program—adhering to the Reagan administration policy of secrecy—refused to show him the audit reports for the previous five years, documents that were public record. He said he had been trying to get the audits for more than a year, and the Department of Health Care Services had given him "a variety of excuses but not one legitimate reason why these important audits should not be made public." Brown, a Democrat who was planning to run for governor, said the administration refused to publish the reports "in an effort to hide what could be a major scandal in the state's health care program. . . . It is outrageous that millions of tax dollars are being spent behind a virtual wall of secrecy."

MOONLIGHTING LEGISLATORS

The insistence on saving money on aid to the poor, the haste in setting up prepaid arrangement, the willingness to contract with profiteers, the eagerness to overlook the program's flaws—all of these might be expected of the conservative Reagan administration, openly hostile to programs that they regard as giveaways to those too lazy to work. But what about the Democratic legislators, men who were publicly dedicated to expanding social programs for the poor? Had the public been aware of the depths of the political intrigue working against reform of the new Medi-Cal program, it would have shocked them.

In 1971, when the Medi-Cal Reform Act setting up the prepaid plans on a broad scale was passed, the issue of medical aid to the poor had been debated in traditional liberal-conservative rhetoric. Reagan accused the poor of robbing the more prosperous. The Democrats attacked him. But the following year, when the legislature had a chance to force the prepaid plans to improve, partisan differences seemed to disappear. An agreement not to reform was arranged between a Republican governor, following his conservative philosophy to its most painful extreme, and liberal to moderate legislators pursuing a quick profit.

For example, to the public Merv Dymally was a liberal. He had all of the qualifications. He was a Democrat. He spoke publicly for the poor. He was black, and the large district he represented in the California State Senate included some of the poorest black slums in the country. He was the senator from Watts, an area still scarred from the 1965 riots. Part of the time, Senator Dymally was in the legislature in Sacramento, denouncing the conservative policies of Governor Reagan in the clipped accent of his West Indies homeland and rising higher each year in the leadership of the Senate Democrats. His position as chairman of a Senate subcommittee on health gave him an opportunity to frequently criticize the governor for denying adequate health services for the poor.

Part of the time, though, Senator Dymally was in business, and he was lucky enough to be able to use what he had learned in the legislature to further his business career. He was a major stockholder in a firm that for a while held a Medi-Cal franchise from the state. Originally, the firm started out in the alcoholic beverage business, as the black-operated Batik Wine and Spirits Company. Failing there, the firm changed its name to Comprehensive Health Systems, Inc., and—with the help of legislation introduced by Dymally—went into the Medi-Cal business, obtaining a franchise to provide health care to large numbers of poor people. Dymally's legislation allowed a profit-making, nonmedical corporation, such as Batik, to own a non-profit medical firm. The Reagan administration, wanting to encourage more people to go into the prepaid health plan business, also favored this legislation. Partisan differences were no obstacle to Dymally's outside interests.

In the summer of 1972, Dymally, embarrassed by the publicity about his involvement in a business having a multimillion-dollar contract with the state, resigned as the firm's board chairman, and later said he was giving away his stock.

Dymally's partner in the health business was Dr. Edward Rubin, operator of a hospital which he leased to another Medi-Cal plan serving 60,000 poor in Los Angeles and collecting $14.4 million a year from the state. Rubin, along with Dymally, had also operated a health plan for 20,000 poor people in neighboring Los Angeles County, and at one point their company received $7.1 million a year from the state. Rubin obtained this contract after dealing with a conservative Republican state assemblyman, John Briggs of Fullerton. Briggs' insurance company sold policies with an annual earning potential of $200,000 a year to Rubin's company after Briggs talked in Rubin's behalf to the state officials who awarded the Medi-Cal prepaid contracts. The officials denied that Briggs' intervention helped Rubin. Later, this contract was one of the few the state took away because Rubin's facilities were inadequate.

Another example of entanglement with Medi-Cal was the liberal Assemblyman Wally Karabian. As a state assemblyman, Karabian had been praised by liberals when he described Governor Reagan's health care advisers as villains who "live life as if it were a John Wayne movie and the guys who aren't bleeding can't really be sick. They just lack the guts to be healthy." But Karabian had a sideline. He was an attorney for firms getting Medi-Cal franchises.

State Senator Al Song was another liberal who criticized the Republican administration. But he was also a partner in the law firm of Masry, David, Song and Cohen in Los Angeles, and the *Sacramento Bee* reported how one of the firm's partners had offered to help a Southern California businessman get a Medi-Cal franchise. The partner denied the story, but Song did not. "I can't stop anybody from using my name in a situation like that," he said. "That doesn't mean I have given my permission to do so." According to a member of a commission supervising the Medi-Cal program, Song's firm told doctors that for a fee it could set them up with a franchise.

The profit hunger among legislators was not limited to the Democrats. A Republican assemblyman, William Campbell, retiring from his seat, planned to go into the Medi-Cal consulting business. Before he left, he introduced legislation that would have allowed profit-making companies to obtain the Medi-Cal franchises directly. That would have simplified things for businessmen, who had to go through a complicated system of private and nonprofit corporations. Campbell managed to sneak his bill through the legislature without hearing or debate. It was done in the confusion of the final days before adjournment, when the number of bills, amendments and bits of legislative business being considered runs literally into the thousands. He explained later his intent had been simply to "clarify" the law. In the end, the measure was vetoed when Reagan's adviser, Earl Brian, who once supported the measure, inexplicably changed his mind. Campbell conceded the bill would have helped his business.

AN ATTEMPT TO REFORM

When facts about the poor medical care given by the plans became known, a move for reform developed outside the capital. As a result, a bill was introduced requiring strictly enforced standards for the prepaid plans. How the legislation was weakened—and nearly killed—is a fascinating study in backroom politics, practiced by men—Democrats and Republicans alike—who put their business interests first.

During the 1972 legislative session, the National Health Law Foundation, a health-care law group financed by the federal government and operating out of the University of California at Los Angeles, proposed a bill placing strict controls on the new prepaid health plan franchise holders. The bill would have required franchise holders to have at least a year's experience in the prepaid medical field, or demonstrate that they have "sufficient financial resources, physical facilities, administrative abilities and soundness of program design to meet obligations." It set down physician-patient ratios and provisions for patients' rights. Every patient, one rule said, was entitled to a doctor of his choice, "and if he is dissatisfied, he may choose another doctor." It set down strict standards of excellence that most of the existing plans did not meet. As we will see, legislators allowed few of these provisions to remain in the final version of the bill; those that were left were so weakened that the law has had little effect on the quality of medical care under the prepaid program.

Two assemblymen, Republican Gordon Duffy and Democrat Henry Waxman were interested in reforming the program. They introduced the law foundation's proposal into the legislature. The Reagan administration opposed it, promising instead to change the administrative regulations to tighten up surveillance of the plans. The Reagan administration knew that the new programs had grown too fast to meet stiff standards. The plans were now controlled by departmental regulations, which could be bent when a prepaid plan operator couldn't meet them. But once requirements were written into law, they became less flexible. It was possible that too stringent a law would put many prepaid plans out of business. It could mean failure or a major slowdown to the medical concept that Reagan and Brian hoped would become a national model.

"I knew there would be some resistance," said Assemblyman Duffy. "I didn't realize that the resistance was going to last as long as it did. To me it was pretty apparent that if you don't have regulations, and everyone says you need them, then you'd darned well better put something into law. I felt rather strongly although, in general, I support the administration. . . . I think I have to worry about whether the next administration is going to do it. This is one of the reasons we do things by law rather than regulations."

The reform bill, at the start, did better than its backers expected. But as it was passed from committee to committee, it was changed. Pat Butler, a young lawyer with the Health Law Foundation, recalled, "The bill sort of lumped along going in and out of committees, and we were surprised because we didn't expect it to get very far. Obviously, the further it got, the more compromises were involved. Originally, the bill required a majority of consumers on the board of directors. Well, as you might imagine, not any provider [franchise holder] or the state was too excited about it, and that got knocked out. . . . They added a lot of discretionary language, like 'to the extent feasible' and 'as the director determines necessary' and that kind of thing. They watered it down by permitting waivers and deviations from the requirements."

Legislative Dirty Tricks

The administration and the legislators with Medi-Cal connections could have simply weakened the bill, but they preferred to kill it. To do this, they resorted to an ancient trick—loving the bill to death.

Every piece of legislation is a compromise between advocates and opponents, delicately balanced to satisfy the conflicting interests of a legislature. A bill can be killed by upsetting that balance, by making it too strong or too weak. When a bill is killed by making it too strong, the killer emerges with the added advantage of appearing to the public as the lonely defender of the moral course.

Since the governor wouldn't sign the bill without some attempt to appease the administration's objections, Brian was included in negotiations on its amendments. He proposed that the bill be strengthened—as he put it—with the addition of an anti-conflict-of-interest provision. It would have made it a crime for any legislator or state employee to even unwittingly hold interest in a prepaid Medi-Cal health plan. The proposal was so stringent that it extended to spouses. And it prevented anyone working for the state to accept anything of value from any of the franchises.

If enforced, such a law could have meant jail terms for the legislators engaged in the increasingly lucrative Medi-Cal business, and Brian knew they would never vote for it. It would have also made criminals out of legislators or state employees who accepted a dinner, or even a cup of coffee, from a Medi-Cal franchise holder.

A veteran of the battle remembered the anger of the legislators, and how they complained to the Democratic speaker of the Assembly, Bob Moretti. "Song, Karabian, Dymally, all the guys who got their fingers in that were screaming like hell," he said. Moretti was not personally involved in the health care business, but he knew his power base was. He approached the author of the bill, Assemblyman Duffy, and demanded, "What in the hell do you mean, putting a thing like that in there without discussing it with me." Duffy honestly replied that Brian had insisted on the unacceptable clause as a condition of Reagan's signing the bill.

But Brian's plan to defeat the bill by making it too strict failed. The bill passed—purely by chance. Loaded down with the conflict-of-interest provisions, it was headed toward a quiet death in the final days of the legislative session. The bill—along with many others—was being considered by the important Senate finance committee, the last step before the Senate vote. The small hearing room was full of spectators—and good representation by the press. But little time was spent on each piece of legislation and reporters had no particular reason to focus on the Medi-Cal bill. This changed, however, when a legislator inadvertently attracted attention to the bill by asking a question about it. Suddenly newsmen noticed the previously ignored conflict-of-interest clause.

Later, Tom Moore, observing the hearing for the Teamsters' California Council for Health Plan Alternatives, said he thought at that point, "We've got them. They don't dare vote against it while the press is sitting there. The bill has to move. And, of course, the bill was approved by the committee unanimously."

That was how a bill—totally unacceptable to both the administration and the legislators involved in prepaid health plans—reached the Senate floor for a final vote. With the conflict-of-interest provision now well-publicized, few legislators would have the nerve to vote against it.

Giving up on the subtleties of the legislative process, opponents of the bill resorted to a final desperate tactic.

The details were reported months later by John Berthelsen in the *Sacramento Bee*. The bill had just passed the Senate Finance Committee. Under normal procedure, it would go to the desk of the secretary of the Senate, who schedules it for the floor agenda. Like a deed or a will, there is only one legally valid copy of each bill. It must be physically in the legislative chamber for a vote on it to take place. In a last effort to do away with the bill, the powerful chairman of the finance committee, Senator Randolph Collier, picked the bill up from the secretary's desk, put it in his pocket, and left the Senate chamber. He took the bill to his office and locked it in his desk. He knew that if he could hold it there until after the session adjourned, it would be too late to vote on it. And any bill not acted on before the end of the session automatically dies.

Collier is a crusty, cantankerous old power vendor. He has been a Senate spokesman for businesses like the highway lobby for years. Although he is a Democrat, he is often on the governor's side. And he was close to many of the legislators involved in the Medi-Cal business. By stealing the bill, he thought he could solve all problems.

But someone told Duffy of the theft, and he found Collier. Duffy demanded to know where his bill was. Collier refused to tell. Only when Duffy threatened to tell the press did Collier confess and produce the bill. But he had one last trick. Instead of returning the bill to the Senate for a vote, he arbitrarily returned it to his finance committee—although it had already been voted on and approved there. Later, he admitted he did this "at the request of some of the members of the legislature," including Senator Song, whose law firm dealt with Medi-Cal plans.

Finally, the bill's supporters pushed it through the finance committee a second time, and it passed the Senate. Duffy personally escorted it to the Assembly for the final vote on the Senate amendments, and it passed by a bare majority.

Failure to Reform

Did the conflict-of-interest clause in the law force legislators to give up their lucrative sidelines of representing and advising the prepaid health plans? It was hard to say since such laws are so poorly enforced. In this case, policing for possible violations was laughable. The state required that each prepaid plan file a statement listing people in its employ or realm of business dealings who might have a conflict of interest. The plans said they knew of no such people. For legislators who had law partners doing business with the plans or who held interests in firms specializing in their

management, the law was vague. The legislative counsel, after
deliberation, said that such an arrangement would be a conflict of
interest. But that was just one opinion, not legally binding.

Even more discouraging was the fact that the legislation failed
to improve health care for the poor. It had gone into effect in mid
'73. But at the end of the year, many prepaid plans were still
delivering inferior medical care. The Assembly health committee
held hearings investigating the plans. It was headed by Assemblyman Henry Waxman, who had been a co-author of the bill
attempting to crack down on the prepaid plans. Waxman explained that the hearings were held because "we are concerned
that the state is fostering 'Medi-Cal mills' which will give recipients
less than the quality of care available to other citizens." He didn't
condemn all of the prepaid plans contracting with the state. But
he said there was still not much evidence the department was
requiring good care for Medi-Cal patients.

The committee paid particular attention to the medical audits
of the plans conducted by the state every six months. This is a
medical inspection by a state team, including a physician, a dentist, a nurse and a pharmacist. The Medi-Cal operators are warned
of the visit in advance.

The medical report that comes out of this inspection is brief
and full of bureaucratic optimism. One team, headed by Dr.
Morris Rubin, chief medical consultant to the State Department of
Health, devoted much of its report to a discussion of the inspected
plan's strong points—a large parking area, a "well furnished and
decorated" building, an uncrowded and orderly waiting room,
"pleasant" personnel, and a general attitude of "pleasantness and
situational satisfaction."

But buried at the back of the report were findings that would
have frightened away prospective enrollees, had they seen it.

Dr. Rubin noted that although 10,000 people belonged to the
clinic, there were only two full-time doctors, and no specialists—
not even an obstetrician. General practitioners took care of
pregnant women, with an obstetrician available on a referral basis
during the last two months of pregnancy. "Most unfortunate,"
concluded Dr. Rubin. Follow-up care, he found, was often "a hit
or miss procedure." He said that at night, "Medical coverage . . . is

minimal and may be potentially dangerous." Hospitalization took time because a chain of command located outside the clinic had to be consulted before admission. Dr. Rubin said he thought this was done to keep hospital admissions down, and that it seemed to be doing the job.

Despite the plan's serious shortcomings, Dr. Rubin found it to be "satisfactory."

The plans were rated in fourteen different categories. These ratings were based mostly on information from the prepaid plans' own records, without much effort to determine if they were accurate. And it didn't seem to matter how many deficiencies were found. Contracts were renewed anyway. Waxman's health committee focused attention on audits of twelve specific plans contracting with the state. Of these twelve, only two passed their audits with no deficiencies. One was deficient in eleven of the fourteen categories, another in ten. Nevertheless, the state had renewed contracts with all of these groups at the end of their first contract year.

At Waxman's request, the legislative analyst A. Alan Post looked into the practices of the prepaid plans. His report found that the deceptive enrollment practices, poor quality care and insufficient monitoring by the state were still plaguing the program. The state had continued its liberal policy toward disenrollment to balance possible enrollment fraud, and recipients were leaving the plans at a rate of over six percent a month. Over a year, that would mean a seventy-five percent turnover. Aside from other difficulties this might cause, it was making preventative medicine—shots, regular checkups and followups—nearly impossible, although these services had been a major selling point of the prepaid arrangement.

PROGNOSIS OF THE CONCEPT

In the narrow sense the Medi-Cal failure showed how legislative manipulation—motivated by greed and ambition—can ruin a program. Medicaid and prepaid health plans, which had started out as pioneering ideas at the national level, continued to founder in

California because those who set up the program cared too little about health care handed out to the needy.

The implications for the future were seen by too few, and it would have taken a major citizen protest to reverse the state's disastrous course. Well-run prepaid medical plans in California could have served as a model for alternative medical care for millions. But the program's record was blotted, and the result could be to sour the nation on this kind of health care.

There is a broader meaning to the California experience. It shows graphically how the bright promise of national policy can be destroyed by the people who actually administer it in the intrigue and secrecy of the state houses of America.

7

The Politics
of Sewers and Garbage

Few realize it, but something as mundane as the disposal of waste can shape a neighborhood, transforming it from a desirable place to live to one that is overdeveloped, crowded and clogged with traffic.

In metropolitan America, garbage and sewage disposal is left to local government, and residents don't give it much thought as long as the garbage is picked up and the sewage is quietly and efficiently carried away. But, while a crew digging a sewer line attracts little notice, it is actually a twentieth-century trailblazer, opening the way for construction of new buildings on vacant fields. As for garbage, no one cares where it is dumped, so long as it is not nearby. Yet—for better or for worse—rotting trash is becoming a building material of major proportions in populated areas.

We underestimate the importance of such decisions because we assume that those who make them are qualified experts, acting on highly technical information. We unquestioningly accept the notion that waste disposal is beyond our understanding, that it has little effect on our lives, and that it is an open-and-shut matter, beyond the realm of political choices.

This blind reliance on government experts is one reason for the decay of the suburbs and for the growing inhospitality of the city. As we pointed out in the first chapter, elected officials often make their decisions in response to hidden pressure from business, labor and other powerful groups—and then justify those decisions with an engineer's report so technical that the average homeowner cannot argue with it. In the game of local government, the unsuspecting citizen is usually the loser. One of the best examples of how it works is in the disposal of waste.

Since sewer lines—more than roads or transit routes—determine where development will take place, a government agency can approve a large sewer line and clear the way for a burst of residential and industrial growth that will radically change the surrounding area. A garbage dump can ruin a neighborhood overnight. With so much at stake, the construction of a sewer line or the location of garbage dumps should be matters of widespread political debate. But under the present arrangement it is impossible for the public to take part in these decisions. The responsibility is usually assumed by one of the least visible agencies in local government, the sanitation district.

THE ANONYMOUS SANITATION DISTRICT

In communities across the country, sanitation districts are in charge of disposing of human waste and garbage for millions of people. Their power is great. For example, in Los Angeles County, local sanitation districts have banded together in one great agency that can obtain private property through condemnation; it decides the paths of sewer lines, the location of treatment plants, and the site of garbage dumps. Each sanitation district can decide the size, capacity and cost of a sewer system. A district can call elections to authorize the sale of municipal bonds to finance the sewer system. Such details can be tremendously important to residents. A large, expensive system can trigger sudden, intense development. In such cases, homeowners can be forced out if they can't afford to pay high sewer assessment costs. An expensive sewer system invites buyers who can afford and make use of the big new sewer system, such as developers of highrise apartments and high-density town houses and condominiums.

The public is given little voice in these decisions. Sanitation district boards are another example of how the average citizen is kept out of local government. It is almost impossible to figure out who serves on the board of directors of each district, or how they got their jobs. Their names are rarely listed in county publications—even on the material given out by the sanitation districts themselves. Despite its importance, most people don't know in which sanitation district they live. The press rarely reports a district's activities—or their significance to those who live in it.

A sewer district cannot be set up without a vote of the people within its proposed boundaries. So, there is some logic to the argument that the residents of a sewer district have the final protection of being able to vote against the district's formation. But this is unlikely, in view of how special local elections work. Few vote in such elections, and setting one up ignores the reality of the voting process. In small elections, such as for the creation of a sanitary district, the precincts are changed from their normal boundaries. The election officials say that since there will be fewer voters, the county will need fewer polling places. Precincts are consolidated, and the polling places are in new locations, possibly miles from where a voter had gone to the polls on previous election days. Voters do receive a postcard telling of the election and the address of the new polling place, but no map showing where it is. That postcard and a paid notice in the back of the newspaper are about the only publicity the election will get.

Difficulty in finding where to vote, as well as public apathy and ignorance, assures a low turnout of voters. Those personally interested in starting a sanitary district will find their way to the polls, and a low turnout gives them the advantage. It is no wonder that an average of ten percent or less of the voters show up for these elections.

MALIBU SEWERS: THE BATTLE LINES ARE DRAWN

One of the few communities that has learned to understand this obscure political game is Malibu in Southern California, where the Santa Monica Mountains reach the sea. There, the canyons widen into the coastal plain and then become part of the beaches. Malibu is almost thirty miles from downtown Los Angeles, and, even today, it still has a little bit of a rural look. But only a little. Just a few feet separate houses on the beach, and during the rush hour and on weekends, the Pacific Coast Highway, which runs through Malibu, is a noisy, smelly tangle of recreational vans, sports cars, camper trucks and sedans.

Malibu is already one of the damaged places on a coastline that is so bountiful in natural resources that its beauty has survived successive attacks by those who believed the trees, the land, the air and the sea were unlimited sources of profit.

Today, the migration to California has slowed. But the desire to develop Malibu has not diminished. There is still vacant land, and the only thing stopping a building boom along the beach and back into the mountains is the lack of sewers.

The Local Resident—Hanging onto the Septic Tank

There was a time when Peggy Callen did not think much about sewers. Ms. Callen, a housewife, lives on Malibu beach with her husband, who is a stockbroker, and their three daughters. She is articulate and well educated. Her deep tan and rounded figure tell of brunches and mai-tais on the wooden sundeck that juts out over the beach from the glass double doors of the Callens' living room.

That sundeck covers a septic tank where sewage from the house is decomposed and purified by bacteria; once cleaned, the water percolates up through the sand. The Callens have had no trouble with their septic tank, but those of some of their neighbors have overflowed onto the beach and backed up into their toilets. While it does its job, the Callens' septic tank prevents them from having the comforts enjoyed by other upper middle-class homeowners—a garbage disposal, a dishwasher. When they entertain large groups, the Callens have to count toilet flushes and pray the septic system doesn't fail during the party.

A visitor's first impression is that Ms. Callen would want something more modern. But she does not. There have been attempts to build a huge sewer system in Malibu that would accommodate ten times the present population. As Ms. Callen recalls, it wasn't easy to oppose "God, sewers and sanitation." But she and her neighbors opposed them successfully at the polls. A look at the history of their fight provides an interesting look at the politics of sewers. The way powerful local officials arbitrarily ignored the will of the people is a sad comment on the state of democracy in local government.

The Local Politician—Pushing for Sewers

The final decision on Malibu's future was not up to the residents. It was largely in the hands of one man, the county supervisor who represented the area, Burton Chace. Supervisor Chace had been elected from a district that extended the length of Los Angeles County's coastline. Chace is now dead. But for many years he represented the state of mind of most local officials. He believed that a property owner had the right to do what he wanted to profit from his property, with a minimum of government interference.

Not surprisingly, Chace's political campaigns received financing from business firms that engaged in development, including those that wanted to develop Malibu. It is difficult to tell the extent of their help because of the weak campaign finance reporting law through much of his time in office. For example, there is an entry in Chace's 1968 report, which merely says "Cashiers checks, donors unknown." The amounts are not listed. Nevertheless, the records do show he received contributions from those who wanted to change Malibu—Pierce Sherman, a realtor-developer; Louis Busch, one of Malibu's busiest real estate men; Merritt Adamson, a major landowner; and the Marblehead Land Company, Adamson's land company.

Until recent years, not many people could live in Malibu and commute to jobs in Los Angeles. But in the sixties a freeway to the coast changed the area's potential in the eyes of the powerful county supervisors. Under 15,000 were living there, but Chace and his colleagues now saw the beach community as a suburb where 200,000 people would live by 1983, and 400,000 by the year 2000. Another new freeway planned along the beach would carry the heavy traffic. They argued, as land developers had done everywhere, that such growth was inevitable, and that government had to prepare for it with sanitation facilities they gave to other suburbs. But the growth, of course, was not inevitable. The population would increase in Malibu only if there were adequate sewer lines to accommodate new residents. Without these lines, the people would live elsewhere.

Chace and the developers wanted to build a huge sewer system to accommodate the densely populated suburb they envisioned for Malibu.

In 1964 and 1966, Chace proposed a bond issue election to build the sewer lines in Malibu. However, he was dealing with an unusual group of homeowners. Well-to-do and well-educated, they took great pride in their unusual environment. As a result, they were quick to realize that the building of a huge sewer line was against their interests. They were disorganized, but they managed to defeat it both times.

In 1968, the supervisor again proposed the same plan. This time, the big property owners hired a public relations firm to plan their campaign. They came up with a unique strategy, to gerrymander the sewer district in a way that would favor the bond issue. Supporters of the measure studied old election results and figured out how to redraw the lines of the district so it would include those who had voted "yes" in the past, leaving out those who voted "no." The idea was to eliminate the potential opposition within the district, and replace it with "yes" votes from other areas.

In this ingenious scheme, people were hired to pass around petitions in "no" neighborhoods, giving the voters a chance to withdraw from the sanitation district. It was explained that if they withdrew, homeowners wouldn't be hooked up to the sewer line, if it were built, nor would they have to pay for it. Understandably, some jumped at the chance. Of course, withdrawing from the sewer system meant they would lose their right to vote in the election that would decide if the sewer line would be built.

Other people were sent to pass petitions in areas that were not in the old sanitary district boundaries, but were nearby and were having sewage disposal problems. These homeowners, likely to vote "yes" on sewer bonds, were asked to join the sanitary district. One such area was on the hills above the beach in Trancas Canyon. The developer of the property had installed his own sewer system several years before, and it was failing. Prompted by the bad smell, Trancas Canyon residents signed the petitions. This brought in a block of several hundred votes—a sizeable number, considering that less than 900 had even voted in the 1966 sewer district election. In other areas within the old district, where some homeowners withdrew and some remained, four houses on a block might be in the sewer district, and four outside its boundaries. The district looked like a ragged piece of swiss cheese.

"Nobody really knew what was happening until people were contacted on a house-by-house basis outside the original district," said one Malibu resident who opposed the bond issue. "And most people were asked the question, 'Would you like to have an election on sewers?' Some people said they could care less and didn't sign anything. Others said, 'Yeah, it would be fun to have an election, we'll vote.' When they signed the piece of paper, nobody understood they were annexing their property to the district. So now they were able to vote, but they were obligated to pay for the sewers if the bonds passed."

Still, these questionable tactics were not enough, and the threat of a big sewer system that would bring crowded living conditions to peaceful Malibu again mobilized the residents. Their campaign also emphasized how the district's proposed sewage treatment plant would empty treated sewage water directly into the ocean. They warned of higher property taxes to pay back the bonds the district would sell to build the lines and the sewage treatment plant. They informed residents living in the hills and far from the road that it would cost thousands to hook up their homes to the sewer system. "By November, we had learned enough on the politics of it, the finances and the ocean outfall," remembers Peggy Callen. "We pulled in enough votes on this enormously technical problem to stop it."

The Developers' Advantage: Time and the Need for Only One Victory

Undaunted by a third defeat, Supervisor Chace and the developers tried again in 1971.

Land was getting even more valuable in Malibu. By this time, the area had the beginnings of a college campus. Pepperdine University, a private, politically conservative, church-related school, was moving much of its operation from the inner city closer to the affluent youngsters of suburbanites, and was building on the hills behind Malibu. Developer Merritt Adamson, veteran of the 1968 fight, was planning homes and apartments near the campus. Alcoa was readying 3,000 nearby acres for housing developments. Alcoa, Pepperdine and Adamson were among the contributors to the 1971 bond issue campaign for sewers. Alcoa alone gave $12,500—$2,500 itself and $10,000 through an affiliate, Century City, Inc. The Beverly Hills Development Company, owners of commercial property in Malibu, donated $7,500; Pepperdine University, $1,000; and Adamson, $7,100.

Proponents based their campaign on a claim that Malibu's septic tanks were unhealthy. They put up a sign outside Malibu that read, "Cesspool City Ahead. The Nose Knows. Vote Yes on Sewers." Their plan would have provided a $16.5 million, 27-mile sewer system to serve 72,000, more than five times the current population.

Homeowner groups opposed it because they said the system was too big. "We're not against sewers, but for sewers only to take care of our needs," said Dr. Charles Cavlieri, representing a group of 1,000 residents. Another homeowner said, "The gut issue here is growth. The high cost of the project anticipates growth, and we don't want more taco stands and gas stations to turn Malibu into an undesirable place to live."

Applying the Pressure

The county supervisors didn't take an active part in the sewer bond campaign, but three weeks before the election, county health inspectors suddenly appeared on the Malibu beaches in great numbers. They were from the county health department, controlled by the supervisors. For the first time, they inspected the beachfront homes' septic tanks, and 123 citations were issued.

Opponents of the sewer plan said the inspection was an attempt by the supervisors to swing the election the way the land developers wanted it to go. "Most of the violations were for laundry water running on the beach" said a homeowners group representative. "But the county has had years to correct this problem. The timing in bringing in a task force to check for violations is an obvious attempt to sway the voters." The homeowners got statements from twenty-three physicians who said there was no health hazard in Malibu and who criticized the sanitary district's plan to dump its treated sewage into the ocean. Opponents cited a 1970 state report declaring Malibu's waters were not polluted, as well as a statement from a marine biologist that said, "In no way does this report establish that there is a health crisis in Malibu. Quite the contrary, in fact."

In March of 1971, the people went to the polls and voted against the sewers again, 2,037 to 340. Sewer supporters had raised about $40,000 for their campaign, and every "yes" vote had cost them more than $100. It was the fourth defeat for the sewer bond and by now Malibu residents had made it clear that they would never vote for a large sewer system.

Disregarding the Election Process

The sewer project was so essential to their development plans that Supervisor Chace and the large landowners persisted. They never considered building a small sewer system that might be acceptable to homeowners, a fact which indicated how little importance the health issue had in their thinking. The next move was to take advantage of a 1913 law which permits a sanitation district to divide into smaller districts. If the owners of sixty percent of the property acreage in one of these smaller districts petition, the county can build a sewer system, assessing all those who live there for its cost. It was not a coincidence that in the first district drawn up most of the land was owned by the firms who had supported the sewer bonds. They were arranging to build the sewage treatment plant and other expensive elements of the system they wanted. Asked one homeowner, "If this were an attempt to deal with the sewage problems in the community, why is the proposed district limited primarily to vacant land?"

An official of the county said that setting up the assessment district on petition of a few major landowners was not an attempt to be devious. "What could be more democratic?" he asked. He said the county's position was to allow expansion of Malibu from

14,000 to 130,000, which the area was zoned for by county planners. "We are trying to get [residents] to separate the two issues of growth and sewers," he said. "The growth that the sewers would allow is not more than permitted by zoning in the area."

The homeowners knew that, but from past experience they understood it was useless to ask the planning commission to change zoning to limit development. The vote on the sewer system had been their last hope, and that had been disregarded. The project would be reviewed by the regional coastline commission, but it seemed unlikely they would intervene. The sewers the developers wanted were going to be built, and homeowners were powerless to do anything about it.

Geared for Failure

The Malibu story shows that in the politics of sewers, the growth-minded official and the developer have an overwhelming advantage. Citizen groups were able to band together to meet a crisis each time they were threatened. But, in many respects, they were terribly weak in the face of the powerful and persistent alliance of businessmen, politicians and technically adept government officials. At one public meeting, a housewife without technical training was one of the few citizens appearing to testify against the sewers. Opposing her was John Parkhurst, the chief engineer and general manager for all the county's sewer districts, who had built sewers around the world. The woman recalled her bewilderment: "They [the officials] asked me, 'What would you propose?' And I thought, 'Dear God, here I am a housewife who's only learned what a sewer is four months ago. How can you ask me to stand up against Mr. Parkhurst and suggest something better?' And that's what you cope with as a citizen unless you can pay." By paying she meant hiring experts, and it costs between $500 and $1,000, plus expenses, to hire an engineer to dispute the county.

Another weakness was the failure of Malibu residents to unite for a long-term fight. After each victory, they went their separate ways only to have to return to combat at the last minute when the county moved to build the sewers again. The land developers, on the other hand, had patience, determination, and professional political help.

Perhaps the failure was in the character of Malibu itself. Many of the residents moved there to escape from the worries of the city—worries due to the strain of living in a crowded, tense community. Racial problems, noise, pollution, crime seemed to abound in the city, and its residents were under constant pressure to solve what appeared to be hopeless problems. Malibu offered peace and solitude.

With so many individuals seeking escape, there was not much to unite Malibu, just a common desire to be left alone on the beach. The only community feeling revolved around the opposition to the sewers. There was no agreement on anything else nor willingness to work out a political coalition with like-minded homeowners in other areas to challenge the county supervisor at the next election.

With each family dedicated to its solitary way of life, Malibu residents missed one other political option. They could have easily stopped the sewers by forming their own city. That would have given them control over their own planning and zoning—a tight rein over everything that would be built there. They, not the county supervisors, would have controlled the sanitation district and could have built a small, limited sewer system if they had decided it was needed. But they were never able to get together on all the other issues involved in setting up a city.

As a group, these homeowners were unusually sophisticated in their understanding of the relationship between sewers and development. But they couldn't overcome the odds against them. Also, they failed to see their fight as just one part of an entire effort to save the remaining beauty of California. There is an argument for preserving the present Malibu for everyone. It has a large stretch of public beaches, and the scenery along its winding roads is enjoyed by people from all over the region. If the mountains are cut away for a freeway and the view obscured by highrise apartments and condominiums, it will be a loss for all of Southern California, not just the few who live here. But Malibu residents failed to see beyond their own septic tanks. By thinking about their predicament in the narrowest of terms, they were unable to ally themselves with other communities who were fighting the system—and sometimes beating it.

THE POLITICS OF GARBAGE

The politics of garbage can be as destructive and wasteful of land as the politics of sewers. Usually, they are both governed by the same agency—the sanitation district—and decisions are made in the same secretive, arbitrary manner.

Garbage has its own monuments scattered around the country. Although Mt. Trashmore is not listed in many guidebooks, it is becoming something of a tourist attraction at Virginia Beach, south of the District of Columbia. It is a mountain made of garbage, the waste of an urban society that has run out of vacant land on which to dump its trash. Each day for five years, according to plan, refuse was dumped on Mt. Trashmore, a nickname bestowed on the creation by Virginia Beach residents. It was compacted and layered with clean earth until it reached a certain height. Then engineers covered it with several feet more earth and made plans for recreational use of the mountain they had built. They are planning a soapbox derby track, a ski run and an amphitheater on its slopes.

Mt. Trashmore is an example of the new technology in waste disposal called "sanitary landfill," the current policy of every community that has rejected the old methods of leaving garbage uncovered in vacant fields. Flies, rats, stench and the danger of disease made these open dumps unacceptable. Just as objectionable was the practice of burning garbage, which increased air pollution. Several alternatives were proposed, including recycling—using discarded goods for manufacturing new materials. But the cost has proved high. In the early 1970s, less than one percent of the nation's garbage was being recycled despite well-publicized volunteer recycling centers in most of the big cities.

Sanitation engineers now favor sanitary landfills in which garbage is compacted and covered with a clean layer of earth each day. They say that when the dump is completed, parks, golf courses and other open-air recreation facilities can be built on top. In some places, this is being done. In the Long Island community of Hempstead, golfers play on the Merrick Road Park Golf Course, formerly a garbage dump.

The new technology is far from problem-free. The daily soil covering makes it cleaner than an open dump, but creation of a sanitary landfill is still a noisy, dusty, smelly and unsightly operation. Because the buried garbage decomposes in absence of oxygen, it produces methane, a colorless, odorless, flammable gas. Methane is the main component of firedamp, an explosive gas found in coal mines. Such gas is emitted from the landfill for the fifty years it takes the garbage to completely rot. Since buildings could trap lethal methane gas, closed structures cannot be built on the dumps. And since the trash sinks as it decomposes, it is difficult to build permanent facilities on top. Landfills are so new a concept, they have not existed long enough for any to have completely decomposed. Scientists have only a theoretical idea of what will happen when the decomposition process is completed.

Sanitation engineers say such fills are the only economical way America can dispose of its waste. But, even the U.S. Environmental Protection Agency, which favors the fills, pointed out their experimental nature when it said of Mt. Trashmore: "We know that trash hills are both economically and structurally feasible. We hope they will be environmentally feasible. To date, we think Mt. Trashmore is." Several artificial lakes dug nearby are being checked to make sure liquids from the rotting garbage do not seep through and pollute them. Despite the risk, Virginia Beach is planning another Mt. Trashmore, and the Illinois cities of Evanston and Wheaton are contemplating resort mountains made of garbage.

What interest do politically influential groups have in the location of sanitary landfills? One group that is a traditionally big giver to local campaigns is trash companies, intent on dumps that are close to the communities they serve, in order to save themselves time, gasoline and money. More than that, land developers are finding the landfills a cheap way to improve and landscape their property. As we will see, some fortunate property owners even receive large sums of money for allowing a sanitation district to fill and landscape their land. Others dealing in housing development near landfills, or proposed ones, put pressure on local government to allow them to continue building homes near the sites, despite the nuisance they will pose to unsuspecting home buyers.

Improving on Nature

The political influence of these groups explains why more and more landfills are appearing in populated areas. One of the biggest is inside the Los Angeles city limits, where engineers are filling mountain canyons with garbage. The canyons are located in the Santa Monica Mountains, which extend from the heart of the city to Malibu and the ocean.

These canyons have their own beauty, with scenery far different from granite cliffs, waterfalls, rapids and snow-capped peaks of more imposing ranges, like the Sierras or the Rockies. They are actually not tall enough to be dignified by the term "mountains." They are hot, dry and filled with brush called chaparral. In the fall, the dry, strong wind called "the Santa Ana" roars through the canyons from the desert. A match, a cigarette or a spark can set the chaparral on fire, and the winds carry the flames down the canyons, burning all in front of them. A fire in 1970 started in the San Fernando Valley, burned through canyons, and did not stop until it reached Malibu beach several miles away. And if the winter following the fires is rainy, the sides of the canyons turn to mud. Stripped of protective vegetation by the flames, the sides slide downward, destroying buildings and streets in their path.

There is danger in the canyons, but visitors can hike among live oak, huge boulders, pleasant-smelling dried grasses and wild-flowers. In short, the canyons are California before man came. They are among the few remaining places in Los Angeles that have not been turned into houses, apartments, office buildings, stores, roads or freeways.

Despite the hazards, the rich have built homes here, some on stilts, others on terraces bulldozed out of the hillsides—precarious perches always threatened by mud and fire. Construction crews have scraped the tops off some of the mountains, and deformed them with terraces, but many are untouched. Now federal, state and local governments are slowly beginning to preserve a portion of them as parkland.

It might be assumed that city and county government would lead the fight to save these mountains. Local politicians have, in the past, voiced general public declarations of support. But, at the same time, these elected officials have quietly cooperated in the scheme to fill a huge section of this canyon land with garbage. And, the project has brought profit to political campaign contributors and has hurt residential areas adjacent to the dumps.

Waste disposal is a particular problem in Los Angeles County. The average man, woman and child in the United States generates almost five and one-half pounds of garbage a day. In Los Angeles County, perhaps in keeping with the California tradition of wasting things, the average is about eight pounds a day for every resident, totaling more than 25,000 tons a year. A third of that comes from households, the rest from business and industry. The amount has increased with the size and prosperity of the population. More people throw away more garbage today than ever before. And, as John Parkhurst, chief engineer and general manager of the Los Angeles Sanitary Districts, said, "Although it may be an oversimplification, it should be recognized that within the confines of the planet earth, there are only three repositories that are available to man for acceptance of this waste. They are the oceans, the land and the atmosphere."

In Los Angeles, the county chose the land, quietly embarking on a policy of dumping the garbage in sanitary landfills in populous areas, despite potential safety hazards. That policy and the decision to transform so valuable a resource as the Santa Monica Mountains should have been well publicized. But they were not.

The decisions were made by the county supervisors, a few sanitation engineers and the Los Angeles City Council, since the sanitation district's canyons were within city limits. The engineers from the sanitation districts favored using the deep Santa Monica Mountain canyons because they would provide an ideal receptacle for the compacted garbage. The location of the canyons was desirable from an economic standpoint, since they were close to well-populated business and residential sections of the city.

A National Example

In the world of garbage disposal, the sanitary landfill in the Santa Monica Mountains has been cited as an example of how it is possible to dump garbage without discomfort to nearby residents. A booklet published in 1972 by the U.S. Environmental Protection Agency said, "As has been demonstrated in the Los Angeles area, refuse landfills can be operated near homes provided a very careful housekeeping job is accomplished. . . . Homes at Mission Canyon were intentionally built overlooking a large sanitary landfill because the owners knew that a park and golf course would be constructed on the completed fill. This is evidence that the public will accept a landfill in their backyard, if the operation is attractive and free of nuisance."

Those who own the homes overlooking the Mission Canyon landfill tell a different story. Homeowners talk about broken promises and government deals that benefited some land developers and allowed others to build homes that would be plagued with nuisances from the ongoing dumping operation.

The story began in 1958, before any of the houses were built. Los Angeles County and the county sanitation districts, which owned Mission Canyon, asked the city of Los Angeles for permission to use the area as a landfill site for fifteen years—until 1973. Since the canyon had been zoned by the city for residential use, the city council had to give special permission before it could be used for any other purpose. The county and its sanitation districts were given the go-ahead, but were specifically told by the city that "filling operations on portions of the property be completed at the earliest possible date in order to permit progressive development of recreational areas."

In the file of the Los Angeles City Planning Department is an artist's conception of how the park on top of the filled canyon would look—tennis courts, baseball diamonds, swimming pools and dressing rooms, several golf courses, a clubhouse—all nestled in some fluffy looking stuff that was the artist's vision of sanitary landfill. The drawing is undated, and there is no name of a government agency on it to take the blame for the overly optimistic view. Closed structures and swimming pools cannot be built on garbage fill, but such details are unimportant, since the park was never built.

In 1965, the county's sanitation districts suddenly stopped dumping in Mission Canyon before completing the landfill, They left it an unsightly mess, and that is how it looks today, with great dirt plateaus where garbage has been covered with a final, thick layer of dirt. Nothing grows there. One upper level near the homes has sprinklers and the start of a lawn, but it has not survived well in the canyon's winter rains, summer heat and Santa Ana winds.

The land on the mountain ridges above Mission Canyon was owned by a housing developer. Acting in line with the proposal for a subdivision around the expected park, the Los Angeles City Planning Department allowed him to begin developing the land for two expensive subdivisions there, Bel Air Knolls and Bel Air Skycrest, while the landfill operation was going on below. Only a few homes had been built up to the time the dumping stopped, by people willing to forgo the temporary noise, dust and mess of a landfill for the future hope of a golf course nearby. Many more homes were built after 1965, until, by the early 1970s, 160 families lived on the ridge overlooking Mission Canyon.

These newcomers believed enough of the fill had been completed to support the planned golf course.

The basis for this belief came from a number of sources: Some said they got the information from the developer and real estate salesmen. A few said that they checked with county sanitation officials—who later denied telling anyone that they were done with Mission Canyon. Finally, in city planning files, is the use permit specifying that the dump had to be landscaped as it was completed, that all dumping must end by 1973, and that a park would be built on top. By the late sixties with no resumption of dumping, it did appear the county must be finished with the canyon.

The first sign of broken promises came when some of the residents checked with the county department of parks and were told there was no money to build the golf course, and there might never be. The city planning file is filled with letters from homeowners telling their disappointment that the park they were promised was never built on top of the landfill.

A Well-Buried Plan—And Its Motive

Not many were aware of what was happening behind the closed doors of local government. Under the original agreement, dumping was to have continued in Mission Canyon until the fill was completed in 1973. Why was it unexpectedly stopped eight years early? The answer to that question illustrates the political aspect of refuse disposal. The dumping operation was moved because the county, the county sanitation districts and a private development company had contracted to fill some other privately owned canyons in an arrangement that was, at the least, very advantageous to the owners.

The Seacrest Company owned these canyons. Five people made up the company: Robert, Richard and Donald Barclay, Mike Hollander and Shirley Curci. Hollander was active in local politics, contributing to the political campaigns of Mayor Yorty and other local officeholders; he served as a member of one of Yorty's city commissions. Together, the five owners of Seacrest also contributed to the campaign of County Supervisor Burton Chace, whose district included the Santa Monica Mountains, as well as Malibu.

The Seacrest Company envisioned putting up an 800-home subdivision to be known as Braeburn Country Club Estates on the ridges of its canyons. The homes would be built around two golf courses, laid out on broad plateaus created by filling four of Seacrest's small canyons. Such construction is tremendously expensive if it is done with soil landfill. Seacrest would have had to bulldoze the sides of the canyons for the fill it needed. Many tons of earth would have had to be moved to create enough flatland for golf courses in the craggy canyon area.

As it turned out, Seacrest got its canyons filled at taxpayers' expense. In an agreement signed by Supervisor Chace, on behalf of the county and the sanitation districts, it was agreed that the garbage that had been going to Mission Canyon would now be put in the canyons owned by Seacrest. In addition, to obtain the dirt it needed to cover the garbage, the landfill operation would take earth from canyon ridges, leaving some of them terraced so that Seacrest could build homes without much extra grading.

A sensible person might argue that Seacrest should have paid county sanitation to fill its canyons. Instead, the government paid

Seacrest over a million dollars for the right to fill. The districts and Seacrest also exchanged some land. Seacrest gave the district some low ground needed for the garbage fill area. The district gave up high ground, which Seacrest could develop. In this exchange, the district also paid Seacrest $900,000 because it did not have as much land to swap as the developer.

That brought the total sanitation district payments to Seacrest to over $1.9 million. Another government agency, the Metropolitan Water District, paid Seacrest $400,000 for some land, too. And these figures do not include the value of some other favors by local government agencies. In filling the canyon, the district placed solid earth, rather than garbage, in areas where Seacrest would lay streets since streets sag if they are built on top of garbage. When the project was completed, the district left it contoured for a golf course, complete with a sprinkler system installed at taxpayers' expense. The sanitation district left a wide access road into the development, built originally for garbage trucks. And, the district paid $213,315 in property taxes to the county on the land while it was being filled. One citizens group estimated that cash and other benefits going to Braeburn Country Club Estates from local government agencies amounted to more than $12.7 million.

The sanitation districts said that the price charged by Seacrest was low, and that the county saved money in the transaction because they didn't have to buy land to fill. But that explanation ignores the great benefits received by Seacrest.

Compounding the Nightmare

Unknown to those who had bought homes overlooking the first, deserted landfill at Mission Canyon, the county sanitation districts planned to return once they were done with the Seacrest project. In 1973, when the city's conditional use permit to dump in the canyon expired, the sanitation districts asked the city for another permit, one that would allow them to resume dumping until the canyon was filled. The engineers seemed to have expanded its capacity. Now it would take another twenty years to fill it. The unlucky homeowners would have to endure the dust, noise, smell and mess of up to 1,500 vehicles a day that would file into the canyon to dump garbage until the 1990s.

One homeowner, Dr. Milton Becker, reasoned that "The city and county, by allowing the building of both Bel Air Knolls and Bel Air Skycrest, implicitly gave the prospective homeowners the belief that they would not be subject to a public nuisance in their immediate vicinity." He also said, "The promise was also, implicitly or not, that the landfill already completed would be used for park area." His argument makes sense. But, along with other citizen complaints, his letter was tucked away in an obscure city planning file folder. Along with the others, it probably will be ignored by the officials who have not yet made the final decision on the fate of Mission Canyon and the problem of where to put the garbage.

Seeing Beyond the Dump

The story is important, not because of the plight of the individual homeowners, but because of what it shows about invisible, unresponsive sanitation districts. Government, designed to serve the citizens, turned out to be an antagonist, an enemy so secretive and powerful that even affluent sophisticated people who lived in the canyons had little hope of beating it. They began to hire experts—a geologist and lawyers—to help them, but their chances of stopping the landfill were poor. While they grasped the technical complexity of the subject, few of them understood the political implications of their fight. Banded together with other neighborhoods, they could have threatened the elected officials who were hiding behind the sanitation districts. Supervisor Chace had died, but his successor seemed to take the same view of the project, and the homeowners said he refused to talk to them or answer their questions.

Meanwhile, the public was unaware that the sanitation districts were buying up land in two other huge, magnificent canyons nearby—Rustic and Sullivan canyons. They planned to hold this land as a preserve to dump trash into the twenty-first century, after Mission Canyon was full. Without public scrutiny or debate, they had made the decision for future generations.

IN FAIRFAX COUNTY: ATTEMPTING
TO REVERSE THE FLOW

On the West Coast, the fight by individual citizen groups was inadequate against the powerful forces who ran the system. On the other side of the country, in Fairfax County, Virginia, the home-owners were more successful. There, people worried about the effect new sewer lines might have on the community's future. Some of them led an organized fight against a county government controlled by land developers. Citizen activists won seats on the county board of supervisors. Unlike their counterparts in Los Angeles, they were able to form a wide political coalition to beat the developers at the polls.

Fairfax County, Virginia, is one of the suburbs of Washington, D.C. It was green farm country until after World War II, with the thick forests and lush fields that thrive in the rain and humid summer heat of that part of the Atlantic coastal plain. After the war, as the federal government grew, many government workers settled in Fairfax County, in subdivisions built on the old farm-land. From a population of 100,000 in 1950, the county grew to 250,000 in 1960. Today, 534,000 live there, most of them crowded into a corner of the county along the highways that lead into the District of Columbia. The people are mostly white and affluent enough to afford homes that cost an average of $41,500—and go up in value every day.

The result of the growth has been a suburban nightmare. School systems build an average of one new classroom a day, but the schools are still crowded. The commuter highways are packed in the early morning and in the late afternoon. Small streams that run through the county are fouled with untreated sewage, and millions of gallons of untreated sewage water finds its way into the Potomac River, the national shrine of pollution.

The politics of Fairfax County are the politics of sewers. In this despoiled land of polluted streams, the newly elected reform supervisors found a new sewage policy was the only way they could slow down unwanted construction.

One of them is Audrey Moore, a middle-aged housewife who got interested in politics when she found out that a group of investors, including Abe Fortas, former associate justice of the United States Supreme Court, was planning to build a highrise apartment near her home on land she thought was reserved for parkland. She protested to a county official. "When I asked, 'How do citizens go about convincing the county to acquire this park land?' The response I got was, 'Hey, Joe, I want you to come over here and meet this funny lady.' [The official] said, 'Don't you know that has all been decided, and they are going to build highrise apartments?' And I said, 'Who is they?' "

She found out. So did another of the new supervisors, Jean Packard, who is chairman of the board. Like Supervisor Moore, Supervisor Packard is a veteran of the League of Women Voters. Both women realized that a group of special interests devoted to growth controlled county government and decided what would be built in Fairfax County. They realized the only way to beat it was to leave the nonpartisan league and run for office.

"The only industry we have in Fairfax County is land and land development," said Supervisor Packard. "So primarily, [county government attracted] the bankers, real estate, insurance, large land owners—all the people whose livelihood and economic interest was tied up in the rapid growth and development of Fairfax County."

Supervisor Moore remembered the corruption of earlier days. Speaking of the late 1960s, she said that zoning officials could be bought. "To get county approval for building permits, sewers, subdivision sites, it was pretty much cash on the line." Eventually, illegal activities caught up with government officials. Four members of the planning staff and six out of the seven county supervisors were indicted on charges of accepting bribes in connection with zoning decisions. Four of the supervisors were convicted.

Gaining a Voice

In this atmosphere, it was not difficult for angry citizens to run for office and win. And in Fairfax County, political campaigns were traditionally less expensive than in more populated suburbs, such as Los Angeles County. Supervisor Packard's campaign, in 1972, cost her just under $2,000. Much of it was raised by selling

$10 tickets to a fundraising reception. One reason for the low cost was that she ran for a seat that was unexpectedly vacated, and the campaign was short. Supervisor Moore's campaign lasted longer, but still cost only $8,000, compared to the $250,000 it takes for a supervisor's seat in Los Angeles County. The two offices have roughly the same duties and powers, but in Fairfax, a supervisor works only part-time and represents 50,000 constituents. In Los Angeles, each supervisor works full-time and represents a million and a half people. Despite the differences in campaign costs and representation, control of local government had traditionally been in the hands of the same business interests in Fairfax County as it had in Los Angeles County. "One of the things I wanted to do," said Supervisor Packard, "was take control of the county away from the special interest groups which have been running every-thing—and this is not peculiar to Fairfax County."

As a first step, the reform supervisors attempted to take away the zoning permission that had been granted by their predecessors for a number of high-density building projects. They said that builders had been given permission for intensive development in another era, when heavy growth was considered good for the county. They insisted that their election meant the public wanted a change of policy. The builders and developers replied that the supervisors were depriving them of something of value—the right to build profitably on their own land. They said they had pur-chased the land with the intent of developing it, and to take away that right would be, in effect, depriving them of property. Attor-neys specializing in land development—many of whom had learned about zoning by working for the county—went to court for the developers. Virginia courts, believing strongly in the rights of property owners, agreed with the builders. Several judges ruled that the supervisors had no right to change the previously granted zoning.

Resorting to Sewers

Next, the supervisors tried to stop big building projects on the argument that Fairfax County's sewage plants were not capable of serving any more people. "I decided to do a little studying and learn a little about planning," said Supervisor Moore. "I began to get very interested in how sewers affect things." She and her colleagues learned that the sewage treatment plants were understating the amounts of sewage they treated, in an attempt to avoid a confrontation with the state water quality control board. "I knew they were overloaded or close to it," she said. Some of the plants tried to increase their capacity by chemical treatment, but it did not work as well as they'd hoped. In the fall of 1972, the supervisors, citing health reasons, imposed a moratorium on building permits in areas served by the overloaded sewage treatment plants, and within a few months the moratorium extended to virtually the whole county.

This time the moratorium was upheld in the courts. The supervisors' success came from the recent passage of federal and state laws regulating the quality of water in the streams. "The courts historically have not considered inadequacy of facilities as a reason to delay development," said Supervisor Packard. "Now, the reason we could do it with sewers is that we have state and federal laws about water quality standards. And the state has said, 'You will not pollute your waters, and if you don't put a moratorium on, we will.' "

But she believes that stopping some kinds of building projects by maintaining inadequate sewage facilities is a bad way to control growth, with evils of its own. For example, land developers began moving into lightly populated sections of the county where they could still build single-family homes served by septic tanks. "It's putting more pressure on low-density land that would normally remain undeveloped," said Supervisor Packard. "So development is sprawling farther out. As long as there is water available—and there is in most places—a man can come in and develop on a half acre lot on septic systems. That's the effect the moratorium is creating on land that normally would not be feeling development pressures if there were sewer construction elsewhere." The result is sprawling suburbs.

Supervisor Packard contended, "We have got to get some handle on growth. Sewers is not a good handle. It's a very bad tool. The best tool would be for us to have the flexibility to decide where the development goes, when it goes, and what type it goes. And that's not in the hands of the people. Right now it's in the hands of the landowner. Now, obviously he's going to develop when it's economically best for him. And I would, too, if I had land. That's common sense. But we have very little way of combatting that except by sewers. It's like using a shotgun when you really want to use a rifle. It's an awkward tool; it's a bad tool. But it's the only one we have, so we use it."

What Was Won

The moratorium didn't stop construction. The previous board of supervisors had given out so many building permits that six months after the moratorium was imposed, construction was under way to house another 5,000 people, with permits outstanding for housing another 8,000 to 10,000. Once this building was completed, there would be a lull in construction, but it would only be temporary because large new sewage treatment plants were being built. And, once these facilities were ready, the courts said private developers had the right to sewer hookups.

There was also pressure both from the building industry and from building trades unions who said the moratorium was creating a recession in Fairfax County, with high unemployment. Even though it was out of political power, real estate was still Fairfax County's most influential industry. And there were disagreements among the supervisors. Supervisor Moore felt her colleagues would begin to surrender to the developers. Supervisor Packard and some of the others wanted low-cost housing in Fairfax County. Builders were hinting that they might be willing to build inexpensive housing in exchange for more sewage capacity—a swap that would mean an upsurge in intensive development and a political victory for the builders.

Fairfax County has not succeeded in controlling the builders—yet. Once the new sewer plants were running, private landowners could still build highrises or condominiums in areas that might best be used for parks or left as woods or farms. And there was, as yet, no way for officials to discourage sprawling suburban developments that used septic tanks. But what Fairfax County reformers had done was to refine the tactics begun in Malibu. By resisting a sewage system, Malibu residents believed they could prevent undesirable changes to their community. By politically organizing around the issue and gaining control of government's power, Fairfax County citizens demonstrated how political dealings over development and waste disposal could be brought out of the backrooms and exposed to public debate.

With this new citizen power, landowners and county officials could no longer quietly deal for a sewage line that would shape the county forever. Decisions of the sanitation district were made public issues—their implications publicized and debated as much as welfare, schools and crime in the streets. And, while it was nearly impossible to reverse past decisions, there was hope that plans for the future would be made by the whole community, not just the few who would profit from them.

8

The Great Stadium Hoax

Would Brooklyn have boomed if the Dodgers had stayed? Will the smelly swamps of New Jersey's Hackensack Meadows equal New York in wealth and fame because the New York Giants professional football team has decided to move there? Will the city of Irving, Texas—population 100,000—rise to greatness on the arid flatlands now that 65,000 come there to watch the Dallas Cowboys play football?

The answer is yes—at least if one of the newest precepts of American business and government is to be believed. We are told that taxpayer-financed construction of a large stadium, a luxuriously furnished indoor arena, or a cavernous convention-exhibition hall will lower the tax rate, provide work for the jobless, save decaying downtowns, restore civic pride, and elevate even the most obscure city into metropolitan greatness. So firmly do local officials believe in the value of a home team, housed in a costly civic stadium, that New York spent $50 million to buy and remodel Yankee Stadium. The city was convinced it would no longer be New York if the Yankees baseball team moved away.

As a result, the new symbol of the American city on the move is the concrete bowl, rising up from an astroturf floor—crowned by a large bar in the Stadium Club and a jumbo scoreboard that illustrates the action with electronic fireworks and cartoon characters.

These are more than civic monuments or showplaces for professional sports teams. Many of them provide clear examples of how the democratic process is sidestepped in local and state government. They show how millions of dollars in public funds can be spent without a vote of the people, despite laws requiring voter approval of the construction of such huge civic projects. And the process by which they are built is another illustration of how, in city hall and the statehouse, decisions are made by relatively few people—business and sometimes labor leaders—acting through obscure government officials whom they control. Together, they form a business-labor-bureaucratic complex that is all but impossible for a citizen who is not part of it to penetrate.

These publicly financed stadiums, sports arenas and convention-exhibition halls are being built in communities all over the nation. The genesis of each project is slightly different, but the result is the same—construction of an expensive civic project, envisioned, planned and built by a small group of people who have the power to set priorities for the entire community.

THE NEW JERSEY MEADOWS: WHAT TO DO WITH A USELESS SWAMP

One such project is going up in the Hackensack Meadows, across the Hudson River from Manhattan, near Newark and Jersey City. The meadowland, despite its name, is a dismal polluted swamp—a place not to visit unless absolutely necessary. But its present condition has not stopped promoters of the project, who are determined to build a civic sports complex that will eclipse the rest in size, cost and scope.

In the past, the meadowland swamp has defied those who tried to reshape it. Nearly twenty thousand years ago, the glaciers of the last ice age receded from this land. During the slow process of geological change, glacial Lake Hackensack disappeared, and plants began to grow. The ocean, its level rising from the melting glacial ice, reached the bed of a river, and the great marsh was born. Fish, crabs, mussels, birds, insects and small animals lived here in an area that had an important natural function, to be the spawning ground for fish and other wildlife of the eastern coast. But only lately has man understood this.

Early Dutch settlers had tried to tame this hostile land by

building dikes to drain it. But tides washed away soil and crops. In 1816, developers tried again, and this time their ditches and dikes fell victim to burrowing animals. Fifty years later, entrepreneurs bought five thousand acres and constructed massive dikes with iron cores, designed to be strong enough to resist both tides and burrowing muskrats. Corn was planted on the drained land. Stalks grew, but never produced one ear of corn. The project was abandoned, and nature took over once more. Within a few years, the heavy dikes sank and disappeared.

The reason settlers felt compelled to do away with the swamp was explained in an 1868 edition of the *Scientific American:* "Such lands are not only unproductive of anything which can subserve important purposes, but they are productive of numerous evils. Teeming with miasma, the home of mischievous and annoying insects, they are blotches on the otherwise fair face of nature."

The New Jersey Meadowland still remains, the largest piece of undeveloped land in a U.S. urban area. It extends over 20,000 acres, an area larger than Manhattan. Yet only 1,000 people live there. Its main value is as a transportation corridor into New York, crisscrossed by railroads and highways, and, in some parts, the site for truck terminals. It is also a garbage dump for surrounding communities. A total of 42,000 tons of garbage is dumped there each week in sanitary landfills. One 7,000 acre portion has been salvaged and developed for industry.

Like other places in the shadow of a great city, northern New Jersey suffers from an inferiority complex. And in many respects, such a complex is deserved. It is a site for New York's bedroom communities and factories, a place for storage yards and train-yards. Although the governor's mansion of New Jersey produced a great American president, Woodrow Wilson, the reputation of New Jersey's state and local governments has been bad. Political machines and mobsters set governmental style in such cities as Newark and Jersey City. During the sixties, unresponsive local governments did nothing for the poverty and despair in city ghettos. In Newark, blacks rioted; racial tension marred city life; whites moved away. Unemployment increased in the decaying inner city, and a mayor was jailed for corruption.

By 1968, the New Jersey legislature had seen the meadowlands used as a neglected backyard for New York City long enough. Government and business interests decided that it could no longer remain undeveloped—and that the piecemeal development that was under way was depriving New Jersey of the chance to create a commercial, residential and recreational center. It was thought the meadowlands could provide the answer to northern New Jersey's staggering economic and social problems. In the late 1960s, the state set up the Hackensack Meadowlands Development Commission to preside over reshaping the area.

Investors for the swampy meadowland were slow to materialize, but a politician named Joseph McCrane, then state treasurer, had a plan he believed would put the area on the road to the prosperity and recognition it deserved. In 1970 he proposed the state build a football stadium and persuade the New York Giants to play their games there. McCrane had been a linebacker on the famous Glenn Davis-Doc Blanchard West Point football teams of the 1940s. After service in the army, he went into private business and then politics. He was a friend of the man who was then the governor of the state, William Cahill.

The Stadium Scheme Unfolds

McCrane suggested that the stadium could be built on the swamp without new taxes—or a vote of the people. He proposed construction of a football stadium and a racetrack. Betting at the track would be a big money-maker. On the prospect of expected racetrack earnings, the $211 million project would be financed through municipal bonds. A New Jersey Sports and Exposition Authority would be created, and it would sell the necessary bonds to pay for land and construction.

A word of explanation about bonds: Most civic projects are financed through municipal bonds that are either general obligation bonds or revenue bonds. Both kinds are attractive to investors because interest on them is exempt from federal income tax. However, general obligation bonds are subject to voter approval and are backed by the full faith and credit of the level of government sponsoring the facility. If such a project fails financially, investors are paid back with tax money. This voter-approved financing is cheaper because it has first call on repayment if the government agency is ever strapped for funds. If a city finds itself short of money, as many did during the Great Depression, it has trouble paying off its loans. But the holders of general obligation bonds are paid first. During the 1930s more than 98 percent of the municipal bonds made good, paying off investors. Since their risk is not as great, those who buy general obligation bonds receive a lower rate of interest than those who buy revenue bonds.

The New Jersey sports complex, however, was to be financed with municipal bonds that are revenue bonds. The purchasers would get their interest and investment back only if the stadium complex earned money. The sports complex revenue bonds would pay its investors about 7 percent tax-free interest, but because they were not guaranteed by the government, they were a highly speculative investment. Most such bonds are rated to show how risky they are. But these bonds had no rating. In the words of one underwriter of the bonds, Merrill Lynch, Pierce, Fenner and Smith, "Moody's [a bond rating company] felt it was too difficult to fairly assess the complexities and various uncertainties of the project."

Although financing the sports complex did not require a vote of the people, it had to be approved by the legislature. Some lawmakers doubted the project's optimistic feasibility study, which showed the racetrack would be a money-maker. Neighboring New York state allowed offtrack betting, and racetrack attendance there had been slipping since 1967. There was the feeling that if the Giants couldn't be persuaded to come—or if the deal fell through— the project would be a financial disaster. But unwilling legislators were persuaded to vote for the project by the wording of the legislation creating the Sports and Exposition Authority. It promised that the taxpayers would not, under any circumstances, be involved in paying for construction, cost overruns or operating losses. Legislation also said that if the Giants didn't come, the sports complex wouldn't be built.

In the beginning, Governor Cahill had been skeptical of McCrane's plan to bring a major league sports team to northern New Jersey. "That's a great idea, Joe, but it doesn't stand much of a chance," he said. But New Jersey was able to offer the Giants a better financial deal than they had in Yankee Stadium. Revenues would be greater because the stadium was bigger, seating 75,000 compared to 63,000 at Yankee Stadium. And, although the Giants would be leaving New York, they would not be far from their New York fans. Times Square is less than fifteen minutes away, and there are seventeen million residents within a 65 mile drive of the planned New Jersey Stadium Complex, including those affluent suburbanites who can afford tickets to professional football games.

The deal to bring the Giants was concluded when franchise owner Wellington Mara signed the forty-five page lease which moved his team from the city of its birth. Governor Cahill said the coming of the Giants would be a catalyst for the development of the entire meadowlands, which he called, "the most valuable piece of real estate in the world." On May 10, 1971, he signed into law legislation creating the New Jersey Sports and Exposition Authority.

The authority was run by men from the state's prominent businesses, and they represented banking and sport-promoting interests better than they did the citizens of New Jersey. There was David (Sonny) Werblin, businessman, former president of the New York Jets and a director of the New Jersey National Bank; Charles Serraino, vice president of Johnson and Johnson; Adian Foley, lawyer; Aubrey Lewis, executive of Woolworth Company and director of Montclair Savings Bank; and John Bell, executive of Trust Company of New Jersey.

A Forgotten Promise

Soon after the authority was formed, the pledge on which the entire project was based—not to use taxpayers' money—was forgotten. In January of 1973, long before the sports complex bonds went on sale, site preparation began. By midyear, $8.6 million had been spent for construction, $39.8 million on land, and an unspecified amount to administer the project.

The money came from $50 million in notes issued to banks by the Sports and Exposition Authority, a state agency, and another

$1.5 million was advanced directly out of the state treasury. This money was to be repaid by the sale of the sports-complex bonds. In addition, $200 million in federal flood-control funds were to be used to drain the swampland around the stadium and racetrack site. Improved roads in the area would cost $38.6 million, but only $6.5 million of the amount would come from the stadium bonds. The rest would be paid by the New Jersey Turnpike Authority and the state. By August 1973, the bonds still had not been marketed, but the authority had contracted out or received bids for half the cost of the project. It was in a rush because its lease with the Giants had pledged the stadium would be ready by 1975.

Just as the bonds were to go on sale, New York state announced that it planned to build its own racetrack complex in nearby Queens. It meant serious competition for the New Jersey project, especially since racetrack attendance in the area was dwindling. It would be nearly impossible to attract investors now, and so the New Jersey Sports and Exposition Authority asked the bond-selling houses to "temporarily" delay the bond sales "with the understanding that a stronger security can be restructured in 30 days."

In order to make the bonds saleable, the sports project needed a better guarantee for investors. But a ballot measure giving the bonds the full faith and credit of the state could not go before the people until November of 1975, which would be too late. Instead, the Sports and Exposition Authority asked legislators to back the bonds with a "moral pledge." This arrangement was a halfway guarantee that the bonds were a safe investment. It meant that the state was not directly obligated to pay the investors if the project foundered financially, but that the legislature could—and promises it would—vote to appropriate tax money in case of default. The risk now boiled down to the chance that some legislators giving their moral pledge might no longer be in office, and a subsequent legislature might not make good the pledge.

The legislature's choice was not clear-cut. It was no longer a simple decision whether to build the stadium and racetrack or not. The Sports and Exposition Authority was already over $50 million in debt, and some state money had already been advanced to begin building. A refusal to back up the bonds would mean this money would be lost. Once the authority had prematurely committed millions, state government had to come across with more money and more guarantees—or lose its original investment.

Legislators were hesitant to back up the project. Said New Jersey Assembly speaker Thomas Kean, "I have in the past been strongly opposed to any moral pledge. The way the project was conceived and sold in the legislature was there would be no obligation. Now I'm reexamining the question of whether a moral pledge is an obligation." Despite doubts, the legislature voted for the moral pledge. With that assurance, the sports-complex bonds went on the market.

The delay had meant it would take a year longer to build the stadium, putting the Giants' lease in danger of cancellation. Costs, of course, had gone up. The complex would now cost $295 million, instead of $211 million. And, there was no guarantee that the price would not further escalate, nor was there any longer a promise that the project would not use tax money. It was still a risky investment, but now the taxpayers of New Jersey—not the private bond purchasers—would be taking the risk.

NEW YORK'S LOSS

At the prospect of losing the Giants to New Jersey, New York had been bitter and angry. Mayor John Lindsay called the team "selfish, callous and ungrateful." Howard Cosell, the sports commentator, said the move was unjustified: the Giants had sold every available ticket for years, and the team's departure would cause economic hardship for the city.

What makes a city a good place to live? How much does the presence of an athletic team have to do with a community's vitality and self-esteem? At least in the minds of baseball fans, the city of New York has been irrevocably identified with the Yankees baseball team, which, beginning in the 1920s, was consistently the strongest in the game until the decline of the team in the mid-1960s. Babe Ruth was a Yankee, and his power, and that of his teammates, made the Yankees synonymous with the home run, the most exciting moment in baseball. In the 1920s, the owner of the Yankees, Col. Jacob Ruppert, built a large stadium in the Bronx to house the team. It cost him $2.5 million, and everyone called it "the House that Ruth built" because the Babe brought in the crowds. Nobody asked the city to pay for the stadium. Col. Ruppert built it and maintained it.

In the late 1950s, the Dodgers threatened to move from Brooklyn unless city government provided help in building them a replacement for their Ebbetts Field. The city refused, and much to everyone's surprise, the Dodgers left. Los Angeles was to be their new home, and through an elaborate land swap, the city provided owner Walter O'Malley with a large and valuable parcel of land for the new Dodger Stadium. With the Giants in San Francisco, it meant New York City had only one baseball team left. City officials and sports promoters felt it wasn't enough. Using a complicated financing scheme that did not require a vote of the people, the city built Shea Stadium for $24 million, and the National League awarded a baseball franchise to John Payson Whitney, who founded the New York Mets. The New York Jets of the American Football League also played in the new stadium, so that New York had two professional football teams. To those who governed New York City, at least, the presence of the maximum number of major league teams was necessary to preserve the city's greatness.

Michael Burke, the president of the New York Yankees, realized that. With the Giants football team moving to New Jersey, the Yankees would be left alone in their old stadium, having to compete with the more comfortably housed Mets for attendance. Burke, too, talked about moving. "My overriding concern is the future of the Yankees," he said. "We shall have to take a new and realistic reading of our options." New Jersey was a potential site for the Yankees, or Texas, or Canada—or anywhere else that offered a better deal. He demanded that the city refurbish Yankee Stadium to put it on the same level as the Mets' $24 million facility. Said Burke, "Parity with the Mets is basic to Lindsay's commitment [to the team]. And Yankee Stadium is basic to that commitment. If that is no longer true, then we'd have to consider our options."

The city agreed and bought Yankee Stadium from its private

owners. It was estimated the total cost of purchase and renovation would be under $25 million, a small amount compared to the $80 million it would cost for a new stadium. In October 1973, after the last game in old Yankee Stadium, 20,000 fans ran wild, ripping up the seats and carrying them home. Within a few days, Mayor Lindsay conducted a ground-breaking ceremony, scooping up grass and dirt in right field with a bulldozer. He said, "Nothing could be more important to the economy and vitality of our city than to assure that the house that Ruth built remain here in the Bronx for future generations of New Yorkers."

By the end of the year, it was apparent that few had understood the cost of that commitment. As usual, the original estimate had been unrealistic. Now, city government was told, the job would cost close to $50 million, and it might be even more.

What would the city gain for its investment? It would keep the Yankees. And Ken Patton, economic development administrator, testified to city council that the city would gain from the renovated stadium $3.6 million a year in taxes, plus wages and employment of 1,500 people. About $10 million of the remodeling money was going into streets, landscaping and other improvements to the neighborhood surrounding the stadium. Conceding that the facility would probably be used only ninety-five days a year, counting games and special events, Patton said, "I believe it clearly worthwhile."

Councilman Matthew Troy argued with this view. Troy is chairman of the city council finance committee and favored tearing down the stadium for a parking lot. "Don't try to put this on a sound fiscal basis," he told Patton. "If you want to talk about the necessity of rehabilitating a section of the Bronx, that's a different thing."

The city council grudgingly approved the additional costs. Like the New Jersey legislators, they had little choice. The Lindsay administration warned that the city had already spent $15 million on property and contracts, and if the stadium project were abandoned, there was no way to get back the money. Furthermore, the city had promised the Yankees to have their stadium ready by April of 1976. Reneging on the pledge would leave the city open to a legal suit and damages.

There were critics who said the project was not benefiting the

Bronx. Planners had put the highway approaches to the stadium through the city's last remaining farmers market. Lamented a *New York Times* editorial, "There is a direct relationship between the quality of life and the quality of a city, and much of it has to do with the quality of planning." It said the project "phases out the real and pleasurable and makes it obsolete."

Even with the Giants leaving, New York still had three of its four professional football and baseball teams, but vast public funds had been spent to keep them—without a vote of the people and with little consideration for the city's other pressing priorities.

WHAT'S IT WORTH?

Voter approval doesn't guarantee voter satisfaction. They may approve a relatively simple project, but by the time the civic boosters in charge are finished, it is a superstadium, a sports palace for athletes and for those fans who can afford to pay admission prices that now average $7 a ticket. A *Fortune* magazine article described the dilemma of such voter-approved stadiums all over the country. In each case, the unsuspecting taxpayers had to pay snowballing costs over which they had no control.

Fortune illustrated its point in detail with stadiums being built in Seattle and New Orleans, where votes had been taken, but the amounts eventually spent were much larger than the figures voters had authorized. The vote in each instance had little relationship to what was built and what it cost. For example, in New Orleans, Louisiana Superdome boosters were carried away with expensive plans, and what began as a relatively modest $35 million stadium now bears a $151 million price tag.

There is a basic question in all of these projects: Does a stadium, an indoor sports arena or a convention center contribute enough to community prosperity to justify the vast expenditures for extravagant extras that were not included in voter-approved plans or—as in increasingly more instances—for a project that has never been put to a vote of the people at all? Even considering intangible gains such as civic pride, the answer is no. An illustration of this can be seen even in the story of one of America's most financially successful projects—a stadium, a glass-walled indoor sports arena, and an exhibition hall for trade shows, located in an industrial city across the bay from San Francisco, in Oakland, California.

SUCCESS ON THE OAKLAND FLATLANDS

The Oakland-Alameda County Coliseum Complex looms unexpectedly in the flatlands that reach to San Francisco Bay. It is a massive, but simply designed stadium and arena, of striking appearance. The passerby cannot help but wonder what these impressive structures are doing there among the vacant lots, factories, and housing projects in a dreary part of a city that looks as though it can little afford such luxuries.

The city's leaders—who are also the stadium's greatest boosters—point to its frequent bookings and big gates as measures of the project's success. Of the nation's new stadiums, it is the busiest, and one of the few able to meet its own operating costs. On fall Sundays, the stadium is full for the games of the Oakland Raiders of the National Football League, and in 1972 and 1973 the World Series was played there, won by the Oakland As baseball team. These were important events in the life of this city of 360,000.

Why was it built? What has it done for the community? Was it worth the $22 million it was costing taxpayers who had never been asked if they wanted the project? To answer these questions, it is necessary to go back to the city's beginnings.

In 1869, the transcontinental railroad was completed, and its western terminus was located in Oakland, then a small town. Those passengers who enjoyed culture, good restaurants, lively theater, extravagant sin and an incalculable number of saloons continued their journey, across the bay on the ferryboat to San Francisco. The trains could go no farther. Eight miles of water separated them from a city that was unparalleled in America for the diverse nature of its sophisticated pleasures. That sealed Oakland's fate as a place for locomotives, freight yards, factories and miles of modest residential neighborhoods for those who could not afford San Francisco or who did not care for its style and its cool, foggy weather.

From the beginning, Oakland was afflicted with a second-city complex, the Newark, New Jersey, of the West Coast. A former resident, Gertrude Stein, who lived there as a girl and never returned, wrote of Oakland, "There is no there there," and today, decades later, the words still rankle civic leaders. But the city had a rough character of its own. Just as it was the end of the line for the westbound trains, the city was the place where much of the western migration of people ended. In small, but successive waves, easterners and midwesterners, Italians and Portuguese, Okies, Arkies, blacks, American Indians and Mexican Americans arrived in the city. Working Man was the city's style, and it was reflected in the plain bars in North Oakland, the inelegant hotels downtown, the old ballpark in Emeryville, and buses filled every weekday morning with men carrying lunch pails to their jobs at the Southern Pacific yards, the shipyards, or any number of small manufacturing plants in the flatlands near the bay.

The continual arrivals made Oakland a receiving station for American migrants and gave the city a feeling of continual change. Neighborhoods never remained the same. A resident might move away and return a few years later, unable to find treasured landmarks of his youth.

But the changes occurred only at the bottom. As in other cities, at the top were a few old families. They were closely allied to the businessmen who owned stores and property in a small but thriving downtown. This combination of ferment at the bottom and unchanging, conservative leadership at the top made Oakland a laboratory of urban studies. It had much in common with other old American cities.

World War II created a huge job market for a new wave of migrants to the West. Before then, California was more of an agricultural state; its coastal cities grew slowly. Its interior valley was scattered with the wandering escapees from the Dust Bowl of the Southwest—the people John Steinbeck wrote about in *The Grapes of Wrath*. As the war began, shipyards were built along the eastern shore of San Francisco Bay, in Oakland, and in neighboring cities. There were finally jobs in Oakland for the Dust Bowl victims and for blacks, too, who came from the South and crowded into the old neighborhoods in the western part of the city. Post-World War II Oakland was a prosperous, growing city.

Death of the Central City

But from the mid-fifties into the sixties, the prosperity was slowly ending. The supply of unskilled jobs, which once seemed endless, vanished. Black and white could not get along. Whites moved to newer homes in racially segregated suburbs. Stores closed. Downtown Oakland, once the busy center for many communities, stood quiet and empty.

It was apparent that Oakland was suffering from sicknesses common to American cities. And like many others, Oakland lacked the elements necessary to democracy—an observant press and civic machinery through which citizens could understand what was happening and make their views known. As a result, the city government chose not to deal with the realities of the new Oakland. Its greatest problems were black unemployment and the terrible social tensions it caused.

Although downtowns in the big cities were dying, California of the mid-sixties was more prosperous than it had ever been before. At least white California was. The shipyards and aircraft plants of World War II had been replaced by aerospace and electronic industries, providing jobs to a postwar generation of Californians, many of them trained in a public junior college, state college and state university system unparalleled in the nation. But, with few exceptions, blacks and Mexican Americans, the minorities in the state, were excluded. The public schools in their neighborhoods were not fit to prepare them to go beyond high school. The children of the ghetto became outcasts in a state booming with new technological industries, offering jobs only to the well-trained.

A White Solution—And a Black One

Not only did two economies develop in California—one for the affluent majority, another for poor minorities—but by the mid-sixties, there were two political systems. One operated conventionally, through the traditional two-party political process. It was for white people. The other operated outside the system, developed by blacks excluded from the normal process. In the 1966 election, the white people elected their governor, Ronald Reagan, who also received support from some Mexican Americans who felt the previous Democratic administration had ignored them while helping blacks. At the same time, a number of blacks formed militant groups that surprised and shocked the white community and even made members of their own race unhappy.

Nowhere was the existence of separate political and economic systems more apparent than in Oakland. In the early sixties, the white system was building the Oakland Coliseum Complex to beef up the city's economy. During those same years, the black system was building a new ghetto consciousness. Each represented one segment of society's attempt to cure the social ills besetting Oakland.

There is an intriguing and important historical note that under-lines the unresponsiveness of local government's business-dominated leadership. In the fall of 1966, while Oakland's leaders were celebrating the completion of their new stadium, two angry young blacks, Huey Newton and Bobby Seale, were organizing the Black Panther Party for Self Defense.

Things were bad in the black community in 1966, just as they had been for years. In spring and summer of that same year, the University of California at Berkeley studied unemployment in the slums of Oakland. In that affluent time, the unemployment rate in the United States was only 3.7 percent. In San Francisco and Oakland, a center of the new electronics industry, it was 4.5 percent, one of the lowest rates in the country for a metropolitan area. But in the slums, which were largely black, 13 percent were out of work. And that 13 percent represented people who had actively sought jobs and had found their way into the statistics. The university study acknowledged that this figure did not include those working part-time, but seeking full-time work; and those working full-time, but earning too little to live on. Nor did it list those who had given up and dropped out of the job market or those in the community who, for any number of reasons, never show up in the census or other surveys. These were the hard-core unemployed. Ten percent of the slum dwellers fell into this category, making the real unemployment rate in Oakland slums 23 percent. Less than half in Oakland's depressed neighborhoods had finished high school.

The Black Panther Party's solution was revolutionary. Its platform called for full employment for blacks, fit housing, exemption of blacks from military service, release of all black prisoners from jails, and black juries to try black people. Less radical was the party's demand for better schools in black neighborhoods. The story of the Panthers is still unfinished. When they first became known to the nation, walking fully armed into the state Capitol in Sacramento, they created an everlasting image of violence. The impression was deepened by their determination to use arms to resist police they considered brutal and repressive. Famous trials followed well-publicized Panther gun battles with the police, trials in which the Panthers won surprising victories.

In 1973, the story of the Panthers took an even more surprising twist. Bobby Seale, wearing a business suit and earnestly talking about ways to find jobs for blacks, ran for mayor of Oakland. He lost to the conservative incumbent mayor, John Reading, but received 37 percent of the vote in a city that was then 34.5 percent black. And both Reading and Seale conducted dignified, high-level campaigns that included serious discussions of the city's problems. The Seale campaign showed that the Panthers were mellowing as they matured. But in the mid-sixties, when our story takes place, the Panthers' emergence and militant stance was frightening to most of the city.

The Men Who Ran the City

The business leadership of Oakland was much like the business leadership of other American cities. The most notable member was William Knowland, former minority leader of the United States Senate and publisher of the *Oakland Tribune*. He was a tall, red-faced, beefy man with a personal manner that was clumsy, blustering and heavy-handed. Knowland's greatest virtue was an old-fashioned sense of personal honesty and fairness.

His greatest failing was a narrow stubbornness, which prompted him to give up his United States Senate seat in 1958, return to

California, and begin a hopeless race for the governorship. It began an intra-party fight that wrecked the state's Republican party for the next eight years.

His father, Joseph Knowland, had been a leader of the Republican old guard that had opposed Hiram Johnson's reformers in the early part of the century. A legacy of California politics is an old photograph showing Joseph Knowland and others celebrating the victory of the corrupt Southern Pacific Railroad at the Republican state convention of 1906. But the senior Knowland also gave the country Earl Warren, whom he sponsored for district attorney of Alameda County in 1925, the first office in a career that ended with his distinguished tenure as Chief Justice of the United States Supreme Court.

Almost as important to Oakland as Knowland was the son of another famous man, Edgar Kaiser, whose father, Henry Kaiser, operated shipyards on the bay during World War II, producing quickly built Liberty and Victory cargo ships at a pace previously unheard of. Like the Knowlands, the Kaisers' life centered in the Oakland area, and in 1957 the city acquired its first highrise—the worldwide headquarters of Kaiser Industries. In an area where there are so few rich and distinguished people, families like the Kaisers and the Knowlands take on even greater importance than they would in other cities.

A major vehicle through which Knowland, Kaiser and other business leaders exercised their influence was through the Oakland Chamber of Commerce, which Knowland once headed. Every city has a chamber of commerce, an organization of businessmen dedicated to improving business conditions in the area, and hence their own profits. As in many other cities, the Oakland Chamber of Commerce served as an informal extension of city government. A small number of large Bay Area firms controlled the chamber, pushing government policies and civic projects that would benefit them and, in their view, the city. They were: Santa Fe Industries, World Airways, Bank of America, Bechtel Corporation, Clorox Corporation, Southern Pacific Railroad, Kaiser, Knowland's Oakland Tribune, Wells Fargo Bank, and the Pacific Gas and Electric Company, which supplied power to everyone.

Ignoring the City's Problems

These major businesses, along with powerful real estate interests and operators of a few remaining downtown stores, constitute a small oligarchy that, with the help of compliant elected officials, has determined city policy for years. The policy of city government in the fifties and most of the sixties was to ignore the problems of the ghetto.

This was well illustrated by a daily reading of Senator Knowland's . *Tribune*. By refusing to run pictures and stories about blacks, the paper pretended there was no black population. And crimes against them were considered beneath the interest of the *Tribune's* readers. For example, in 1956, a young reporter was sent to the West Oakland ghetto early one morning, to an old housing project where a black man had killed his wife, three or four small children and then himself. The bodies were scattered around the small cluttered rooms in a scene which even affected Oakland policemen usually unmoved by death, particularly black death. The reporter did not know why the man had murdered his family, whether it was despair, anger or insanity. He knew that he had seen something important, but he lacked the skill and experience to understand and describe it. He returned to the paper and told the city editor. "What color were they, kid?" the editor asked. "Black," was the answer. The city editor held his thumb and forefinger two inches apart in a gesture meaning that was the length story he wanted.

As a result of the paper's refusal to print black news, its readers received a picture of a peaceful, all-white city that did not exist. Unaware of changes, discontent and despair, white citizens never understood the city had deep, festering problems that would some day have to be dealt with.

But the departure of business from downtown and the increasing flight of whites to segregated suburbs convinced the Oakland oligarchy by the beginning of the 1960s that something had to be done to save the city. In the minds of civic leaders, building the coliseum complex was the answer. Part of the motivation was commercial. The *Tribune,* for example, depended on the city's businesses for advertising and circulation revenue, and Kaiser had invested millions in its two large downtown headquarters buildings that were to start the revival of the central city. But part was civic pride, and the feeling that rank imposes obligations.

Chamber of Commerce—Spur to Progress

Oakland businessmen had been talking about building a stadium for years. They saw it as a means of boosting profits and community spirit, but had never been able to persuade the rest of the citizenry to support the plan. In the post-World War II boom year of 1946 when crowds were filling the community's small minor league baseball park, the city proposed a $1.5 million bond issue for a modest 40,000-seat stadium. It was defeated, 53,000 to 45,000. That was the last time city government asked the voters about it.

Through the years, the idea was studied by both the city council and the chamber of commerce stadium committee. The two groups had many of the same members, and they often met together. But in all of the discussions about the stadium, it was always the attitude of the city council that it should follow the lead of the chamber of commerce.

Several times plans for another stadium bond election were unveiled. But the matter did not go on the ballot. Many reasons were advanced publicly for not putting it to a vote, but city officials agreed privately there was only one real reason: an electorate which was turning down financing plans for schools and other projects would not approve spending public money on a stadium. As a result, the city's leaders devised a way to build the stadium without an election.

The man who got the stadium project going was Robert Nahas, a developer of shopping centers and other property. He was also the president of the chamber of commerce. The others behind the project were Kaiser, Knowland and George Loorz, president of the Stolte Construction Company, a large firm with a stake in the development of Oakland and the surrounding communities. Following the local custom, the plan was outlined to city and Alameda County officials only after it had been devised by the business leaders of the chamber of commerce. Government accepted the scheme willingly and without question.

The Nonprofit Stadium Corporation

Nahas and the others used a financing plan adopted by many other communities who want to build stadiums or similar facilities, but cannot count on the voters to approve general obligation bond financing. It is called "lease purchase." A private, nonprofit corporation is formed, and it is authorized by local government to borrow money to build the project by selling tax-exempt bonds. It owns and runs the stadium until the bonds are paid off. At that time, usually, ownership of the facility is turned over to government. Although the bonds are not voter approved, they are actually backed up by government's good credit. That is because the arrangement hinges on a city, county or state's promise to pay off the bonds and the interest on them in the form of "rent" paid to the stadium corporation. The city's and county's payment of rent is justified by the argument that the community is gaining a public facility. But in this case, the benefit is indirect. Government is renting the stadium's presence in Oakland. The rent comes from taxpayers' pockets, but they still have to buy tickets from sports promoters and other show backers to gain admission.

As the *San Francisco Chronicle* financial editor, Sidney Allen, explained, "The Coliseum project is to be financed by lease purchase. That's the process of getting a third party to do the job on the assurance that the municipality will lease it at a rate and for a length of time that assures the facility will be fully paid for, with interest.

"Lease purchase commits the credit of all the municipality's taxpayers, of course, without taxpayer approval."

As in most such schemes, stadium backers insisted taxpayer support would be minimal since Coliseum, Inc., would get income from the stadium's users—shows, ballgames and concessions. Theoretically, this amount was supposed to eventually make the stadium self-supporting and allow it to pay off its own bonds.

To build the Oakland Coliseum Complex, a nonprofit corporation, Coliseum, Inc., was created and was authorized to borrow $25 million by selling revenue bonds to lenders. The city and county each paid $750,000 a year—a total rent of about $1.5 million out of their current budget to Coliseum, Inc. It was hoped the coliseum's revenues would soon be enough to pay back the city and county their investment. However, even the most optimistic stadium boosters conceded that—at least in the beginning— the project's income would not be enough to pay operating expenses, much less the lenders. So, in addition to the $1.5 million, local government agreed to pick up any operating deficits until the coliseum could become self-sustaining.

As in the financing of the New Jersey stadium, the interest on the revenue bonds was higher than it would have been on voter-approved general obligation bonds. In the case of the Oakland-Alameda County Coliseum Complex, interest on the bonds was $4\frac{1}{8}$ percent—a full percent more than general obligation bonds would have paid. In comparison to the high interest rates of the seventies, the $4\frac{1}{8}$ percent sounds low, but over the twenty to thirty years it would take to pay off the bonds, that extra one percent would cost the taxpayers several million dollars.

The general public was only dimly aware of the complicated financial arrangement, and the city, the county and Coliseum, Inc., in advancing the project, minimized what it would cost taxpayers. For example, in November 1960, the *Oakland Tribune* merely said, "The city and county would sign a long-term lease with the nonprofit corporation, guaranteeing to help meet the debt service required on a loan the corporation would obtain from private financial sources," and "if the net income were not enough to meet the required payment in a given year—and it is unlikely that it would be for the first few years—then the city and county would share equally the cost difference out of their general fund revenues from taxes and other sources." Even so, instead of raising taxes, the stadium would, in the words of the Oakland city manager, "bring income and tax relief to our city."

Getting It Rolling

The board of directors of Coliseum, Inc., turned out to be the same civic leaders who had been boosting the stadium project through the chamber of commerce. In no way was Coliseum, Inc., required to be responsive to the citizens who were footing the bill. Since the corporation was a private organization, business leaders—rather than elected officials—selected its members on an informal basis. "We hope to enlist the active participation of community leaders from all sections of the county," said the corporation board's first member, Robert Nahas. "We want men of vision and experience in development who recognize the economic impetus for the entire Eastbay . . . at long last we are on the move." After another builder, George Loorz, joined Nahas on the board, Knowland and Kaiser followed. A few days later, the board had lunch at what was then Oakland's most exclusive businessman's club, the Athenian Nile, with directors of the Port of Oakland and the East Bay Municipal Utility District, all part of the chamber of commerce-government oligarchy. They arranged for these two government agencies to sell land to the corporation for the stadium.

The whole operation was planned without the benefit of public scrutiny. Not until six months after the architect was selected were public hearings called to get citizen reaction to the project.

As plans firmed up, the *Tribune* carried statements by the coliseum's backers telling what the project would do for the community. The reasons were the same as those given for similar projects across the country. Civic leaders claimed it would increase business and income for the city's businesses:

"Oakland needs a stadium to generate more economic activity," said William Knowland.

"Day after day, Oakland money is being spent elsewhere for sports events which could be held here if we had adequate facilities," said the mayor.

"This is how we can stop the flow of dollars out of Oakland," said the city manager. "It is a generator of economic activity, a money maker to bring income and tax relief to our city."

"It is bound to mean more business for the entire community," said Edgar Kaiser.

And, the general manager of the chamber of commerce predicted that the stadium's first year would produce $10 million in business revenue for the area. "The complex will have the effect of a major new industry," he said

Construction went well. Kaiser's firm and the Stolte Construction Co., headed by George Loorz, provided free assistance in planning. Recognizing conflict of interest, they refrained from bidding on the job. Costs were far below those of most other new stadiums. Cost overruns were almost nonexistent. The stadium, the adjoining indoor sports arena, and an underground exhibition hall cost $22 million, low by today's standards when a stadium alone can cost over $100 million.

In 1966, the Oakland Coliseum Complex was completed—and the project had cost just about what backers said it would. The nonprofit corporation had done its job well. Compared to such projects elsewhere, the complex was a commercial success. Across the nation, expensive new stadiums stood empty much of the year, unable to attract events and professional teams. But in 1970, there were 1,400,000 paying customers for 225 separate events at the Oakland Coliseum. The Coliseum, Inc., board reported that the project was paying its own operating costs from the beginning.

Nevertheless, revenues were never enough for the city of Oakland and surrounding Alameda County to suspend their joint payment of $1.5 million a year rent. By 1973 the amount invested by the city and county taxpayers was about $12 million. That year, for the first time, the nonprofit corporation made enough from its users to turn back $350,000 to the city and county. But that still meant taxpayers had thus far paid over $11 million for the facility. The lease-purchase agreement had more than fifteen years to go.

THE COLISEUM'S CONTRIBUTION TO OAKLAND

Questions remained about the backers' original promise. Had the project contributed to a revival of the city and the surrounding area and to tax relief and increased employment?

One measure of the prosperity of a city is whether the assessed value of the land has increased. Backers of the stadium said that the project would guarantee increased property values. But there has been only a modest increase in Oakland's assessed valuation over the past few years, and today's county officials attribute the increase to inflation. In the 1969-70 fiscal year, assessed value of property in the county was $949,785,978. In the 1971-72 fiscal year, it was $996,799,747. By 1973-74, it had risen to only $1,101,652,276.

Backers of the stadium claimed it would reduce property taxes. But while taxes in surrounding Alameda County have declined slightly, those within Oakland, which provided the impetus for the coliseum, have gone up.

Unemployment and poverty are just about as bad in Oakland as they were before the stadium was built. And blacks, 34.5 percent of the population, and Mexican-Americans, 9.8 percent, receive a disproportionately small share of whatever new prosperity is available. Median white-family income was $10,766 in 1973, compared to $8,782 for Mexican-Americans and $7,400 for blacks.

The construction of the coliseum complex had done nothing to end the decay and despair of a growing black ghetto that was at the heart of Oakland's basic dilemma.

What improvements there were in the economy came from other projects—an expansion of the airport and industrial lands by the Port of Oakland. The coliseum was near both the airport and the new industrial tract. Land assessments had greatly increased in that area, and several hotels were built. But their clientele was more apt to come from the airport and industries than from the coliseum. An attempt was being made to revive downtown, with new office buildings and stores in a redeveloped area. But, again, this had nothing to do with the stadium. Neither did the civic project that could do the most to shape the area, the Bay Area Rapid Transit commuter train lines.

Even the Oakland Coliseum's most fervent supporters now say there is really no way to measure its direct benefits. Instead, they say, there are intangible things—a boost in civic pride, the creation of a feeling that Oakland is not dead. It is a place for athletic teams around which citizens, white, black and brown, can unite, temporarily putting their differences aside. "People from the East Bay, when they were in the East, would say they were from San Francisco because no one ever heard of Oakland," said Jim Coward of the chamber of commerce. "Now, they say, 'I'm from Oakland, California.' " David Johnson, assistant to Mayor John

Reading, said, "The World Series generated a community feeling in the city not seen for years. There was even a parade in downtown Oakland, the first one since the early fifties, and thousands came."

Still, there were those in the community who were questioning its value. In 1971 an Oakland city councilman, John Sutter, told a council meeting he was surprised to learn that the city's share of the coliseum lease-purchase rent that year was still $750,000, when the stadium and arena were so successful in attracting attendance. And after the 1973 World Series, the city council tried to find out why the stadium had collected only $2,000 a game in rent when 150,000 people paid from $6 to $15 for tickets. The World Series rent was "not impressive" said Councilman Sutter, considering the million dollar gates. American League playoffs paid a higher rent of $6,000 a game. But another critic pointed out that while the city and county were paying $750,000 a year each in rent for vague benefits, the Coliseum's food and parking concessionaires, who paid Coliseum, Inc., a low rent, were netting from $5,000 to $6,000 a game.

Was the operation a giveaway to the businesses that were using it, at the expense of taxpayers who had to pay to get in? Was it booked up with attractions because it was charging less rent than other similar facilities? In Texas, for example, the Astrodome had charged $35,000 rent for a single big event, the Super Bowl.

It is clear that those who benefited financially from the Coliseum complex were the few entrepreneurs who put on the games and shows there. The taxpayers were footing the bill, but all they gained was an intangible pride in local teams. And for those in the poor minorities, there were few benefits. Most other government-funded recreation facilities—museums, beaches, parks, planetariums—are free or available at nominal cost to the taxpayers who made them possible. Although the coliseum was built with tax money, tickets are no less expensive than those sold at privately built facilities—averaging $5 to $7 for sports and other events. Not everyone who paid a share of the lease-purchase fee through city and county taxes could afford tickets.

The Oakland Coliseum was one of the few such projects in the nation that was busy and paying its own operating costs. Elsewhere, in Seattle, New Orleans, Hackensack, San Diego, and other

American cities, taxpayers were footing the bill for stadiums that were recently built or under construction. Few had hopes for attracting the number of teams and events that the Oakland Coliseum is host to. The Houston Astrodome—generally regarded as a huge success—was built on taxpayers' money and lost nearly $600,000 in operating costs in 1971. Even Oakland's limited success story shows what is wrong with building great athletic edifices with public money.

We found no proof that any of these stadiums add enough to the prosperity of their communities to justify their cost to the taxpayer without his consent. If voters refuse to approve such a project, the few private businessmen who stand to benefit can finance the stadiums themselves. It has been done. For example, in Los Angeles, Jack Kent Cooke, unhappy with the way the publicly owned Los Angeles Sports Arena treated his Los Angeles Lakers basketball team, built his own arena with his own money. It is a great commercial success.

These are not projects for the public good. They are commercial enterprises, planned in private meetings, subsidized by the taxpayers with the approval of compliant local officials, and operated for the benefit of a few. The voters, not a few businessmen, should be the ones to decide if this is the best way to spend their money.

9

Waiting for

the Transit Revolution

Like most days in Canoga Park, a suburb of the Los Angeles San Fernando Valley, it began with sunshine. And like most commuters in big cities across America, Hal Block started his daily ordeal. Hal was thirty-nine and he had settled in Southern California because he felt it could offer him and his family a better life. But he had no time to enjoy the weather or the pleasant suburban surroundings. He said good-bye to his Japanese-born wife and his two daughters. His mind occupied by his immediate difficulties, he settled behind the steering wheel of his three-and-a-half-year-old Impala and drove away from the ranch-style house on the tree-lined cul-de-sac.

Carefully navigating the city streets, with the nervousness of someone who battles daily traffic jams, Block soon reached the Ventura Freeway, the first leg of his trip to downtown Los Angeles. The Ventura is an eight-lane marvel, but it was clogged with early morning traffic. He coasted along, waiting for an opening in the main traffic lanes and then dashed in between two other cars. A tailgating driver moved closer to Block's rear bumper, and occasionally Block glanced at the rearview mirror, half expecting a rear-end crash.

Tense, aggravated, he listened impatiently to a radio commercial. An auto manufacturer was describing the Southern California freeways as the greatest testing ground for motor vehicles and picturing the Southern Californian as some sort of superb test driver, in love with his car. Not Block. An accountant by profession, he had meticulously added up the cost of owning two cars. He figured that the slow, frustrating twenty-eight-mile journey downtown ran close to $1,800 a year—an amount that was escalating because of the increasing cost of gasoline.

Block is not alone in his agony. Dependence on the auto can exhaust many people trying to reach their jobs. A few years ago, the University of California, testing middle-aged executives for stress, found that the worst time of the day for the managing editor of the *San Francisco Examiner* was not at his high-pressure job of putting out a daily newspaper, but when he drove to work and back on the Bayshore Freeway.

Across the nation there are fifty million people like Block who commute to work by car. Only eighteen million ride buses and trains. A handful of big cities like New York, Philadelphia, Boston, and Chicago, have kept their old transit lines intact, still running and serving commuters. And, while a few places—Washington, D.C., Atlanta, Baltimore—are building rapid transit systems, San Francisco is the only city with one of these new lines in operation. For the most part, Americans face backward, unresponsive public transit systems that make it impossible for them to do anything except what Block is doing every morning.

Commuters are marooned in traffic jams not because of their love affair with the internal combustion engine—a theory widely used to explain America's dependence on the automobile—but because they have no choice. The truth is that the transportation system was shaped by forces outside the motorist's control.

Exposing these forces is becoming increasingly important because America is beginning a transportation revolution as great as the one that occurred with the growth of the freeway system after World War II. In this revolution, huge government-financed rapid transit systems will be built in our large and middle-sized cities.

Today, Americans could have a rare opportunity to shape these systems, which, after all, belong to the public. The public officials who run transit agencies owe their allegiance to the voter and taxpayer. But the same forces that made the freeway system unworkable at rush hour are now determined to influence future transit plans. Before the voter can exert pressure on transit officials, he must understand the politics of transportation and how it. caused the predicament of today's commuter.

This chapter deals with two transportation systems that show the game at work. The first tells why Los Angeles doesn't have rapid transit, and the second tells why San Francisco does. Ironically, the same forces that kept it out of Los Angeles put it in San Francisco.

THE BUSY SIGNAL AT THE OTHER
END OF THE LINE

Once, Hal Block had tried to do something about his own personal transportation problem. He called the Southern California Rapid Transit District, the public body that operates the buses in Los Angeles County. Asking what bus he could take to get to work, he learned he would have to drive several miles from his home to the nearest commuter bus stop. Then, he could take either a local or another slow bus, called, with unconscious irony, the Freeway Flyer. He asked for a schedule. "But I never received it," he said. He called again, "but their lines are always jammed. You get a recorded message." When he finally did get a schedule, it told him that his commuting time would be increased to three and one-half hours a day from the two hours it took by car. A few months later, the transit district—in a highly publicized move— offered faster buses running directly downtown from Block's stop. But it was·on a prepaid, reserved-seat basis and ran only at a time convenient for people working from eight to four.

An unresponsive government agency denied Hal Block a choice of transportation, and it was costing him money he wanted to put away for his daughters' education. And because of the way the transit district was run, he was not even permitted to exercise what every American believes is his due—the right to vote his tormentors out of office.

Block had tried to find someone who would listen, but failed. "On the way home one night, I heard about Congressman James Corman making waves about the transportation problem in the valley," said Block. "I called his office and the secretary suggested I call my local city councilman." The fact was that no elected official would admit responsibility for bad transit. They could all blame the appointed transit board, an obscure group of officials who ran the transit district.

But the responsibility belonged to state and local political leaders—and the men who backed them. They had decided that transportation would depend on the motor vehicle. The decision was based on the view that post-World War II America, free from wartime restrictions, was ready for a long drive. The choice had been heavily influenced by businesses that drew their profits from the highway program—oil companies, trucking firms, construction companies and the others that were called the highway lobby. These businesses contended that prosperity lay in highway growth, and their proposal was endorsed by those who were to build new communities in the areas opened up by the freeway system.

Their estimation appeared correct. America did want to drive— to work, to homes in new suburbs, on long vacations in camper trucks and huge gas-consuming vans laden with cooking ranges, refrigerators and showers.

But in building the motor vehicle society, government officials and their backers had made a miscalculation that Americans were learning to regret. While building the roads, state and local governments had allowed the disintegration of most public transportation systems. The flaw in the plan did not become apparent until the late sixties, when smog and traffic congestion became severe. Finally, in the early seventies, the oil shortage revealed the gravity of the mistake. Faced with unacceptably high fuel prices, Americans found they were prisoners of the freeways they had paid so much to build.

THE NEW TRANSIT LOBBY

The fact that the highway lobby had one of the greatest voices in shaping America in the fifties and sixties has been well documented. Less publicized is the recent birth of a new lobby, intent on shaping public transit of the future—and with it, the communities it will serve. For today even the highway lobby concedes that the boom in freeway building is over. America still must travel. But state and local governments have to find a new way to do it.

Under pressure from powerful forces, cities from Los Angeles to Boston are preparing to gather billions in federal dollars which, added to state and local money, will revitalize public transit. In the sixties, the federal government gave $1.5 billion to local transit. So expensive is mass transit, that this subsidy had little effect. Now federal legislation has pledged $10 billion over the next ten years, but that, too, is just a beginning. Transit for a city like Los Angeles, for example, could alone cost as much as $7 billion. The price of Washington, D.C.'s Metro has climbed close to $4 billion, and may go higher. The cost of putting the cities on the move will exceed the $25 billion the country spent to put a man on the moon. The race to the moon had made an economic giant of the aerospace industry. By coincidence, commitment to space exploration dwindled at the same time highways had peaked. In the 1970s, the aerospace and construction industries joined in a search for a new source of income, and found it in the construction of rapid transit lines. Land developers were interested, too, in the profits the systems would bring them. This coalition is the new transit lobby.

WHY THERE IS NO TRANSIT IN L.A.–YET

The best place to see how the forces shaping transportation work is in the ultimate city of the automobile. Los Angeles—its sprawl, its freeways, its smog—is considered an aberration by other communities. But by the end of the sixties, most cities in America were well on the way to becoming like Los Angeles—totally dependent on the automobile.

There was testimony before a U.S. Senate committee in 1973 that General Motors bought and deliberately dismantled many rail rapid transit systems all over the county in order to cash in on the company's virtual monopoly in bus manufacturing. Los Angeles' reason for lacking good public transit is a variation on the same profit-motive scheme.

Like other big metropolitan areas, land speculation shaped the city's growth after World War II. The business interests that profited from the speculation decided that a freeway system would serve their interests best. And since leaders in business were also civic leaders, the public officials whom they influenced abandoned a well-developed rail system, the Pacific Electric red cars and the Los Angeles Railway, and failed to replace it with a workable form of mass transit. There were buses, but they were scarce, and many lines didn't connect or run during the night or on weekends. Except for the downtown area, bus service was poor and only for the desperate who had, literally, all day to wait.

The social implications were dangerous. For the middle class, it meant the forced ownership of two or three or more cars by a family, eating up a substantial part of its income. It also converted the middle-class housewife into a chauffeur, spending weekday afternoons driving station wagons filled with children to little league practice and ballet lessons.

For the poor, lack of public transit was even more unjust. There is a huge black ghetto in Los Angeles, stretching from the south central part of the city westward toward the Pacific. The poorest and most famous part of the ghetto is Watts, where, during the sixties, the first major racial outbreak of violence outside of the South occurred. Without transportation, Watts is doomed. Like the rest of Los Angeles, it sprawls, and the red trains that once served it have been junked. Churches and stores are often beyond walking distance. Jobs are usually far away too.

A commission appointed to investigate the Watts riot found that one of the causes was the lack of transportation. Only fourteen percent of the population there had automobiles. It took an hour and a half on three separate bus routes to reach the nearest state employment agency. The county hospital closest to Watts was a two-hour bus ride away. There is a county hospital in Watts now, but joblessness there is still the highest in the city, and a number of chain food markets closed after the riots have never opened, making the lack of transportation even more of a problem. A few improvements in bus service have been made, but they are pitifully inadequate to cure mobility problems in the city-sized slum.

The Transit Board

On the surface, the board of the Southern California Rapid Transit District, which operates buses in Los Angeles, seems to be democratic, designed to serve the public's needs. Its members are appointed by locally elected officials. Serving part-time, they are members of the community. The meetings are held in public, under the terms of a state law passed with much fanfare several years ago, aimed at opening the doors of every government agency to the inspection of its citizens.

But few people attend the meetings of the district's board, which are held at transit district headquarters downtown. It is difficult to find the place, or to park once there. The press rarely comes. And when citizens, finally aroused by bad service, find their way to the meetings, they have difficulty understanding the bureaucratic jargon and procedures used by the board members and transit officials. Such behavior is common to government agencies in areas such as transit, planning, and smog control. It is an attempt to make the public believe that the board and staff are the experts and that only they can understand the reasoning behind transit decisions. In fact, such decisions often involve political choices. Why, for example, should the downtown Los Angeles business center have ten-cent minibus service when Watts does not? But transit officials prefer that the public not understand the priorities involved in such decisions.

Even if the public knew what the board was doing and decided to throw the members out, they had no way of doing it. Created by the California legislature while it was firmly in the hands of the highway lobby, the transit board is made up of a strange hodgepodge of appointees, with no common goal. They are, almost without exception, wealthy businessmen who never ride public transit. Not one has a personal stake in whether the bus system succeeds or fails.

Five of the transit board's eleven directors are appointed by the Los Angeles County Board of Supervisors, who are elected. If the public didn't like their transit board appointments, conceivably the supervisors could be punished at the ballot box. But it costs more than a quarter of a million dollars for anyone to run a campaign seriously challenging a supervisor. The mayor also appoints two directors. But through the years of the transit district's decline in the fifties and sixties, no one blamed former Mayor Yorty. Finally, the remaining four members of the board are elected by the League of California Cities, a semiofficial organization of city officials. The league is dominated by the smaller communities surrounding Los Angeles. Such regions are traditional opponents of mass transit for the big cities.

As the district is run, the board members are not held accountable to the public. They are also insulated from events. A few days after the Federal Environmental Protection Agency threatened big cities with gas rationing, the transit board considered selling some older buses. Thinking of the need for public transit if there were rationing, the general manager said, "We might want to consider keeping those buses." The board ignored him and, without any discussion, voted to sell the buses. Later the general manager admitted that gas rationing would be a disaster for the area because the district did not have enough buses for increased patronage.

A Half-Hearted Attempt

The transit district had once proposed to build a rail rapid transit system. In 1967, as the district was preparing to take this plan to the voters, a bill was introduced in the California legislature to open the highway fund, made up from gasoline taxes, for rapid transit. The bill was motivated mainly by the needs of San Francisco's Bay Area Rapid Transit District, which had stopped building its new rail system midway because it had run out of money. If the bill passed, the gas tax would also be available to the Los Angeles transit district.

The powerful business leaders of Southern California—eyeing the proposed new use of the gas tax money—decided to fight rail rapid transit. Their decision was not a philosophical one, based on an idea that this form of transit wouldn't serve the community. Instead it was motivated by a fear that financing would be taken out of the money paid by highway users—gas taxes from truckers and motorists—that had been used exclusively for the building of roads. The highway lobby was strong enough to get the legislature to say no to using gas taxes for rapid transit.

The Members of the Club

It was in California that the highway lobby first came into power, controlling the legislature as tightly as the railroad barons controlled it a century before. In Southern California the highway lobby is a gentlemen's club, and its members are the most respected members of the community. They are sons and daughters of old families—old only in a special Los Angeles sense, for their forbears came west in the last part of the nineteenth century and got control of huge tracts of land. Growth, based on the increasing value of land, became their way of life. Bound by common interests, the leading families supported public works projects that tended to increase the value of land—an aqueduct to bring mountain water to Los Angeles, a huge state water project, and the freeway system.

There is an interlocking relationship in this gentlemen's club that can be seen among the people running the organizations most heavily influencing state and local government in Southern California. Two of these groups are the California State Chamber of Commerce and the Southern California Automobile Club, both powerful members of the highway lobby. The directors of the two groups were, in 1967, virtually the same businessmen. For example, Asa Call, a former president of the state chamber of commerce, was for years the president of the Southern California Auto Club. He is a rich businessman, who rebuilt a failing insurance company in the mid-thirties and became a great influence in the Republican party. If he is remembered by history, it will be because he and his wife thought highly of the young Richard Nixon, then an obscure lawyer who wanted to run for Congress, and they were among those who put up the money for his first campaign.

It was Call who used his influence, as one of the state's most successful political fund raisers, to lobby through the legislature the bill that in 1947 launched the California freeway system and established the highway lobby as a permanent political force. It increased the tax on gasoline and set aside the proceeds in a special trust fund, to be used only for highway construction. "There are so many economic advantages that come from freeways that the disadvantages are so small as to be insignificant," Call predicted at the time.

Formalized in later years as the California Highway Users Conference, the highway lobby eventually grew to include more than 180 business members, among them the Motor Car Dealers of Orange County, the United Auto Dealers, the Asphalt Institute, the Southern California Ready Mixed Concrete and Rock Products Association—even the California Funeral Directors Association, which is not so puzzling as it might at first seem. They are pleased by the ease with which hearses can travel from funeral home to graveyard by freeway.

Strategy I: The Campaign against Transit

Call, the auto club and the state chamber of commerce emerged as powerful foes against use of the highway fund for rapid transit in Southern California. A group called the California Freeway Support Committee was formed by the state chamber of commerce. The committee launched a campaign to educate the public on the value of the freeway system.

Although the Freeway Support Committee was designed to give the impression of having risen from the grassroots, more than half its members were highway lobby regulars, including the president of Union Oil, the president of Western Transport Company, a Los Angeles trucking firm, the chairman of Standard Oil, and the president of Consolidated Rock Products, which provides building materials for freeways.

The committee hired the public relations firm of Spencer Roberts Associates to run the $200,000 campaign. Using expensive, well-designed brochures, the public relations firm told Californians that they had more freedom of choice because of the freeway system and that they benefited by the mobility given by freeways and private cars. The committee distributed the results of a survey by pollster Mervyn Field showing Californians actually believed their lives were different, and that good roads were one reason for it. Ninety-three percent agreed that "freeways give more people freedom to live as they choose." Seventy-four percent disagreed with the statement that "freeway traffic creates noise, pollution and dirt." More important, virtually all said they believed there should be no cutback in freeway building. The auto club also joined in, sending letters and literature to nearly a million members.

When questioned about the ethics of using the money of auto club members—most of them working-class people—to lobby for the interests of the oil and highway industry, the club replied it was representing its members' opinions. It claimed to have taken a poll of 16,000 representative members, but refused to show anyone the poll.

Ethical or not, the highway lobby's tactics worked. The bill proposing the use of gas taxes for rapid transit failed to get enough votes to pass.

Strategy II: The Campaign for Transit

Later in 1967, when the preliminary transit plan was unveiled to the public, it was apparent that the rapid transit district didn't need powerful enemies. Since the project wouldn't be receiving gas-tax money, it needed voter approval of a revenue bond measure. But the transit agency was so insulated from political reality that it had designed its own defeat. The plan was the largest single public works project ever proposed, costing $1.5 billion, but it was too small for the sprawling metropolitan area, and it neglected areas such as the San Gabriel Valley, the San Fernando Valley and the Pasadena area—packed with voters who were needed to obtain the 60 percent approval required for the passage of the revenue bonds.

Community groups and chambers of commerce from every outlying district spoke against the plan. But the district seemed to respond to only one set of complaints, those voiced by the Los Angeles Chamber of Commerce, composed of downtown businessmen, land developers and others who had a stake in the central city's well-being. This group said that they hoped to spearhead a successful vote for the measure, but that they couldn't do it unless the district corrected some "serious flaws" in its plan.

Early in 1968, when the transit district's final plan appeared, it contained many of the Los Angeles chamber's requests, including a line to the airport and an extension of a costly subway line through the Wilshire business district. Originally a financing scheme had been proposed using property taxes to pay off the revenue bonds. But the Los Angeles business leaders had suggested the district find another means of financing. Since they were big property owners, they were opposed to paying for transit through their taxes. By summer, a few months before the bond election, legislation was passed to finance the revenue bonds with a new sales tax. This would put the total cost of the system on the average citizen, hitting the poor harder than anyone else.

Meanwhile, the transit district did little to appease the outlying suburbs. The San Fernando Valley association of chambers of commerce, composed of small businessmen, opposed the measure. They contended that while the valley was paying for a large percentage of the system, it was getting little in return. They also were angry that they were getting an unsightly elevated line while the Wilshire corridor was getting a subway, at three times the cost per mile.

The campaign for the bond issue did not get started until too late, because of delays in the legislative approval of the sales tax financing. But the list of contributors offers evidence of the coalition that was emerging to work for such projects. Surprisingly, many of the donors were members of the highway lobby, who had opposed transit earlier. Their earlier opposition had been based mainly on the fear that rapid transit would endanger highway building. But once the gas tax was safe, many of these businesses saw the transit system as a good thing that would increase business and the land values in its path. The campaign raised $433,480, an impressive amount at that time, and the size of the contributions showed that many contributors seriously hoped the measure would pass.

Those who gave were businesses with big real estate and highrise interests, such as the Transamerica Corporation, Title Insurance and Trust Company, Century City, Inc., and the Los Angeles Clearing House Association. There were businesses that would be in on the actual building: Kaiser, the project engineers on the preliminary plan; and the Bethlehem Steel Corporation. There were the unions: carpenters, electrical workers, operating engineers, laborers, and iron workers. There were downtown retail businesses. There were the airlines who had benefited from the line to the airport. There were the members of the highway lobby—the oil companies, Consolidated Rock Co. and the cement companies. The freeway construction companies gave too. And, finally, there was a new element, contributions from aerospace companies who hoped to build the trains and the controls—Lockheed, Westinghouse Electric, Westinghouse Airbrake, and North American Rockwell.

In spite of all this support, the measure was overwhelmingly rejected. It received only forty-four percent of the vote. The transit district blamed it on "clouding by unrelated controversies." For there had been a variety of issues that detracted from the measure. One was a scandal involving the district management a month before the election. And Los Angeles voters were aware that San Francisco's rapid transit project had run out of money, and there were serious doubts that it would ever be completed. But the one factor that guaranteed the measure's failure was that the district had ignored its need for votes. It had refused to give lines to outlying suburbs, where many of the voters who were to pay for the system lived. The officials who ran the district thought it would be improper to redraw their routes to attract voters. But they saw nothing wrong with making many of the changes suggested by the big downtown business interests that would run the election campaign.

Settling into Failure

With the failure of the rapid transit plan in 1968, the transit district gave up the idea of expansion and settled into a struggle with declining numbers of bus riders and the rising costs of running the existing system. That was the last year the system broke even. Occasionally, there were public demands for more service, but even when persuaded to try out a new line, the transit district quickly removed it when, in most cases, it was not self-supporting within a few months. The district had no government subsidy, and the board was incapable of getting additional financial help.

Even more discouraging was the behavior of the board in the early seventies, during America's great environmental revolution. This was one of the broadest-based political movements in history, supported by both conservatives and liberals. Yet the Southern California Rapid Transit District remained completely unmoved by it, painful proof of the unresponsiveness of obscure government bodies to the will of the people.

Community groups around California, increasingly inconvenienced by auto travel and worried about smog, finally forced the state legislature into allowing a small sales tax on gasoline, with the proceeds to go to local areas for rapid transit. In Los Angeles, the voters were informed that this was the first step toward building a rail rapid transit system. The Southern California district would receive about $40 million a year. The money was intended to be used to apply for newly available federal funds that had to be supplemented with local money.

But in the end, not a penny of this money was used for new rapid transit in Los Angeles. The only innovation the public got for its increased tax was a bus lane added to a freeway reaching from the center of Los Angeles to the suburbs of the San Gabriel Valley. It turned out that most of the gas sales-tax money was used to underwrite losses for the existing system. "They are sweeping the needs of the people and the mandate of the legislature under the rug," protested a state senator.

It seemed that the transit district had learned nothing from its past defeat at the polls. In mid-73 it came out with a new preliminary transit plan it hoped to put on the ballot. But again it ignored the same regions that had defeated it in the past. Within a few months of its announcement, it had been denounced by Pasadena, the San Fernando Valley communities, and eight cities to the east of downtown.

But commuters were desperate. And, with the further decline in highway construction and cutbacks in the space program, the coalition of transit builders were getting ready to offer the consistent support that the rapid transit proposal had lacked five years before. As the plan was announced, several oil companies began running television commercials promoting the concept of rapid transit and blaming the public—rather than themselves as members of the highway lobby—for not supporting it in the past.

THE FIRST OF THE FUTURE

Four hundred miles to the north, in San Francisco, is an example of what happens when business wholeheartedly endorses rapid transit. Then almost nothing can stop it. BART, the Bay Area Rapid Transit District, offers a unique glimpse of the American transportation future—of people riding cheaply in comfortable, quiet, high-speed, automated trains. And it provides a glimpse of something else—of a government-aid program to business that eclipses anything conceived by NASA.

A project of laudable ambition, BART was planned by business interests trying to increase the value of their downtown real estate holdings. It was also supported by construction firms and labor unions interested in jobs and by suburban business interests who anticipated real estate windfalls along the new lines. Not surprisingly, it was vigorously promoted by electronic and aerospace firms, who had the foresight to see government-sponsored transit lines as a substitute for decreasing military and space business. Finally, BART was being built because of the peculiar nature of the San Francisco Bay area, itself.

Edmund (Pat) Brown, who served as governor of California from 1960 to 1968, believes the state should be divided into two political jurisdictions, Northern California and Southern California. More than geography divides the two areas. San Francisco, like Los Angeles, has a social and business establishment. But San Francisco's society is older, a cosmopolitan blending of immigrant cultures, dependent on trade in the seaport city. Many of its leading families trace their ancestry back to the gold rush of 1849—ancient by California standards; their fortunes reaching back to gold and silver mines, the Pacific trade, lumber, Levi pants, and the railroads. Only later did the Midwestern farmers—

encouraged by landowning railroads—settle in agricultural Southern California, bringing with them their narrow outlook and disregard for cultural amenities and urban tradition. In San Francisco there is a long history of excellent Italian and French restaurants, the opera, the ballet, the theater. Parks and old buildings have been preserved, and entire streets of Victorian row houses still stand, restored and revered by the affluent people who can afford to live in them. More important is the San Franciscan's desire to hold onto the unique beauty of his city. This has meant that a huge, land-consuming freeway system could not be permitted within its narrow boundaries.

San Francisco's geography is different from that of Los Angeles. "You've got the bay, a hilly terrain and the bay plain, with Mother Nature's transportation corridors, which are the only way to move people," said Bill Stokes, the general manager of BART. "In San Francisco you can't use up all the land for freeways. But Los Angeles is like Kansas; you can lay down freeways all over the place. LA lacks cohesive regional concerns. Here the idea sprang up from local businessmen and local topography. It was an orderly process." Stokes is right. The San Francisco establishment dictated the need for good public transit, just as the same forces had been able to bring about Los Angeles' freeways for its transporation.

After World War II, San Francisco, backed by the business community, took over all the city's privately owned transportation systems. In 1953, the transit system on the eastern side of the bay went under public ownership too, largely because of the support of one of the most conservative of the old Bay Area families, the Knowlands, owners of the *Oakland Tribune*.

The area had just suffered through a fifty-three-day transit strike against the private transit company, hurting business and affecting their newspaper's advertising. The strike convinced the Knowlands that publicly owned transportation was badly needed. About the same time, San Francisco business leaders, concerned about the downtown area's loss of business to new outlying shopping centers, began to think seriously about the future. In Los Angeles, fortunes were made in buying land in the suburbs. In the north, they were made downtown in trade and commercial enterprises, and life was centered there.

Thus, by the mid-fifties the business communities of San Francisco and Oakland were actively supporting the construction of a rapid rail system linking San Francisco to the eastern side of the bay through an underwater tube and connecting the scattered suburbs of the East Bay.

The Campaign

Business went to extraordinary lengths to see that BART got started. For a few years, transit engineers were quietly studying the kind of system that would be built, its routes and finances. But by late 1957, the San Francisco Chamber of Commerce president announced that his organization would begin a two-year campaign to educate the public on the advantages of rapid transit. As it turned out, a bond issue for financing wasn't ready to go on the ballot for another five years. But the chamber and other downtown businessmen's clubs continued promoting the concept of BART during that time, planning and pushing for details, such as the downtown subway, through their own rapid transit study committees and through polls of their members.

A formal campaign took place before the 1962 bond election, conducted by a group of citizens who also happened to run the city's banks and other big downtown business interests. San Francisco financier Mortimer Fleishhacker, Jr., headed the group, and Carl Wente, then chairman of the board of Bank of America, was in charge of fund-raising. Campaign contributions came from the businesses that would eventually profit from building BART or through increased land values. Among them were some of the same businesses that gave late in the campaign for Los Angeles' rapid transit: Westinghouse Electric Company, which received a $26 million contract for BART's automatic controls; Bethlehem Steel Corporation, a $23 million contractor for part of the BART tube under San Francisco Bay; and Kaiser Industries, whose subsidiaries received contracts for work on the tube, for cement and for a tunnel through the hills. Wells Fargo Bank, Bank of America, and Crocker Citizens Bank—three banks owning downtown property benefiting from the system—gave their help. And there were the project engineers: Parsons, Brinckerhoff, Quade and Douglas; Tudor Engineering Co., and Bechtel Corporation, who also made millions on the project. Many of these same firms also had buildings downtown—offices serving as financial bases for their extensive holdings in the Far East. These buildings would be served by the completed BART system, bringing thousands of employees to work and making possible a great West Coast highrise center, increasing land values for the owning companies.

Approval was needed from the county supervisors of the three participating counties to get the BART measure, financed by a property tax, on the ballot. Some politicians objected. But as business was behind it, so were important politicians willing to use political muscle to push it through. Governor Brown, a Democrat, called up one supervisor—a Brown appointee—and persuaded him to back BART. The mayor of San Francisco, Republican George Christopher, hurried across the bay to the small city of Martinez to persuade another recalcitrant supervisor to vote yes.

Socialites as well as labor unions supported BART during the election campaign. One night, as a publicity stunt, a member of the wealthy Zellerbach family drove up to the carriage entrance of the San Francisco War Memorial Opera House in a 1931 Lincoln and announced to newsmen and photographers, "This Lincoln is antiquated. I contend traffic congestion and the freeway explosion in the Bay Area even more outmoded."

San Francisco voters, repelled by the ugly Embarcadero Freeway, were deep into a freeway revolt, and even natural events seemed to be working to shape public thinking. A few weeks before the election, a fierce rain storm not only forced postponement of the World Series in San Francisco but blocked the tunnel between a huge East Bay suburban area and the bridge to San Francisco. For days commuters had to spend two extra hours each way driving a narrow, winding road. But the most important single factor was the long-term barrage of support from the civic-business leadership. BART was approved by sixty-one percent of the vote.

The Cost of Building It

BART's next stage was construction, and it illustrated a fundamental truth about government—if businessmen benefit directly from a project, they will tolerate waste, inefficiency and great cost, as they did in the case of Southern California's freeway system. Complaints come only about spending for public schools, welfare or other areas where there is no direct benefit in the form of business profits.

Costs began increasing immediately after the election. Suits by taxpayers who opposed BART delayed work. Cities could not agree with the district on the location and design of stations. The city of Berkeley objected to an elevated line, and work was delayed until the city and BART agreed to split the cost of a subway. And inflation, fed by the Vietnam war, drove costs higher than ever expected. By the mid-sixties, BART conceded it would cost $1.5 billion to finish the system, instead of the $795 million approved in 1962.

Knowing the public would never agree to pay for the gigantic cost overrun through another bond issue, BART approached another source of money—the California legislature. Some legislators urged that the property owners and other businessmen benefiting from the new lines be assessed for the added costs, but neither the majority of the legislators nor the governor would support that. Others wanted a portion of the tax on gasoline used, but the highway lobby opposed that. Finally, the highway lobby's spokesman in the legislature, Senator Randolph Collier, supported a bill raising the BART area local sales tax by a half cent—putting more of a burden on the poor and middle class than the rich, and virtually exempting giant corporations from sharing the added costs. Reluctantly supporting the new tax, Mayor Joseph Alioto of San Francisco said, "The sales tax imposes the added cost of transit on those least able to afford it. We have no notion of giving up fighting for a more equitable financing plan, but we must take a hard headed view of practicalities." The sales tax prevailed.

The Finished Product

As BART neared completion, investigators for A. Alan Post, financial analyst for the legislature, said the new system was as inefficient as it was expensive. Called in to investigate an accident when a train failed to stop at the end of the line, Post decided BART's management had been wasteful, careless and incompetent.

The automatic equipment could not detect dead trains on the track; computerized stop-and-go commands were often ignored by the equipment on the train, or were incorrectly sent.

While there was no evidence of dishonesty, the liaison between BART management and those it bought services from had become very cozy through years of association. Post said he believed that manufacturers had overcharged BART for goods and had not been penalized enough for defective work. Finally, the loose arrangement between BART and its engineering-management firm, Parsons, Brinckerhoff, Tudor and Bechtel, was criticized. Stephen Bechtel, president of the Bechtel Corporation, had been one of the influential men who had launched the BART project in the beginning, and it was Bechtel's vice president who ran Parsons, Brinckerhoff, Tudor and Bechtel. BART had paid them too much money, said Post, and he asked the attorney general's office to look into some of the overcharges. Also, in a number of messy transactions, the engineering firm had sat down to negotiate payment disagreements with construction contractors—without any member of BART's staff present. "This practice," said Post's report, "appears to be commonly permitted by district management."

Stokes, BART's general manager, said Post's report was "an example of A to Z critical overkill and skewed perspective." But there was no doubt the new system had flaws. Stokes, himself, was at a stop near BART headquarters when one of the trains passed by at thirty-seven miles an hour, the computer failing to stop it. "Hit the stop button," Stokes shouted to the passengers. He waved excitedly, as the train passed the station's platform.

Flawed as it was, the system was rushed to completion. More money was spent to correct the automatic equipment. There were real estate profits to be made in rapid transit. As an example, in Canada, four years after completion of its subway system, the Toronto Transit Commission printed a promotional booklet that boasted of the $10 billion in new construction along the subway route. "If an urban rapid transit system never earned a dime," it said, "it would pay for itself many times over through its beneficial impact on real estate values and increased assessments. . . . Toronto has not experienced the flight of commercial and retail business from the downtown area that has occurred in some cities. On the contrary, it is in the midst of a downtown building boom that is the envy of many larger cities."

Even before BART trains were operating in San Francisco, there were five hundred new floors of office building space downtown with another $400 million worth of construction under way. And all of it was within five minutes of a BART station. Market Street, San Francisco's broad central avenue, had been losing its glamor to penny arcades and cheap movie houses, but with BART nearing completion, it was being converted to a handsome shopper's mall with voter-approved money.

THE AEROSPACE FACTOR

BART had to be completed, no matter what the cost. It was the first transit system in the nation to use all the hardware of the electronic age—light metals, computers, remote control guidance systems and the rest. An example of the aerospace industry's transformation to rapid transit manufacturing can be found at the Rohr Corporation's world headquarters in Chula Vista, just south of San Diego. Rohr was, and is, the nation's largest manufacturer of jet pods, the aluminum housing for jet airplane engines. But with the decline in the aerospace business in the mid-sixties, Rohr decided to diversify. A tour of the enormous installation, with acres of hangar-sized buildings, shows the wisdom of the decision. Rohr's first transit contract came from BART in 1969, building the cars the system's engineers had designed, and Rohr is still busy building them. Seeing a trend toward refurbishing existing transit systems, they bought a bus company. They also now own two concrete companies, to provide prefabricated concrete structures for rapid transit tracks.

The Chula Vista plant is just one of fourteen Rohr factories, and Rohr officials say that nearly half of their $400 million a year in business is now in rapid transit. The Georgia plant is manufacturing D.C.'s Metrocars, and is hoping to win contracts to build trains for the new system under construction in Atlanta, as well as new trains for upgrading by the Chicago Transit Authority.

Aerospace companies like Rohr, Boeing, and General Electric are using their technology to make mass transit competitive with the automobile in speed, convenience and comfort. One huge building at Rohr is dedicated to displaying what is in the works for the future. One is the Monocab, a taxicab-sized, driverless vehicle that floats along an overhead glide. At stations along its route, passengers order a cab through the system's computer that calculates where to send the cab, where it is going, and the number of riders. With this information, it tells the patron how much the ride will cost. When fed the correct amount of money, the system instantly issues a ticket and dispatches a cab. County government has already approved the financing of a twenty-two-mile, $100 million Monocab system in Las Vegas. Denver and Minneapolis-St. Paul are both considering building similar systems.

Another project on display at Rohr is a low, wide-tracked bus. It represents Rohr's entry in a design competition of the federal Department of Transportation. The other big bus companies, General Motors and American Motors General, are also competing to set the standards for new city buses. The federal government plans to give money to the cities to help them improve their existing bus systems over the next few years, and it hopes to encourage them to buy faster, nonpolluting, more comfortable vehicles.

Even more impressive are designs for the future. One is Romag, a train that has no moving parts but can run at supersonic speeds along an electromagnetic rail. Of all the new transit systems, Rohr says this uses the least power. It is not a theoretical concept, but is already operable, although not ready to be marketed. As with the other new rail rapid transit, the Romag is run by remote control, piloted by computers, like a space ship.

Federal money is beginning to flow. And the Auto Manufacturers Association—sensing the end of the highway era—dropped its opposition to federal aid to rapid transit, and is helping the President's $10 billion transit aid program become law. The industry realized it couldn't expect an ever-expanding auto market. General Motors, Ford, Chrysler, and American Motors changed their policy and supported legislation in Michigan allowing the state to use part of its gasoline tax for mass transit.

What the industry had in mind was apparent at Transpo 72, an exposition of transit rolling stock at Dulles International Airport outside Washington, D.C. As the Goodyear blimp flew overhead, more than a million people saw how the auto industry, aerospace companies and other businesses were preparing to profit from the government transit programs of the future. Ford Motor Company, Bendix Corporation, and subsidiaries of Rohr and the Otis Elevator Companies showed off people movers, like Monocab. General Motors, Twin Coach, and American Motors General displayed new hardware for carrying passengers.

TODAY

It is already clear what rapid transit will do for the business community. What will it do for the average citizen? That depends on his ability to force transit boards to give him a role in shaping the new systems.

There are some encouraging signs for the transit riders. In 1973, San Francisco made its transit board elective—the first step in making it responsive to the public instead of to the big businesses whose representatives traditionally have served on the board. And Atlanta, analyzing its 1968 transit bond defeat, took an interest in the voter's opinion. It had lost heavily in the poor, black areas. Resubmitting the issue to the vote, if offered incentives for poor people's votes—fifteen cent fares and routes that would carry inner-city dwellers to jobs at suburban factories, a switch from the usual arrangement. The new Atlanta transit authority was approved. Its operations are far from satisfactory to its riders. However, community groups are finding the board more responsive than it was in the past.

But there were bad signs as well. When we visited Metro headquarters in Washington, D.C., officials told us how they had benefited from BART's mistakes and were avoiding them. But later in the year it appeared they hadn't. The opening date was delayed for the third time; costs had escalated from $2.5 billion to $3.5 billion, and officials admitted that it could be more; equipment was outdated before it was received. When the *Washington*

Post forced Metro management to reveal a secret list of people who awarded Metro contracts, improprieties were revealed. Even more discouraging was the fact that riders on the district's current bus operation were declining. And, while service remained poor, taxpayers had to absorb losses that were 20 percent higher than had been estimated. Real estate speculation had already begun in some areas close to metro rapid transit stations, threatening to disrupt existing neighborhoods. But local officials did little about it, and Metro officials denied it was happening.

The coming of rapid transit could be a good thing for urban areas. The unrepresented—the poor in the ghettos and the middle class in their suburbs—need trains or modern buses with low fares subsidized by the government. The poor would be able to leave the ghetto to work. The middle class would no longer need two or three cars. It would mean a decrease in smog, and discourage urban sprawl.

But the transit lobby—which will grow as big as the highway establishment—could nullify all of these benefits to the average citizen. Unless the public finds its way into the decision-making process, special interests will design transit systems. If the transit lobby is allowed to take over, it is easy to predict what will happen: Huge systems will be designed solely for economic motives, with the social implications ignored. Old neighborhoods will be split by elevated train lines, just as they were by freeways. There will be huge cost overruns, paid for by the average citizen, who has no choice in the selection of routes, schedules or design. Lines will run where speculators will profit most. And unresponsive public boards will make their decisions, oblivious to what the people want and need.

10

Too Many Agencies,

Too Much Smog

Marlene Behar watched her children, Victor, 5, and Solomon, 2, play in the family room of their attractive, rambling tract home. Outside, the setting was rural, for the house was located in the hills around the University of California campus. It was a warm, sunny autumn afternoon in Riverside, the kind of weather for children to play outside. But that was impossible. The air was too polluted.

This is the blight of the new California. The causes seem obvious—packing new freeways with motor vehicles, allowing politically influential industries to pollute the air. Like other functions of state and local government, the highly technical matter of smog control is run by secretive and unresponsive officials. As in planning, waste disposal, transit and the rest, a low priority is given to the people's welfare and their right to know what is happening. But in the regulation of air pollution it is even worse. Obscurity and secrecy are multiplied by a myriad of independent local and state agencies. Authority is so split between different levels of government that very little is being done to clean up the air.

California claims to have the toughest and best-enforced smog regulations in the nation. But proof of their inadequacy hovers visibly over the state most of the year. Smog and government's failure to deal with it are not limited to California. There are many smoggy areas like Riverside, visible as one flies over the nation.

Brown air now lingers over the once sparkling western cities of Denver, Colorado, and Phoenix, Arizona. A pamphlet published by the U.S. Environmental Protection Agency included the following cities in its list of areas subject to serious air pollution: Baltimore, Birmingham, Buffalo, Charleston, Chattanooga, Chicago, Cleveland, Detroit, Houston, northern New Jersey, New Orleans, New York, Philadelphia, Pittsburgh, St. Louis, and Washington, D.C.

In neighborhoods across America, secret pressure on government has made life inconvenient and uncomfortable. In the case of smog, it has made life downright dangerous. A recent unpublished federal report concluded that laws in communities throughout the country are too weak to protect the public's health. The figures predated the energy crisis. Faced with a shortage of low sulfur oil, many communities have now relaxed smog rules and now permit industries and power plants to burn dirtier fuels, compounding the problems of air pollution.

AGE OF THE SMOG ALERT

Life in and around urban America is living under something called a "smog alert," as familiar to children in places like Riverside as practice air raid drills were to youngsters growing up during World War II. A smog alert means that breathing the air is hazardous. It is a warning for people to stop exercising and go indoors.

Ms. Behar is aware of the danger. Her husband, Joe, a Ph.D. in chemistry, is an air pollution specialist employed by the city of Los Angeles. Until recently, he worked near his home at the Statewide Air Pollution Control Center on the university campus. But the Behars have decided to leave Riverside. The smog—and the hopelessness of the fight against it—were part of the reason.

On bad afternoons, Ms. Behar calls a local telephone number and listens to a recorded message of the local smog control agency. It is a forecast for the day's smog level. Sometimes she runs her own check, looking out the front door at the gray haze. If she cannot see Boxspring Mountain, a block away, she doesn't bother to call the Riverside County Air Pollution Control District. She knows the smog is severe, and she keeps the children inside. "That air is dangerous," said Joe Behar. "It isn't right. It isn't fair. They're only children once, and they have a right to fresh air."

Despite a proliferation of smog-regulating agencies, there are still smog alerts in Riverside. One reason is that the city is located at the extreme eastern end of the geographical basin that contains the Los Angeles metropolitan area. Almost ten million people live in the basin, owners of seven million motor vehicles that disgorge exhaust fumes into the air. To the west, thousands of factories add to the pollution, and it is all blown eastward by the ocean breezes. Riverside, itself, adds more pollution with its own factories and a growing number of automobiles.

What We Don't Know . . .

Unlike the Behars, most people pay little attention to smog alerts. While they are unhappy about the air, they do not understand the deadliness of it. There is undisputable evidence that a high level of smog damages lungs. A recent federal report estimated that it costs Americans from $1-3 billion a year in medical bills. "These estimates are probably conservative," the study said.

As a relatively new phenomenon, smog has been subjected to little long-range research. Scientists are not yet sure how harmful it is in constant lower concentrations. Nor do they completely understand the nature of smog itself. Researchers are just beginning to learn how smog travels from city to city, even hundreds of miles across state lines. They know that it is changing, that on days when the air looks clear, it can be poisonous. Most important, there is evidence that smog is getting worse in some ways, spreading to new areas where residents had previously enjoyed clean air.

Those studying smog admit that new technology can only provide a limited improvement as long as cars, factories and people continue to multiply in crowded urban areas. Meaningful solutions have to come from tough legislation, relentlessly enforced by state and local smog agencies. As we have seen, these levels of government are particularly susceptible to influence from those who have a vested interest in pollution—a highway lobby whose profits increase with the number of cars; developers who need population growth to insure sales of houses and condominiums; factory owners who resist the high cost of cutting down noxious smoke-stack emissions.

CALIFORNIA—NATION'S FOREMOST SMOG LABORATORY

In California, researchers are closer to an understanding of the complex problems that make up air pollution. California is the nation's best laboratory of smog, especially in the Los Angeles basin. Southern California holds the per capita record for auto-mobiles. The Los Angeles basin is surrounded on the inland side by mountains, and the air is trapped by the mountains and held down by a ceiling of stagnant air known as an inversion layer. This combination makes the basin particularly susceptible to air pollution.

Because of this problem, Los Angeles County was the first area in the nation to impose strong regulations on industrial air pollution. State government followed the example, and today California has the most highly developed smog regulation structure in the nation, at both state and local level. It has served as a model for federal legislation. Yet, after a promising start, the polluters—through persuasive lobbyists—have quietly stifled the effectiveness of the regulation machinery. They have done this by encouraging the legislature to create a smog-control system in which responsibility is hopelessly fragmented among many agencies.

The solution to smog is complex and difficult both on political and scientific levels. Cleaning up the air will involve changes in the American lifestyle that will be unpopular with voters as well as with special interest campaign contributors. Elected officials have been able to avoid taking the blame for unpleasant decisions by simply not making them. In the process, they have confused the public with a muddle of jurisdictions divided between agencies and layers of government.

The First Layer: The State Smog Board

Despite feuding and continuing debate between smog officials, all agree that most of California's smog is caused by the internal combustion engine. In many states, all sources of air pollution are

handled by the same state-level agencies. But in California, authority is divided. It is the job of the state agency, the Air
Resources Board, to control auto-caused air pollution. The Air
Resources Board is headed by five members who are appointed by
the governor. Unlike most appointed boards, they are not free to
serve out a specific term of office but can be—and have been—fired
by the governor when he is displeased with their performance.
Their authority is weak because of this and because the board has
to get approval from the governor's cabinet before it can act. To
make matters worse, many of its programs need to be imple-
mented by the Democratic legislature—which views the Republican governor's rubber stamp Air Resources Board with surly
distrust.

Understandably, most of the board members have been inde-
cisive about tough smog controls. In 1966, a state law was passed
requiring emissions devices on cars, but it failed to clean up the air.
The device only cut down one element of smog, hydrocarbons,
while increasing another, more poisonous, element, oxides of
nitrogen. It was an error in legislative judgment, influenced by
heavy lobbying from highway interests. This group was opposed to
more complex devices which would have posed technological
difficulties for auto manufacturers.

Even after the flaw in the auto emissions devices became apparent, the Air Resources Board was slow to require installation of
a second device on the post-1965 cars to correct the mistake. The
board delayed action for nearly three years, from 1970 to 1973.
During this time, the powerful highway lobby remained strongly
opposed to the measure. When the Air Resources Board finally
voted to make it mandatory, the governor nullified their decision
by replacing four members of the board. The administration said
its stand against the smog device was based on the fact that it
would reduce gas efficiency. The governor's press secretary explained, "The governor wanted to reconstitute the board to take a
fresh look at the air pollution problems confronting California,
particularly in light of the energy crisis."

Despite these weaknesses, California's standards for new cars are
the highest in the nation. But the Air Resources Board's method
of inspecting new cars to determine whether they meet the stand-

ards is so inadequate and superficial that it is almost a joke. For all but a few cars, the tests mean monitoring tailpipe emissions for a few seconds on the assembly line. Tests at this point in a car's use are meaningless. People familiar with the tests agree that a new car's emissions will drastically change before it has gone a hundred miles.

Another job the state has is to oversee the many county smog agencies, called air pollution control districts, or smog districts. This, too, is a job that requires a hard line from the state board, but it lacks the statutory power to take it. One person who can explain the Air Resources Board's failure is Gladys Meade, a unique public-minded citizen who was a member of the state board until Governor Reagan fired her. She believes the legislature, afraid to be tough on polluters, withheld the necessary power from the state board. Its power over the local districts is almost nil: "There can be an exchange of letters," said Ms. Meade. "The state Air Resources Board will write to a local agency and say, 'Well, you fellows are not doing a good job in this area; we suggest a need for improvement.' The county district will, on the other hand, write back and say, 'Why, we can't understand your concern. Obviously we are doing the very best job possible.' Then will follow several pages of justification of their program. We, then, have the authority to write back and say, 'We disagree.' All this can go on for a period of two years." Eventually the state board can hold a public hearing on the presumed failings of a county smog district, but in recent years few have been held. The board's power is limited because the governor and the legislature, who created it, didn't want to take the blame for strong smog controls that were sure to make enemies.

The Second Layer: The Local Air
Pollution Control District

The state board has jurisdiction over motor vehicles, but not over factories, garbage dumps and other nonmoving sources of air pollution. These are regulated by the county smog districts, and there are about fifty such local districts throughout the state. California has more local districts than any other state. But this is no guarantee of success. With few exceptions, these agencies work independently of each other, sometimes at cross-purposes, even waging public relations campaigns against each other and against the state board.

For example, in 1972, scientists released brightly colored particles in Orange and Los Angeles counties. Within hours they had traveled eastward into Riverside County. Researchers felt this was proof that smog was a regional problem. But the Los Angeles County Air Pollution Control District officials insisted that the long flight of the particles was due to unusual weather conditions. The Riverside smog district believes it is the victim of pollution from Los Angeles and Orange counties, too, but it is powerless to fight smog in other jurisdictions.

Besides the fragmentation of power, another result of the multi-agency approach is that the county smog district, like most agencies of local government, is subject to local political pressure. In some counties, the job is handled by the public health department, an agency of county government. But in most cases, the local district board is run by the county board of supervisors—the same growth-oriented supervisors we looked at in Chapter Three. Their reluctance to regulate big polluting industries is evident in Los Angeles County, where the head of the county Air Pollution Control District in 1973 was County Supervisor James Hayes. When he was elected to the board of supervisors the year before, Hayes received campaign contributions from industries listed by the smog district as some of the county's major polluters, among them Shell and Standard Oil companies. In addition, he received help from labor unions involved in smog producing industries, such as power plants.

A study by a faculty-student team at the California Institute of Technology saw the dual role of the supervisors—serving as elected county officials and as air pollution control district board members—as a conflict of interest because the supervisors needed the financial and political support of business polluters to win reelection. Even in Riverside County, where the smog district officials complained bitterly about industrial pollution from other counties, they were lax in carrying out their own regulations. Ron Hosie, a reporter for the *Riverside Press Enterprise,* wrote a story explaining how smog control regulations were relaxed for certain industries. He concluded that the local district appeared to allow "some polluters the freedom to violate the law."

Other Layers of Smog Regulation

There are a number of other government agencies also responsible for at least part of the fight against smog, such as the State Department of Transportation, the State Department of Motor Vehicles and the Highway Patrol. They, too, tend to work independently of each other and everyone else in the field.

The inconsistency in enforcement and the bickering between agencies is endless. The Los Angeles County Air Pollution Control District participated with the Southern California Rapid Transit District, a few years ago, in a study funded by the federal government to see if it would be beneficial for the transit district to convert its buses to clean burning fuels such as propane or natural gas. It decided it would be a good thing. The study ended, but the transit authority never did make the fuel changeover. Similarly, both the Los Angeles county and city officials made public statements endorsing the concept of converting fleet cars to natural gas, but neither level of government did it.

And, while it constantly criticized the state Air Resources Board's failure to clean up auto-caused smog, the Los Angeles County smog district lobbied against state legislation that would help do it. One bill it opposed would have required all fleet cars to use clean fuels. It supported another bill that would have allowed county supervisors to decide for their own county if citizens should be required to install the retrofitted auto smog devices. This was because the Los Angeles smog district board—whose members were also the county supervisors—opposed the devices and did not want to require motorists to install them. Despite evidence to the contrary, local smog officials said the devices wouldn't work. Their opposition was difficult to understand. "There won't be much of a change" (if the devices are required), said an official of the district, "but the change will be for the worse.... Ordinary logic does not will you the right path—you have to have a deeper understanding." A cynical view of this attitude would be that they didn't want to see a decrease in auto-caused smog. Then industrial smog—their responsibility—would become the focal point of public criticism.

Carping at Each Other

Aside from hopelessly fragmenting the responsibility for cleaning up the air, the confusing division of authority gives government at each level the opportunity to blame others for the smog. For example, in 1971, A.J. Haagen-Smit, who was then chairman of the state Air Resources Board, commented that in the state's area of responsibility, auto-caused smog, things were well under control. On the other hand, he said, local smog agencies were falling down on their job of regulating industries: "I still say let's keep the pressure on the auto, but we are solving that problem with new regulations. It's the stationary sources that are becoming an increasingly larger part of the problem now. . . . If we don't stop this trend now, we'll be back in the fifties."

Local districts took a different view. None was as vocal in its criticism of every other smog control agency than the Los Angeles County Air Pollution Control District. Most of its literature detailed what a bad polluter the automobile was. The message was clear: Citizens must force the state and federal governments to clean up moving polluters, since they are out of the county's jurisdiction. The Los Angeles district consistently claimed that cars cause 90 percent of the smog. Experts disputed this figure, since it considers only the total weight of pollutants, not how poisonous they are. Taking that into account, industry plays a bigger part in health-damaging pollution—up to 40 percent.

A colorfully illustrated cartoon booklet distributed by the Los Angles smog district is typical of the propaganda. The auto is shown belching fire and smoke monsters from its exhaust pipe and engine. The booklet says that the Los Angeles Air Pollution Control District's laws "are the strictest and toughest regulations found anywhere in the world," but that federal and state "government levels have taken away the County's right to control the emissions from moving sources. . . . The County Board of Supervisors, since the early 1950s, has demanded that tough and effective regulations be adopted by government and met by the auto industry." But it says that state and federal officials, as well as the auto industry, have refused to do this. Finally, the booklet shows a businessman wearing a huge diamond ring. He is astride a car that reads "auto manufacturers." The man is dropping a hot potato. "DON'T LET THEM DENY US CLEAN AIR AGAIN!" it' warns—"them" being the auto manufacturers, the Federal Environmental Protection Agency, and the state government.

By attacking other agencies, the county smog district was diverting attention from the industrial pollution it was supposed to control. Its literature ignored the fact that the district's regulations are not the strictest in the world and that other agencies know as much about smog as they do. The purpose of the propaganda was to blame everyone else for the smog.

An Area of Agreement—Ultimate Victory

What officials at both state and local levels have in common is an optimistic view of the smog situation that is contradicted by the murky air that greets urban Californians on most days. Their motivation is clear. It is the bureaucratic urge for self-protection. By saying the problem is nearly solved, they are showing what a good job they are doing.

"We have turned the corner on smog," said Governor Ronald Reagan in 1970. "We are doing all that I think can be done at the present time."

"The worst is over, there will still be plant damage and health effects, but it is not as bad now as a few years ago," said another state official in 1973.

In 1972, the Los Angeles Air Pollution Control District published a newsletter talking about a downward trend in smog. But at the end of an article full of statistics, it was apparent district officials were talking only about one ingredient of smog, ozone. Buried on a back page was the admission that the more toxic pollutant, oxides of nitrogen, was increasing.

Robert Lunche, administrator of the Los Angeles County Air Pollution Control District, said in 1973 that smog was decreasing everywhere in the Los Angeles Basin: "It's more apparent in Los

Angeles. It's already beginning to show in Riverside, though the amount is small."

The evidence of one's eyes said otherwise, as did more scientific proof. Information from the Riverside County smog district showed the smog season was starting earlier each year. Smog alerts there were lasting longer. The head of the Riverside district said the smog was spreading "like a fog that creeps along the ground and keeps covering more territory."

Joe Behar's research at the Statewide Air Pollution Research Center in Riverside revealed that high levels of smog are lasting longer throughout the Los Angeles Basin, with the exception of one element of smog, ozone, on the west side and downtown. The number of hours in smog season is increasing. "We are dramatically exposed for more hours," he said. "How can they tell me it's getting better. . . . We've looked at the information every possible way, and we couldn't see any way it is getting better."

Behar's former boss at the center, Dr. James Pitts, testified to a congressional committee in 1972, "The state of California has had controls on exhaust emissions for six years, yet air quality has not improved in many areas in the state. In fact, during this period, it became significantly worse in much of the South Coast [Los Angeles] Air Basin."

The Big Surprise: Federal Intervention

The doomsday predictions of conservationist groups and people like Joe Behar had been regarded as the protestations of a lunatic fringe. But in 1973, the public was surprised to hear the Nixon administration's Environmental Protection Agency agree with critics of both state and local smog agencies. The federal government was now saying that the air was unhealthy and that present state and local programs to clean it up simply would not work in the foreseeable future. The federal EPA, tired of delays by the smog agencies, ruled that California would have to meet new 1971 federal clean air standards, stricter than those of the state, by 1975. To do it, drastic changes would have to be made. One judgment was that auto travel in the Los Angeles basin would have to be reduced 80 percent in smoggy months—but federal officials later backed down on this demand because it was impossible to carry out in an area where state and local government had insisted on substituting freeways for mass transit.

When the federal government announced its deadline, Southern Californians were incredulous. They had wanted to believe what smog officials had been telling them for years—that they were on the verge of solving the problem. The federal Environmental Protection Agency—required by the 1970 Clean Air Act to step in when state and local levels failed to provide a plan for ending smog—found itself being criticized by California officials for being unreasonable. Even Tom Bradley, the reform mayor of Los Angeles, said the agency was too harsh.

The reaction of Californians was not surprising. For the entire structure of smog control in the state was shaped in such a way that it reinforced citizens' blindness toward official misbehavior and the resulting dangers around them.

The job of reporting the day's smog level falls to the county smog district. In Southern California, local officials consistently deny the public enough information to give a complete picture of how bad the air is. For example, the Los Angeles district gives out daily smog information, much like a weather report. It is carried by newspapers and broadcast stations. But it reports only the day's high reading of a few key pollutants. This is meaningless. Federal and state health standards for clean air are based on how long the high level of smog lasts—not just the peak reading. A low level of carbon monoxide might be safe for an hour, but dangerous over a twenty-four hour period.

And the district's smog prediction speaks only of eye irritation as a side effect of air pollution. It does not mention other, more serious known effects, such as impaired breathing, headaches, aggravation of lung and heart conditions, and changes in blood chemistry impairing some brain function. Thus, when the public hears the smog prediction on radio or television, it appears to put smog in the category of a nuisance rather than a health hazard. Local district officials consistently deny there is "hard medical knowledge of any more serious effects," even though state and federal agency booklets specifically list the kinds of health damage smog can cause.

Residents have been told by the Los Angeles smog district that their senses are not a reliable gauge of the smog level. But on the worst days, a commuter—trapped on a crowded freeway, heading into the brown haze that hides the new buildings downtown—knows he has to keep his windows closed and car air conditioner on. If he opens a window, he knows he will feel sick. And he knows, too, that by the time he reaches home in the evening, he will be drained of energy. What he doesn't understand is why a day of work at the office makes him so tired. He is tired because of the bad air he breathes. Yet, over the car radio, he hears the report of the Los Angeles County Air Pollution District: "Light to moderate smog in the basin, with moderate eye irritation."

The local smog district—the only agency with current information on smog concentration—is unwilling to admit how bad it is. Bureaucratic survival dictates that it delude the public into believing smog is a minor problem. If it admits things are not under control, it fears it will threaten the well-entrenched power of the agency. As we will see, this attitude made the agency regard the public—especially those who demanded more information—as the enemy.

THE SIGNIFICANCE OF THE SECRECY

The story of Leonard Levine illustrates this tendency toward secrecy and misinformation—and how the district gets away with it year after year.

Of all the smog control agencies in the nation, none is more important than the Los Angeles County Air Pollution Control District, for it claims a reputation as the first and the toughest smog regulation agency in the country. And it is in charge of the area that has become a national symbol of smog. That is why, when Leonard Levine found himself choking with asthma outside his office building, he went to the district for help. He didn't get it. Instead he found the district protecting the polluters and consistently denying access to the smog information it supposedly gathered for everyone—the public, the academic world, and even other agencies of government.

Levine is a family man in his mid-thirties. An electronics engineer, he designs computer memories for Xerox Corporation. He is serious and reserved, until he begins telling about his long battle with the Los Angeles smog district. Then he becomes animated and paces about. It is a subject of endless fascination to him—a cause that has changed his life. After seeing the gap between the intent of the law and its actual enforcement, he has begun studying at night school to become a lawyer.

In the fall of 1968, Levine and the rest of the Xerox data systems staff had just moved to a new building in El Segundo, south of the Los Angeles International Airport. For the first time in his life, he began to get asthma and serious headaches. In the parking lot one day, he smelled something he recognized, and it explained his sudden illness. It was the same smell given off when a match is struck. From college chemistry, Levine knew it was sulfur dioxide, poisonous to humans. And he, in particular, was highly allergic to it.

El Segundo is on the west side of the Los Angeles Basin. It is near the ocean, and, logically, it should not be as smoggy as inland areas. But it is in a pocket of heavy industry. Less than a mile from Xerox was a Standard Oil refinery and the Allied Chemical Company plant. Allied was in the business of recovering usable chemicals—sulfuric acid and sulfur products—from a poisonous gas, hydrogen sulfide, that was a by-product of the Standard Oil refinery. An underground pipe brought the hydrogen sulfide from Standard into the Allied plant, where another poisonous gas, sulfur dioxide, was produced. Levine decided that he smelled gas that Allied was emitting during the manufacturing process.

Other Xerox employees were getting sick too—coughing, suffering from headaches, nausea and sore throats. They too felt worse in the parking lot, where they could actually smell the sulfur dioxide. Their reaction was typical of unorganized citizens. "For a while we did nothing but complain to each other," said Levine.

But the smell got worse, and on a particularly bad day, Levine called the Los Angeles Air Pollution Control District. He was switched to the public relations department, which handled complaint calls. To Levine's surprise, he was told that there probably were sulfur dioxide and hydrogen sulfide in the air and that he probably could smell it. But the district said it would do nothing because the amounts were well within the limits of the smog district's regulations.

Puzzled by the district's attitude, Levine obtained a copy of its regulations. Then he went to a law library and read the state health law which forbids emission into the air of anything "unsafe, noxious or unhealthy." The smell in the Xerox parking lot, he felt, was definitely noxious and unhealthy, and he was afraid it was unsafe. Leonard Levine, engineer, suddenly became Leonard Levine, battler against bureaucracy.

He knew he needed help, from fellow employees and from experts. "At Xerox, I was there eight hours a day, facing a health problem, which threatened my livelihood and my health every day, so I was strongly motivated," he said. Levine started going to environmental organization meetings. There he met Gladys Meade, active in the clean air fight and later to be appointed and fired as a member of the state Air Resources Board. She told him about the Beverly Hills Bar Association, which had a committee on environment and ecology. Through the bar association, Levine was introduced to Norman Zafman, an attorney who had once been an engineer. They joined forces in a battle that was to go on for years. Their object first was to force the county smog district to crack down on Allied and Standard Oil. Later their aim was to destroy the secrecy behind which the smog district hid.

"Levine turned to the district for help as naturally as one turns to the police following a crime," wrote attorney Zafman in the *Beverly Hills Law Review*. "What happened to change Levine's view of the district from protector to adversary is a story, in microcosm, of how a governmental agency loses the confidence and trust of the public in whose interest it is created and which it ostensibly serves."

Measuring the Danger and Hiding the Results

Levine first asked the district to test the levels of sulfur dioxide by installing a monitoring device in the Xerox building. The district refused. Levine persisted, and finally the district agreed. The first day Levine saw that the levels recorded by the machine were dangerously high. The sulfur dioxide concentration was four times the level listed as harmful to health in a booklet put out by the state. On the second day, Levine could see nothing. The district had covered the gauge that showed the level. Levine demanded the figures. He was refused. But the level must have been high, for the district filed an injunction against Allied, asking it to stop polluting.

A victory for Levine? Not at all. What happened next again shows the difference in the way the law is enforced for major business and the way it is enforced against citizen-lawbreakers. While the injunction sought an end to the pollution, Allied was not closed down during the litigation. When the pollution continued, the district attorney of Los Angeles County filed charges against Allied and Standard for violating air pollution laws. Had they been tried and found guilty, the law was so weak that the companies would have been fined only a few hundred dollars. But the two firms were never brought to court on these charges. They filed delaying motions, and, in 1971, charges were dropped when Standard announced plans to build a new sulfur recovery plant that would replace the Allied operation. But the new plant would not be finished until 1973. "Meanwhile," said Levine, "we continued to be gassed by Allied."

All through the fight, the district refused to provide Levine and Zafman with any of the information about industrial pollution they sought: the specific pollutants each industry was emitting and the data on which the district based such information. Were tests being performed near polluting industries or in their smoke stacks? What did such tests show? The agency refused to give any of this information for a most interesting reason. They said to divulge any of it would reveal trade secrets of the corporations involved and would give their competitors an unfair advantage.

"The most significant issue is the secrecy," said Levine. "This is the most powerful lesson I learned from this whole experience. That becomes the central issue. Once the public has access to the data and can understand and evaluate the decisions, the policy making and the activity, then they can make intelligent decisions. They can see what the policies and priorities should be, and they can participate in the process. The agency doesn't want that because they are fundamentally opposed to strict regulation of large polluting industries. They will regulate the hell out of a small polluting industry. But the larger industries represent enormous political power.

"Look at the oil companies, who contribute significantly to, not only the president, but the governor, the county supervisors. They have a powerful financial interest there. And if the agency were to actually make measurements as to what the air quality was near these sources, they would find that they're in violation of the state and safety standards. They would have to enforce them or they would be in violation of the law. The best thing they could do is not know."

Faced with the attack by Levine and Zafman, the district responded by trying to portray them as pests. County air pollution control officer Robert Chass wrote to the county supervisors, who were also the members of the smog district's control board, about Levine. The letter said he was "an unreasonable, chronic complainant." Chass admitted the Standard Oil-Allied Chemical operation was polluting, but said the problem would continue until the new plant was built. He said justice would not be served by prosecuting the polluters. He concluded the letter, "Allied Chemical has been kept under surveillance for more than a year and a half and constantly in recent months corresponding to a resurgence of complaints by Mr. Levine. The results of our constant surveillance and investigations do not substantiate his charges, and I believe most of them are exaggerated." But Chass didn't give any figures to back up his statement. He still wouldn't say what the district had found out about the specific levels of pollution from Allied.

Trying to Get Help Through the Machinery of Government

With little money available for a big public fight and with few committed allies, Levine and Zafman decided to study the state law and methodically pursue the smog district through the machinery of government. In January 1972, they sent a forty-one page letter to the state Air Resources Board formally requesting a state investigation of the Los Angeles County Air Pollution Control District. They wrote, "A significant health problem presently exists" in the county, and the district's "priorities, policies, emission control regulations and enforcement record are inadequate with reference to what can and should be done to meet state and federal air quality standards." Levine and Zafman obtained endorsements of the letter from several citizens' environmental groups, including the Sierra Club.

Action was slow, but after six months of looking into the matter, the state board held a public hearing. Testimony at the hearing told of a smog control district so secretive that it would not even share its information with other government smog-regulating agencies. One witness testified that he had a contract with the U.S. Environmental Protection Agency to study smog, but that the Los Angeles district refused to provide him information about industrial pollution. The district again insisted that to reveal emissions data—even about a government-owned power plant—would reveal corporate trade secrets.

A state college engineering professor told how officials of the Los Angeles district refused to attend a federal workshop intended for the exchange of information with other government agencies. Jack Green, who headed a neighboring government air pollution control district in the Coachella Valley, said he had observed "a continuing disregard for the public on the part of the [Los Angeles] district personnel that is unbecoming for any agency. It is particularly astounding when that agency is legally public in nature. In the absence of a proper answer to the question regarding public access to APCD records, we must conclude that the Los Angeles Air Pollution Control District is intentionally and purposefully violating state law, an incredible indictment."

The state Air Resources Board said it would not pass judgment whether or not a smog health hazard existed in Los Angeles County. Illogically, the state board went on to say that if one did exist, the Los Angeles smog control district was not to blame for it. The Air Resources Board criticized the county district for having a bad attitude toward the public and for refusing to open its records, as required by the state public records act.

But a major part of the board's criticism was reserved for

citizens who complain. "Another [reason for polarization between citizens and the county district] is the tendency of some citizens to assume that the information supplied by the district is wrong, even purposely wrong. . . . The citizens must recognize that the district is technically competent and that it is not trying to mislead them. It is impossible to work with someone if you mistrust him and tell him so in the bargain."

Citizens did not follow the state board's advice. Soon complaints were coming in such numbers that the county supervisors held public hearings on possible reorganization of the county smog control district. One witness was Dr. Arthur Atkisson, professor of urban health at the University of Texas. Atkisson was in a unique position to criticize the district. He had once worked for it and was familiar with its reputation. Among the nation's smog experts, it was known as secretive and uncooperative. "I think you've got to restore the capacity of the agency to criticize and change itself," he told the county supervisors. As for the district's secrecy, he said, "That's been so well documented, I guess that isn't even an open question." And he said the district had come to think that citizens, especially those organized in groups, were the enemy instead of the smog. "I submit letting the public in, letting researchers in, causes you lots of inconvenience. There isn't any question about that. But if you don't let them in, the inevitable price you pay is a loss of public confidence in your operation. . . . If you are unwilling to expose yourself to censure, then the public sadly will always conclude that you are as guilty as hell."

Early in 1973, the district finally released some of the information sought by Levine and Zafman. But when the list of major polluters and what they were emitting was made public, the information was still far from complete. For one thing, the district refused to disclose the research upon which they based their information. Engineering estimates, not air monitoring tests had been used. But there was no information given to show how the district knew this information was accurate. Nor would it release data that industries had been required to give the district when they applied for permission to operate. That meant there was no way for Levine or any member of the public to check the truth of what the district was saying.

The Price of Not Letting the Public In

The attorney general of the state, Evelle Younger, then tried to force the district to open its files. While agreeing that some of the information might include real trade secrets, protected by state law in certain instances, Younger said the district had to prove their secret nature or "show that the public interest served by not making the record public clearly outweighs the public interest served by disclosure of the record." He added that it was his belief that the entire Standard Oil file could not consist of trade secrets, yet "it is our understanding that requests for some or all of the above information have been denied by the district."

Still the district refused. It asked Standard Oil to turn over to Younger whatever information it chose. But the district itself would do nothing. The legal process was painfully slow. By fall of 1973, the attorney general's office was still evaluating whether or not this answer was satisfactory. Levine and Zafman didn't think so. They were getting ready to sue for the information.

In his long fight against the district, Levine learned some generally unknown facts about smog in Los Angeles, facts which tended to destroy the district's rosy contention that it was the best and toughest such agency in the nation. He learned:.

The district waited too long to declare a smog alert. For example, a federal health study showed that changes in blood chemistry occurred when the air contained thirty parts per million of one pollutant, carbon monoxide, over an eight to ten hour period. But the district did not call an alert until the level had reached fifty parts per million. A state Air Resources Board publication indicated there is respiratory irritation when the sulfur dioxide level is as low as .04 parts per million over a twenty-four-hour period. But the local district did not ask factories to shut down until the level of sulfur dioxide reached five parts per million.

Contrary to the Los Angeles district's claims, other districts had tougher laws. For example, the smog district in the San Francisco Bay Area limited plant emissions of sulfur dioxide to less than half what Los Angeles allowed.

The district measured plant emissions indirectly, from mathematical models of how plants operated. Air around the factories was not checked routinely, nor were the smokestacks, except when a plant first received a permit to operate. The district refused to reveal how it devised its mathematical models. "You have a major source of pollution, yet you don't go to the trouble of measuring what people are breathing," said Levine.

The district had a well-publicized program of surprise early morning raids on polluters. When the raids were held, inspectors cited only those places where emissions were visible, even though it was well acknowledged that many poisonous emissions could not be seen. "They have a surprise raid where they find one smoky school bus and one smoky train," said Levine. "But if they would put a single instrument in a stack they'd find plenty. And if they'd put instruments on the ground in the vicinity of major polluters, they'd find plenty."

Variances—permits to operate while exceeding smog regulations—were regularly given to polluting industries that said they needed time to develop or install antipollution equipment. These variances were renewed— sometimes for years—with few questions asked.

Levine and other critics of the smog control district came to believe it was incapable of controlling smog for a number of reasons. A major factor was the political power of the polluters, as campaign contributors to the county supervisors. Another, more subtle reason, was that the district—once a pioneer—had grown old as bureaucracies tend to do. "I think the agency has aged so much that their behavior is actually senile," said Robert Doty, a graduate student at the University of California at Riverside and a member of an environmental group called Clean Air Now. "They view the public as an antagonist, an outsider to the agency rather than the basis of their support."

Entrenched as it was, resistant to change, there was nothing that could be done to the district except keep hammering away, hoping for small victories. What had Levine gained in his five-year battle? "We have had a regulation changed that makes a significant reduction in one pollutant. Yes, we've gotten one company closed down in one situation where it was intolerable. It's still intolerable in other areas. . . . I think we have been very effective, considering the resources we have had. Compared to what could be done and what should be done, we have hardly scratched the surface. I think if *we* had an agency like the APCD and that budget and that staff, I think we could clean up the air."

But smog was such a complex problem that it was beyond the capacity of a single agency to cure it without the coordinated backup of all levels of government—tough state and federal laws forcing business and individuals into compliance, along with government funds and cooperative effort to produce a workable mass transit system. To make these things possible, smog agencies first had to admit that smog was not getting better, that it was a problem, and that something had to be done about it.

THE VALUE OF CANDOR

There were local smog agencies outside of California that were admitting such things. In the Washington, D.C., area, the fall of 1973 brought an unprecedented two-week smog alert. Officials admitted that the smog was a threat to public health and that while they didn't understand it, it might be getting worse. One official, interviewed by the *Washington Post*, commented, "It's a helluva thing, but I can't get a handle on it. I don't know what it means, do you?"

The Metropolitan Washington Council of Governments, the agency responsible for monitoring smog in the area, released its information—and what it meant—to other government agencies, to health officials, to the academic community. It was not a secret, and from talking to many representatives of different agencies, John Saar of the *Washington Post* was able to write a story explaining what was happening. The smog experts were concerned because air quality was deteriorating in some suburban areas of the metropolitan complex—just as it was in areas of the Los Angeles basin. They admitted that their present programs to combat air pollution might be totally inadequate.

There was still some equivocation by those in charge. The Washington Council of Governments' smog chief, David Di Julio, still maintained his faith that the agency's programs would work: "It should be going down now. Our best calculations are that although car owners and mileage are going up, emissions are going down." And the man who directed the district's department of human resources refused to tell the *Post* if there had been a rise in deaths during the long barrage of smog: "If there was a 500 percent increase in deaths, I'm not going to release it and cause public alarm unless the deaths are firmly related to air pollution." In other words, regardless of the public's right to know, those in charge were still trying to withhold information they felt would panic people.

But' there were enough public officials in Washington who had the smog information, and they could draw their own conclusions. Gilbert Hahn, a city councilman who had been working on the smog problem, said that the long smog alert was "deadly serious," and concluded that the problem will worsen until "unfortunately people will get sick and die from it.

"There are certain areas like F Street," he said, "where they check for carbon monoxide and it goes off the scale. Well, you may have to close down F Street for health reasons."

In D.C. there was a relatively free flow of information, and the smog officials admitted they didn't have all the answers. The dangers of bad smog and the sacrifices necessary to clear it up were becoming matters of political debate.

That couldn't happen in Los Angeles. There, realistic solutions were not discussed because those in charge refused to admit there was a problem. For people who understood what was happening, the last hope was that the federal Environmental Protection Agency would make good its threat of forcing a cure on the area. But Congress, too, had its pressures, and deadlines for compliance were being postponed.

The California experience showed how the failings of government can actually endanger the health of millions, without their being aware of it. Nobody, of course, wants air pollution. But in the short run, the costs of curing it are so tremendous that polluting industries want the public to continue to tolerate it. And since those industries have a strong measure of control over the agencies that regulate pollution, the war against smog is lost almost before it begins.

WAITING FOR GOVERNMENT TO CORRECT ITSELF

As with campaign contribution laws, it can be a waste of time waiting for politicians to impose strict regulations on themselves or their fellow officials on another level of government. This is especially true when powerful business interests are dead set against reform. Occasionally the structure is tinkered with, but serious moves to change things are usually defeated. In 1973, for example, both the Assembly and the Senate of California passed a bill that would have eliminated the county air pollution control districts, like those in Los Angeles, and replaced them with regional agencies that could operate across county lines. It was a small start, undertaken because legislators saw growing voter resentment against smog and against the Los Angeles district, in particular. If the bill were signed into law, industry's influence on smog regulation through the county supervisors would be gone.

The Los Angeles County supervisors have little influence in Sacramento. But they moved quickly in an attempt to defeat the bill and stay in control of smog enforcement.

Some of their maneuvers were discussed at a county supervisors meeting one morning, after they whipped through their agenda. It was a meeting much like the one described in Chapter Three: people were refused permission to speak; business was taken up that had not been scheduled. The supervisors—since they also functioned as the board of the air pollution control district—adjourned as supervisors and reconvened, a minute later, as county smog officials. Although they hadn't announced the matter in advance on their printed agenda, the supervisors—turned smog board—began talking about how they could save the Los Angeles County Air Pollution Control District. Their discussion was an illuminating example of the difference between public debate and private action. Publicly, the district portrayed itself as a powerful foe of industrial polluters, its agency as a victim of wheeling and dealing state legislators. Privately, it was known to play the same political games.

An employee of the smog district, Robert Barsky, who lobbied legislation for the district in Sacramento, appeared before the supervisors to report how he had so far been unable to stop the bill abolishing the county's air pollution control district.

"Do you mean the big corporations who have had to meet the strict standards of Los Angeles County are working in the background with their powerful lobbies to dilute the whole air pollution program?" asked Supervisor Kenneth Hahn.

"No," replied Barsky.

"Who is?" said Hahn.

Barsky truthfully answered that it was the environmentalists who wanted to dissolve the county districts, specifically the Planning and Conservation League, a lobbying coalition of environmental groups. Among Barsky's fellow lobbyists against the bill in the legislative hearings had been the California Manufacturers Association, the lobbying organization for big industries. In other words, those being regulated by the Los Angeles County smog district were fighting to save it, illustrating the way the system actually worked.

Nevertheless, Supervisor Hahn continued to argue the board's public stance—that the district was feared by the big business polluters. "They're railroading a bill through both houses," he said. "And to think the Republicans as well as the Democrats knuckle in to this kind of pressure. . . . It won't do anyone any good. It won't do those senators any good, no matter how much campaign funds they're going to raise, if the people know they just horsetrade the people's health and good for their own political advancement."

In the end, the supervisors won, a surprise victory achieved when Governor Reagan vetoed the bill.

The process of an executive veto is a private one. Legal and political advisors provide memoranda, and the governor studies them. In this case, the governor had a large number of bills before him, sent to his office after a final, all-night session of the legislature several days before. Reagan also had a political problem. He was campaigning for a tax plan on the forthcoming November ballot, and he was generally opposed by representatives of local government, who said the tax plan would cut state taxes at the expense of local government. Reagan badly needed some local government representatives to step up and defend his tax plan. He got one from the Los Angeles County Board of Supervisors, Supervisor James Hayes, who served as head of the county smog control district board.

Had the old custom of the legislative trade been adopted by the governor and the supervisor? Since it happened in private, the truth will never be known. What is known is that the county smog control districts were saved. The governor vetoed the bill that would have replaced them with regional districts, saying they would create another level of government with taxing powers, which he opposed.

No Options

But if the local smog control districts were going to keep on operating as before, and if the federal government was delaying intervention, that meant it would take years for the haze to clear up. Politicians could continue to dodge the issue and its unpopular solution, just as they had in the past.

Dr. Pitts, the Riverside smog expert, explained the problem of not putting the choices before the public: "Now the problem is, the public has never . . . had brought to their attention [by government] the options they have, putting it in terms of the science involved, the health effects involved, and what you have to pay [to correct it]. What we desperately need now are sets of control options that we can present to the public and say: 'Here are the options':

"Option one: Don't do anything.

"Option two: Let's have mandatory vehicle inspection; let's put NOx [oxides of nitrogen] controls on. Let us require [that] all stationary sources have modified combustion, and let's put some buses into L.A. This is going to cost the following amount. You know what the improvement is going to be. You are going to be a little bit disrupted, maybe.

"Option three: Let's go forward. We're going to do better than that. Let's think in terms of rationing of fuel. Or voluntary shift to smaller cars of the kind that pollute less.

"Now, I'm not saying I advocate any of that. What I advocate as a citizen—I wish to heck I had in front of me some of these options, based on the best evidence that government and the academic communities can develop.

"... I don't want to criticize an agency. No, let me tell you; they're on the firing line. They're getting it from all directions. I would rather say I would hope that they'd provide data. I think it's crucial. I think the days of saying, 'Everything's fine. Don't worry. It's perfectly controlled'—when the public themselves look out the window, and they don't see the mountains, and they're choking. Their kid has been sick, and they know. . . ."

But do they know? The public has been confused by the barrage of conflicting statements from official agencies. And before anything can be done, voters have to understand that smog is bad and force the structure to do something about it. When state and local government are susceptible to special interests, polluters make intelligent choices impossible. In the case of smog control in California, the program has been subverted by regulation machinery so complex that its main function is to hide its own impotence. We know the danger of having no regulatory agencies. We are learning the danger of having too many.

11

Why You Don't
Read about It in the Papers

At their best, newspapers, magazines, television and radio represent the public in the clash of special interests competing for a voice in government. By disclosing what happens in the backrooms, journalists can prevent the secret exercise of power by business, organized labor, and the bureaucracy of government itself. This way, the press can be an invaluable ally to the citizen.

At their worst, those who communicate in print and by electronics are a party to the backroom system of government, either as passive partners—guilty of sins of omission—or as willing participants in cover-ups. When they fail to report government news thoughtfully, aggressively and completely, the print and electronic press betrays the citizen who subscribes to a newspaper or spends the dinner hour with a vacuous news telecast.

This is especially true about state and local government coverage. Most citizens will probably never encounter a national magazine story, a network television special, or a book dealing in any depth with specific problems of their community. Only the local press can do that job. As Ben Bagdikian, a commentator on the American press, has said, "We need local papers because our society concentrates more responsibility on a local level than does any modern state. We do not have national papers as do other countries that have a few huge papers blanketing the country. We have local papers because our localities control their own schools, police, taxes, highways, welfare distribution and other functions handled in other countries by centralized government. No matter how much we admire *The New York Times,* the *Wall Street Journal,* and the *Christian Science Monitor,* and no matter how quickly they can be delivered to other cities, they cannot tell the local citizen what he needs to know to govern himself intelligently in his own town."

THE ADVERSARY PRESS

The Constitution gave the press protection in the First Amendment, which guarantees freedom of speech. That special status permitted it to undertake a special role in our democratic system of government, as watchdog and critic. In that uncomfortable position, it has never been beloved by public officials.

Printers putting out their own newspapers helped inspire and further the cause of the American Revolution, but later the critics among them faced the retaliation of the Federalist Party of George Washington. Benjamin Franklin Bache, grandson of Benjamin Franklin and an anti-Federalist Republican, revealed in his *Aurora* that Washington had received $11,200 in expense reimbursements from the federal government instead of the $6,250 authorized by law. When Washington was succeeded by John Adams, another Federalist, Bache's attacks became stronger. Adams' wife, Abigail, unhappily wrote, "We are now wonderfully popular except with Bache and Co. who in his paper calls the President old, querulous, bald, blind, crippled, toothless Adams." The First Amendment stopped the Federalists from acting against Bache and the others, but in 1798, the Adams administration persuaded Congress to pass the Sedition Act. This law made it a crime to print "any false, scandalous or malicious writings" about the government, and it was used to censor the President's critics. It was enforced against Republican editors like Bache until the election of Jefferson's Republican administration in 1800.

The Industrial Revolution, European immigration and population growth changed the press from a collection of relatively small party organs, like Bache's *Aurora,* to large mass circulation papers, costing only a penny and written to appeal to the majority of working people. The complex new times eventually brought more complex journalism. After the Civil War, crusading, perceptive reporters began to examine the institutions of the new America, the giant corporations and the governments they controlled. Lincoln Steffens, Ida Tarbell and other journalists at the turn of the century discovered corruption in the system. Some of their writing so angered Theodore Roosevelt, who was a reformer by the standards of the day, that he called them "muckrakers," and he did not mean it as a compliment.

Until relatively recently, those who ran the government had a limited adversary. Not everyone read newspapers. Television, however, has made the distribution of news something of a monster in the minds of officials. For today, reading skill has little to do with the power of the press. Even the most illiterate watch the news on television and it has become the dominant force in shaping the view Americans have of their elected officials. Confronted with television, those who exercise governmental power now view reporters with more distaste than ever before.

Throughout this book, we have seen how government likes to hide the decision-making process. The most important part of hiding information is keeping it from the press. Secret meetings are illegal at most levels of government, but state and local officials are often able to conceal their important decisions behind a network of agencies, commissions and committees. Officials can also use the mechanical limitations of newsgathering to their own advantage. With so many separate official groups meeting at the same time, handing out complex decisions, reports and press releases, it is almost impossible for reporters to keep track of it all and what it means. Even the most responsible news agencies must be selective.

THE MECHANICS OF NEWSGATHERING

Despite a large number of potential stories on a given day, the same few events that are covered in newspapers tend also to be found on radio and television broadcasts. This is no accident. It is due to the mechanics of getting out the news and the close relationship between newspapers, radio and television. All are in the business of distributing information, and while the techniques of each are different, they subtly influence one another. Television, with a screen full of exciting images, has forced more newspapers to adopt interesting writing styles and to provide stories with depth and analysis that go far beyond the limited broadcast news accounts. Television and radio, on the other hand, are guided by newspapers. Their executives base their assignments largely on the stories that have been featured in that morning's major newspapers or on information received over the wires of the two national news-gathering agencies, the Associated Press and United Press International. The wire services, in turn, are guided, to a substantial degree, by what has appeared in metropolitan newspapers.

The mechanics of putting out a visual newscast make it difficult for television to initiate a story, as a newspaper can do. Television news reporters complain they seldom can do exposés or explain in detail how government really works. TV news has a transient quality, seeming to go from one unconnected event to another, forgetting yesterday's news as today's unfolds. There are good reasons for this. The economics of television dictate that news staffs be kept fairly small. And to cover a story, television requires more than a single reporter. A well-paid cameraman and soundman must also go along. A TV news staff generally has just enough reporters to provide the necessary number of stories for that day's show. Rarely is enough money included in the budget for specialist reporters, experts in a field who have the time and knowledge to outwit the bureaucrats who prefer to hide from publicity. And even if such reporters were retained on television news staffs, there wouldn't be time to show all their stories. News segments must be short and pictorially interesting. Producers find it hard to illustrate a story obtained by dull digging through documents— even when it exposes secret government activities. As a result, television reporters tend to flit from story to story: a murder on Monday, a flood on Tuesday and a battle in city council on Wednesday. Even if disclosures of corruption are made, television has even more trouble following up on them, obtaining new information, digging deeper, keeping the story before the public.

This is especially true when a local government story drags on day after day without a change in its scenic possibilities.

The printed press, then, is left with the job of initiating exposés of the activities of city councils, county supervisors, state legislatures, and, as in the case of Watergate, the political operations of the President of the United States. In the vast majority of cases, only the newspapers can uncover the story and keep it alive until it reaches some sort of conclusion. When newspapers are performing well, they are uniquely equipped for this sort of muckraking. In judging their effectiveness, we must consider a basic fact of American journalism, the monopoly press.

NEWS MONOPOLIES

In 1910, when the United States' population was 92 million, there were 2,600 newspapers. Today, with a population of more than 200 million, there are only 1,761. Decades ago, most places had several competing newspapers. Now, for the most part, competition has gone. Most cities have one newspaper. If there are two, they are usually a morning newspaper and an afternoon paper, not in direct competition. Often a single owner puts out both of these papers. Or, if there are separate owners, they may share printing plants and the cost of maintaining the business portion of their staffs.

Thus in hundreds of cities and towns throughout America, only one newspaper voice speaks about the concerns of the citizens. This is particularly damaging in the coverage of local government, the level of government providing the most direct services to the people. Network television, while unable to investigate, covers the major national government and political stories. In the most populous states, big city television stations send reporters to the state capital. But in most of America, the only reporter at city hall or the county administration building is the representative of the local monopoly newspaper. The amount of news the reader gets depends to some extent on the reporter's skill. But mostly it depends on the skill and courage of editors and the determination and integrity of the publisher.

But too often, the publisher is part of the backroom crowd that runs the city or county, a businessman who feels his fortunes are tied to those of the real estate, industrial or business interests of the area. As a particularly reprehensible example of this, press critic Ben Bagdikian cited the *Wilmington* (Delaware) *Morning News* and the *Evening Journal,* both owned by the DuPont Company, the most powerful corporation in the state. When Bagdikian made his study, members of the DuPont family manipulated the news content of the papers to reflect their own political and economic interests. Political stories were slanted toward Republicans; and locally the DuPonts objected to the reporting of public charges of mismanagement of the local airport, which had dealings with a private aviation corporation partially owned by a DuPont. (Bagdikian's study was done a few years ago. Since then, the DuPont papers have changed. In his 1973 critique of the reporters covering the 1972 campaign, *The Boys on the Bus,* Timothy Crouse said that the reporter for the Wilmington papers was free to write stories as he saw them and was one of the few campaign reporters who wrote critically of President Nixon.)

In Jackson, Mississippi, one family, the Hedermans, monopolizes the city's newspapers, owning the morning *Clarion-Ledger* and the afternoon *Daily News.* In a 1970 study for the *Columbia Journalism Review,* Edwin Williams told how the papers' stories inaccurately gave the impression that the police had no responsibility for the killing of two young blacks and the wounding of twelve others when officers fired into a girls dormitory at Jackson State College. "The Hedermans, staunch Southern Baptists and political conservatives, epitomize the white power structure in Mississippi," wrote Williams. In a summation that could apply to scores of newspaper publishers around the country, Williams concluded, "The Hedermans and their allies are the Mississippi establishment. If they want change, they seek it through the application of political and economic power at the top, not through investigative reporting and newspaper editorials. The police and highway patrol are part of the establishment. If the patrol, for instance, must be dealt with, it will be dealt with in the councils of power, not in the pages of the newspaper."

Yet there are monopoly newspapers that are courageous and

fair. "Some of our greatest newspapers exist in towns where the ownership is limited to one firm," monopoly newspaper owner John Cowles correctly wrote in 1951. He cited his own *Minneapolis Star* and *Minneapolis Tribune* as well as the *Louisville Courier-Journal*, the *Atlanta Constitution* and *Atlanta Journal*, and the *Kansas City Star* and *Kansas City Times*. What is important are certain qualities, described by Theodore White in his *The Making of the President—1972*. He was explaining why President Nixon was estranged from the owners of the nation's great newspapers, which the President lumped together as "The Liberal Press." They were, said White, *The New York Times*, the *Los Angeles Times*, the *Washington Post*, the Field Papers in Chicago, the *Louisville Courier-Journal*, the *St. Louis Post-Dispatch*, the *Boston Globe* and *Newsday* on Long Island, all of them owned by old, but still vigorous, families.

"What characterizes these hereditary newspaper barons is something not too difficult to define," said White.

"The families that own the great newspapers of The Liberal Press have the taste, and the purse, for the finest newswriting; they invite from their staffs elegant, muscled investigative reporting. In this field, they outclass all other newspapers; they have survived, and their competitors have perished, because of this quality. These families regard their star reporters as almost sacred—as great racing families regard their horses, horse handlers and jockeys."

The same could be said for other, lesser-known, papers around the country. Unfortunately, they are in a minority. In most cities in 1972, the President's public relations emissary, Herb Klein, was welcomed in the publisher's office when he toured the country complaining about the liberal press.

A Particular Monopoly

In 1970, I went to work for what amounted to a monopoly paper, the *Los Angeles Times*.* It provides a good example of the strengths and weaknesses of such a system. My experiences and

*Portions of this chapter are based on Bill Boyarsky's experiences as a political and government reporter and thus are told in the first person.

views are not too different from those of a reporter working in a similar situation in Minneapolis, Louisville, or any other city.

The *Times* is published in the morning, and the only other daily newspaper in Los Angeles, the *Herald Examiner,* comes out in the afternoon. The *Times'* circulation is 1,226,132 on Sundays and 1,036,911 on weekdays while the *Herald's* is only 483,649 on Sundays and 474,020 on weekdays. The size and quality of the *Times* staff so far overwhelms that of the much smaller *Herald* that, in most areas of news, the *Times* is dominant. There are smaller papers, some of them good, in surrounding suburban cities, but their staffs and circulation are so small that their presence is felt only in their immediate area.

The *Times* demonstrates all of the advantages of a monopoly newspaper. Over a decade ago it went through a historic change. In 1961, the Chandler family, which controls the paper, had closed their afternoon paper, the money-losing *Mirror.* The Hearst Corporation had shut down its morning paper, the *Examiner,* and monopolized the afternoon field with its merged *Herald-Examiner.* At about the same time, Otis Chandler succeeded his father, Norman, as publisher of the *Times.* A period of expansion began, with the Washington bureau greatly increased in size, and bureaus opened in other cities and nations. He turned what had been a dull, provincial newspaper into one with national stature.

More than increase the size, Chandler changed the tone of the *Times.* For many years before, the *Times* had been closely involved in California and local government and in the affairs of the Republican party. In the thirties, forties and fifties, California politicians believed that an axis of three newspapers, the *Times,* the *Oakland Tribune*, and the *San Francisco Chronicle* helped establish policy in the Republican party and slanted their news coverage in favor of the Republican candidates. But under Otis Chandler, the political writers were independent. The first election covered by the new *Times* was in 1962 when Richard Nixon unsuccessfully challenged Governor Edmund G. Brown for the governorship of California. The *Times'* political reporters Carl Greenberg and Richard Bergholz trailed both men up and down the state, pointing out in their stories inconsistencies in the candidates' statements. Nixon, since he had spent eight years as

Vice President and had been a presidential candidate just two years before, was unfamiliar with the state and the issues. He was the most inconsistent and ill-informed of the two gubernatorial candidates, a fact that showed up regularly in the *Times'* stories.

The day after he lost, Nixon berated the press in the famous "You-won't-have-Nixon-to-kick-around-anymore" press conference. Nixon praised Greenberg as a fair reporter, much to Greenberg's embarrassment. But many of the newsmen familiar with the campaign felt that Nixon's tirade was, in part, a bitter reaction against the coverage of the *Times,* which had once protected him.

Today, the *Times* continues to permit its political reporters to operate independently of the paper's editorial views. No reporter sits on the board of editors which decides what candidates the paper will endorse. Politicians supported by the *Times* on the editorial page have complained to the editor about what they considered unfair stories on the news pages. Political writers are never expected to favor endorsed candidates in their stories. When they unearth stories damaging to the candidates endorsed by the *Times,* such stories are printed in prominent spots in the newspaper.

The Bad Side of Monopoly

But the lack of newspaper competition in the city has bred evils of a different kind in the coverage of local, political and governmental news. Knowing nobody else is interested, the *Times* pursues local news and local government scandal at too leisurely a pace. Broad areas of government activity can be neglected by editors and reporters who know that the other Los Angeles paper, the *Herald,* or the radio and television stations, with their limitations, will not inquire into them.

In the *Times'* Washington bureau, the editors and reporters read national political and governmental news in *The New York Times* or the *Washington Post.* They are unhappy when other newspapers beat them on a story, and they feel victorious when they are ahead. The reporters know that if the *Washington Post* comes up with a big story, and it is repeated on television, with the *Post* given credit, their editors will ask about it, and *Times* readers will wonder why they did not read it over breakfast.

But the *Times* metropolitan, or local, staff is under no such gun. Rarely does the *Herald-Examiner* or the surrounding suburban papers come up with anything new. When they do, television—relying on the *Times*—usually ignores them. Knowing they will not be beaten by rivals, the *Times'* staff seldom reads other local papers. The only competition felt locally by the *Times* is from television. And because of TV's limited news staffs, it is not competition for individual stories. It is a more subtle competition for the attention of the reader-viewer and for the dollar of the advertiser.

This is true of most aggressive newspapers, monopoly or not. The most creative of today's journalists understand they are in competition with television for the reader's attention, and the only way to succeed is with new forms of newspaper journalism, with stories in the style of magazine articles. That is why the *Boston Globe,* the *Los Angeles Times,* the *Miami Herald,* and other successful newspapers often have the look of magazines.

At the *Times,* readers are given long, in-depth stories about subjects the editors believe are of interest to the Southern California community. They are deliberately written in a lively or dramatic style by reporters chosen as much for their writing ability as their reporting skill. Reporters, themselves, think of many of these stories, and their suggestions are usually accepted by editors who pride themselves on running what is known as a "reporter's paper." As a result, the staff spends long hours on a relatively small number of stories that interest the reporters or editors. The day-to-day run of news is often neglected in favor of a lengthy piece on a single subject.

This means that citizens interested in government reforms are left ignorant of many important government actions. And, knowing *Times* reporters will not be observing routine meetings, members of many boards and commissions feel free to act without much thought of public reaction. Only two reporters cover Los Angeles county government, compared to nineteen in Washington and five in the state capital. Only two covered Los Angeles city government for years, until mid-1973, when a third reporter was added.

This, in turn, affects the presentation of news in Los Angeles on television. For, while the newspaper prints a story first, television's version of the event has the most direct impact. The newspaper's influence is indirect—on television news executives who schedule their own reporters' assignments. In the case of a monopoly newspaper like the *Times,* when it misses a story, the television news executives have no guide to follow. If the *Times* does not cover an event, probably no one will.

Understanding the news situation in a city like Los Angeles, the politician and bureaucrat can adjust to it. Important matters sneak through in government meetings, unnoticed because they are sandwiched between overwhelming amounts of trivia. Operating unnoticed, county supervisors turned over land of unparalleled beauty to favored land developers, doing it in bits and pieces, in actions recorded only briefly in the *Times* and with a few exceptions, untouched by the powerful television stations.

CHICAGO—THE ADVANTAGES OF COMPETITION

No newspapers in the country do a better job in showing up local corruption than those of Chicago, a place where competition is still alive. Chicago has always been unique in American journalism, the great Midwestern city more interested in what is happening within its own boundaries than in the power centers of the East. That might have been because life was more interesting in Chicago, the home of Capone, the mob, and the machine. The city's newspapers produced talented people to describe Chicago, from Carl Sandburg to Mike Royko. Two of them, Ben Hecht and Charles MacArthur, wrote about the city's newspapers in their play, *The Front Page,* which established the image of the reporter as a scruffy, fast-talking fellow who was always kidnapping key witnesses or stealing prized family photographs from grieving widows.

Chicago's newspapers have dwindled to four, but it still has more than any other American city. The *Chicago Sun-Times* and the *Chicago Tribune* compete in the morning; the *Chicago Daily News* and *Chicago Today* in the afternoon. Field Enterprises owns the *Sun-Times* and the *Daily News,* and the *Tribune* owns *Chicago*

Today. But the staffs are separate, and there is genuine competition between all of the papers.

Mike Royko, the *Daily News* columnist, talked to us about it one morning in the small, cluttered office he occupies, separated from the *Daily News'* large city room by a shoulder-high partition. Like most city rooms, the main newsroom of the *Daily News* is a messy reminder of the old days of journalism when employers supplied old typewriters, dilapidated desks and put sheets of rough copy paper in bathrooms for reporters to dry their hands. The reporters treated their surroundings with the disrespect the dirty rooms deserved. Cigarettes were tossed on the floor. Desks were never cleaned.

Today, wages have greatly increased; there is a measure of job security and news reporters tend to be college-educated men and women who want as stable a life, and as good a pension, as anyone else. Working conditions are better. But in the hierarchy of the newspaper business, the city room employees are still the "grunts," the infantrymen who do as they are told by the city editor, who stands over them as if he were an officer. Grunts never achieve the status and pay of editors or correspondents overseas or in Washington. And while most newspapers now supply paper towels in their washrooms, even the best city rooms tend to be littered, noisy and undignified places to work.

Royko seems to be a man who remembers the bad days, who has served his time as a grunt and still retains the admirable quality of viewing with suspicion those above him in rank. Despite the national popularity of his syndicated column, he remains part of the *Daily News'* working staff and a leader in the city room.

Royko told us that competition is the reason for the vigor of Chicago journalism—the reason why muckraking is still popular there. "Exclusives have died out in journalism [elsewhere] but not in Chicago," he said. He believes that television has killed the old-fashioned kind of exclusive—getting the first story of a fire or a murder. Exclusive stories on disasters and crimes were part of an earlier era, when most people heard the news first from the papers. A paper that could break the story of a kidnapping an edition before its competition was money ahead. Radio, and then television, killed competition on police stories as one way for Chicago papers to fight each other for circulation. What remains is fierce competition for another kind of local exclusive—the exposé of government misbehavior.

The tradition of muckraking in Chicago, Royko said, is carried on by city editors trained by muckraking city editors of days past. And that type of reporting is helped by the conduct of the machine and public officials, engaging in activities that are either corrupt or questionable. Chicago papers are blunt in their accusations, often drawing damaging conclusions about public officials that papers in most cities would refuse to publish for fear of lawsuits. But in Chicago, the heat of daily competition forces publishers to be more courageous. "The fact of the matter," explained Royko, "is that it is damn hard to libel people."

In Chicago, reporters use techniques abandoned by their more gentlemanly colleagues in other cities. Chicago newsmen put on disguises, act as undercover agents and take physical risks for stories. In 1970, *Tribune* reporter Bill Jones and William Rechtenwald, an investigator from the Better Government Association, a privately financed watchdog organization, worked as ambulance attendants. Along with other investigators, they found that city-regulated ambulance crews refused to move patients unless they were paid first. Attendants were unqualified; conditions were unsanitary, and equipment inadequate. Ten Chicago policemen, five ambulance company executives, two employees and two companies were indicted as a result of the *Tribune*'s series. Jones was awarded journalism's highest honor, the Pulitzer Prize. He was promoted to *Tribune* city editor and now has between seven and ten investigative reporters and other staff members who move in on major stories. Once a reactionary paper whose stories were shamelessly slanted to reflect the views of the publisher, the late Col. Robert McCormick, the *Tribune* is behaving with integrity and independence. It has the largest investigative staff in the city because it has more reporters than the other papers. But the *Sun-Times,* the *Daily News* and *Chicago Today* all have investigative forces, and some Chicago television news shows employ investigative reporters.

In uncompetitive Los Angeles, only the *Times* has full-time investigative reporters, and it has only two on the metropolitan staff. One member of the Sacramento bureau staff spends the bulk of his time on investigations, and a second Sacramento reporter uses part of his time for investigative work. That is virtually the only journalistic investigative force on the most influential paper of the nation's third largest city. Even worse, no newspaper in the state has as many investigative reporters as the *Times*. In San Francisco, most government exposés are done by the *Bay Guardian*, a small, fortnightly muckraking newspaper. The morning *Chronicle* and the afternoon *Examiner*, while taking occasional in-depth looks at the way the city is run, have no full-time investigative reporters. As a result, these influential papers can usually cover only the surface news of the city.

In the years it has engaged in investigations of local government, the *Los Angeles Times* has uncovered major scandals, winning the Pulitzer Prize in 1968 for disclosures of irregularities in the city's harbor department and in zoning. But if there were other papers doing the same thing, the *Times* would have to allocate more resources to investigative work. Doing exposés takes a tremendous amount of time. It involves countless man hours to check and recheck obscure records, to draw conclusions from columns of hard-to-decipher figures and to scrutinize government contracts worded in nearly incomprehensible jargon. With many reporters working on a single project, their combined efforts would uncover more scandal, incompetence and waste in government. Newspapers can't catch every crook, but exposés serve as warnings to officials who are afraid of being caught.

A Day of Competition

In Chicago, we saw coverage of local government news at its best and most exciting. The vitality of Chicago investigative journalism was in evidence on an early spring day of 1973, in the offices of the Better Government Association. The Better Government Association is financed by businesses and individuals interested in uprooting corruption in Chicago. It was founded forty-eight years ago by ministers who used it to break up speakeasies, a formidable job in Chicago. Over the years, it turned to municipal corruption. Much of the time, it was regarded as a mouthpiece for Republican businessmen trying to break up Democratic control of the city. But today, it has bipartisan support, and the majority of the Republican businessmen in the Loop back Mayor Daley's machine, rather than the Better Government Association, so the GOP taint has faded.

The association employs investigators, who work with the investigative reporters of the Chicago papers. Under the ground rules, the newspaper that cooperates with the association on an exposé is permitted to first print the details exclusively, with the other papers receiving the information later at a press conference. The BGA takes turns working with the newspapers so that each one gets a chance at having an exclusive exposé.

On that spring day, the BGA was holding a press conference to announce the latest in a series of exposés by the association and the *Chicago Sun-Times* on the activities of Alderman Thomas Keane, a friend of Mayor Daley and chairman of the city council's important finance committee. In charge of the press conference was J. Terrence Brunner, the executive director of the BGA. He had been head of the Justice Department's Organized Crime Strike Force in Pittsburgh, the youngest man to head such a group.

Tacked to a display board in back of Brunner were headlines from BGA exposés. They told the story of what had been happening in Chicago:

"How Keane Group Piled Up Profits"

"Tax Breaks Come Easy for Keane Cronies"

"City Land a Bonanza for Keane Combine"

"Keane Called to Face Grand Jury"

The *Sun-Times* had been doing much of the work with the association on this particular story, but the other papers had been following up with investigations of their own. Rivalry was intense.

The competitive atmosphere showed at the morning press conference. Before that meeting, the *Sun-Times* had printed another chapter of the Keane story. But only a few hours after the morning *Sun-Times* came out, the afternoon *Daily News* printed a similar account in its first edition. Although it is an afternoon paper, the *Daily News* puts out its first edition early enough so that morning commuters can buy it on the street on their way to work.

Brunner was aching with strep throat and swallowing penicillin pills, but he still had the energy to be angry at the *Daily News* for what he felt was a violation of the ground rules—not waiting for the release time which would give the *Sun-Times*, as the investigating paper, a chance to print the story first. Brunner believed that the *Daily News* had merely rewritten the *Sun-Times'* story, without waiting for the Better Government Association press conference, in order to have a story for the first edition street sales that would match the one in the *Sun-Times*.

The back of the small room was crowded with television cameras and crews. That pleased Brunner, for one purpose of the press conference was to give television an opportunity to cover the story that had already appeared in the papers. Later in the day, the most enterprising stations would go out and film the real estate from which Keane was alleged to have profited.

As the news conference went on, Charles Nicodemus, political editor of the *Daily News* and author of the disputed Keane story, questioned Brunner sharply on details of the investigation. Brunner seemed to resent his questions. He accused Nicodemus of trying to get more details of Keane's real estate transactions "so you can go back and reinvestigate it and label it your own as you did today." Nicodemus replied, "There was a lot of material in our story that wasn't in the *Sun-Times.*" Brunner renewed his accusation. And Nicodemus, as angry as Brunner, ended the exchange by saying "That's a crock."

Later, Ron Dorfman, who edits the *Chicago Journalism Review*, assessed what competition over local government investigative stories means to the papers and their circulation. The journalism review is a uniquely Chicago institution, a magazine created by young reporters to muckrake their employers. Dorfman told us the *Sun-Times* had planned to use its investigation of Keane as a circulation promotion in its war with the *Tribune*. The *Sun-Times* had been planning to break the Keane story on a Sunday. Dorfman said, "It was because they were raising the price of the Sunday paper, and they wanted a big *do* to get folks over the hump." In other words, the readers, fascinated with a new sensation, would not mind paying the higher price. But the *Tribune* got wind of the story early and published what information it had on Friday. Unfortunately, the *Sun-Times* had already printed vending machine advertising cards that promised, "The Keane Combine Begins Sunday."

The *Sun-Times'* distress over being beaten; Nicodemus' and Brunner's argument; the whir of TV cameras at the Better Government Association press conference; the *Chicago Journalism Review*—all were testimony to the good health of Chicago journalism in covering news of local government. It is a competition badly needed in Chicago for it seems to have an unusual number of questionable officials. But it occurred to us that other cities might well be as corrupt. It was just that nobody ever looked into it. We were reminded of what happened early in this century when Lincoln Steffens visited Los Angeles, just after a municipal scandal had been exposed in San Francisco. Los Angeles has always suffered from blind boosterism, wanting to push scandal under the rug so that tourists and new residents would not be frightened away. For many years, this boosterism governed the city's newspapers, which did not like bad news about Southern California.

Steffens found Los Angeles' leaders smug about the lack of exposés in their own city. "Soon," he wrote, "there was a group of 'knowing' Los Angeles business leaders deploring the conditions of politics and business in San Francisco. Los Angeles was, fortunately, not like that. I thought they were joking.

" 'Wait a minute,' I said. 'I know that you know, and you know that I know, that Los Angeles is in the same condition as San Francisco. The only difference is that San Francisco has been, and Los Angeles has not been, shown up.' "

Without investigative reporters or something like the Better Government Association, how do newspaper readers and television news show audiences know their town isn't another Chicago that, as Lincoln Steffens said, "has not been shown up"?

THE MINOR LEAGUES OF JOURNALISM

Lack of competition and the weakness of publishers are not the only reasons why city hall and the county administration building are not covered as thoroughly as the Pentagon. There are other, more subtle reasons. Much of the blame rests on the hidebound practices of journalism and on the attitudes of reporters and editors toward local government news.

There are as many upward strivers in journalism as anywhere else, young men and women who battle each other for better jobs and wage increases. On their way up, they follow a path laid out generations ago. Beginning reporters are given short, unimportant stories at first and are expected to learn without much instruction. Often, the newcomer begins with coverage of local government. Having learned to meet deadlines and to produce usable copy without guidance, the reporter goes on to other stories. After three or four years, skills in basic techniques are mastered, and the reporter looks for better assignments. With talent, he can advance beyond basic reporting of news. He can carve out a specialty if he has a flair for dramatic or humorous writing, a gift for analysis or a tenacious ability to dig out facts. But only a few are fortunate enough to move into the spotlight. Most plug along for years as journeymen reporters, writing routine stories without high pay or personal glory.

Once the reporter has mastered the techniques of the craft, he—or she, if the employer is one of the rare newspapers which promote women to executive positions—feels impelled to move up. That means becoming an editor. For reporting, like teaching, can be a dead end for those who want an important-sounding title, prestige, and pay increases. If an ambitious reporter wants to remain a reporter he often feels the need to move to a news field that offers more prestige than the local scene. If the specialty is government or politics, the young man or woman maneuvers a transfer to the state capital and from there to Washington. Salaries in Washington are among the highest in news writing. Expense accounts are the most generous. There is an opportunity for travel and making a wide range of contacts, both for news stories and for better job opportunities.

So ingrained is the idea of moving on that editors and reporters wonder about someone who has chosen to remain covering city hall. He soon becomes known as "good old_____." He is referred to in such damning terms as "steady" and "reliable," while younger reporters come along and attract attention with their fast pace, flashy writing styles and consuming ambition.

On some papers, the editors treat their local government reporters well. The editors consult the reporters about news coverage and give them praise and considerable freedom. But even under these favorable conditions, most reporters feel the need to leave a local government assignment because their colleagues consider city hall and state political news "the minor leagues of journalism."

This attitude is almost universal in American journalism. Ms. Jean Packard, a county supervisor in suburban Fairfax County, in Virginia near the District of Columbia, saw it at work in the *Washington Post,* which does a better job than most papers in covering the residential communities outside of the district. "Fairfax County government is kind of low on the totem pole of training," said Ms. Packard. The *Post*'s suburban government reporters want to leave, hoping for a place on the paper's national staff. By the time they learn the intricacies of their assignment, they are promoted. "Generally speaking, I think they are very good," said another supervisor. "But usually, they don't stay more than a year, and it takes six months to learn the lingo. . . . As soon as a new reporter gets here, [the county's public relations man] does his best to brainwash them into thinking the way he thinks the majority of the board sees things." Both supervisors felt the inexperience of the *Post*'s reporters showed in their coverage of suburban government.

Another difficulty is "the loneliness factor." Since few reporters cover local government, those assigned to it work pretty much alone. They are denied the camaraderie and exchange of ideas that are just as important in journalism as they are in the academic or political worlds. Local reporters find themselves facing news sources alone, the object of attack from both sides in a controversy. Instead of encountering several reporters on the attack, the news source meets only one reporter. In addition, the local government reporter, as a member of the community, constantly meets news sources—in restaurants, at parties, or at the supermarket. For the people he writes about, he is as close as the telephone, and calling the reporter at home—evenings, weekends—does not even require a toll call.

In 1971, I was assigned by the *Los Angeles Times* to cover a local election for city council and board of education. I had written about presidential and governorship campaigns, but this was my first experience with local politics for a local paper. At many events, I was the only reporter. A few weeks into the campaign, I was surprised to find myself emerging as a personality in the fight between the candidates. Two neighborhood newspapers carried statements by a city councilman attacking me. On weekends, candidates and their managers telephoned me at home to complain of coverage. When I met new people at dinner parties, the evening invariably ended in a long argument over the quality of the *Times'* coverage of the election. In 1973, a colleague covering a similar election was the target of a hate mail campaign. Constant harassment and the lack of companionship of fellow reporters takes its toll. Covering local political news can be a singularly nasty experience.

Chained to the Desk

But even when the reporters are willing to go out and report the inner workings of government, old-fashioned attitudes of editors can make it impossible. Too many newspapers still suffer from one of journalism's greatest ailments, the dictatorial city editor syndrome. It is hard, looking back on it, to describe the admiration and fear with which I viewed my first city editor, Al Reck of the *Oakland Tribune*. He would not tolerate failure. As a young reporter, I was sent to a hotel, where a physician had been arrested for possession of drugs. The physician was a fairly prominent man, and the police would not permit me or a photographer to go upstairs to the hotel room where he had been caught. I returned to the paper, and reported this to Reck. "Kid," he said (he called everyone "Kid"), "go back to that hotel, and go up to that room, even if you get arrested." I returned and persuaded the police to let me upstairs since I would rather have been arrested than go back to the paper without having seen the physician.

Reck once became mistakenly convinced that the body of a well-known coed murder victim had been found and that the police, for some reason, would not announce it. The police denied it, as did the coroner. The reporter handling the story was so afraid of being wrong, that he went to the morgue and looked at every body. Only when he saw that the coed was not among them would he tell the city editor that the body was not there.

As a boss, he inspired such intense personal loyalty that, on the day he left the paper to retire, the staff stood and applauded. But he was of a time when the editor held unimaginable power over his reporters, the power to capriciously fire, to humiliate with public tongue-lashings, to destroy with degrading assignments or to elevate with prestigious ones.

Because he was a decent man who led by example and through some intangible quality of command, Al Reck did not engage in the commonly practiced cruelties of many old city editors. However, like the others, he had his reporters sit in front of him at desks, as if they were school children waiting for the next assignment. Only his most trusted employees would approach him with ideas for stories, and these were usually rejected. His goal was to have enough reporters in front of him each day so that if a disaster occurred, it would be adequately covered. As a result of his attitude, members of his staff spent much of their time with nothing to do, waiting for a big fire or an exciting murder story. The old city editor's desire to have a fully staffed emergency crew always ready to go made investigative or analytical writing an impossibility—even if the publisher of the newspaper had allowed it.

Today, the old-fashioned dictatorial city editor is vanishing, but his influence lingers on, stifling initiative. Too many newspaper staffs wait around like firemen, instead of going out of the office and mingling with the community. Too many editors still want their reporters in the office, ready for the rare disaster.

This attitude is related to another failing that frustrates the imaginative coverage of local government news. Editors become so preoccupied with the mechanics of putting out their newspapers or assembling the news that they put little thought into the content. I saw how this frustrated aggressive reporting while working at the Associated Press capital bureau in California.

The Associated Press is a cooperative organization of newspapers and broadcast stations. Each newspaper and station pays a membership assessment which helps support the worldwide news-gathering organization. For a comparatively low assessment, these members receive news from around the world. The small paper uses a wire service as a substitute for foreign correspondents and out-of-town bureaus. In addition, each member supplies news and pictures to the cooperative.

The executives of the member newspapers and stations meet frequently around the country to discuss the operations of the cooperative, and we in the Sacramento bureau were often invited to attend. Newcomers to the Sacramento staff went to these meetings with high hopes and fears—hopes for an intelligent discussion of how we could improve coverage of government news, and fears of scathing criticism of our work. The staff soon found out that the fears were unjustified and that the hopes would never be satisfied. Most of the discussion was about the mechanics of newspapering.

A perennial topic was why the stock lists arrived at the papers so late, and explanations about the hours the stock market opened and closed never seemed to satisfy the editors. The other main topic was the arrival times of baseball box scores on the Associated Press wires. There was seldom criticism or praise of government news, although some of the editors did place our stories on page one. After a number of meetings, we were no longer nervous; we realized that too many of the editors were more interested in the mechanics of the wire than the contents of our stories. They had the same attitude back at their own newspapers, concerned with mechanical problems more than with the quality of reporting.

Mechanics—and editors' subjective judgments—explain much of what happens in the press: why one story is featured on the front page, while another is buried inside, and a third is ignored or dropped after the paper's first edition. The competition for space, or for time on the air, dominates discussions in the newspaper city room or behind the scenes in the television newsroom. The reporter fights with his supervising editor for priority treatment of a story. Once convinced by the reporter, the supervising editor must then argue with his superior, the city editor or, in some cases, the managing editor. The person in charge of the local news staff must compete for space with editors who supervise national and foreign news, with the managing editor the arbiter. The final decision is seldom perfect, for the judgment of news is subjective. In this competition, local governmental news often loses out. It bores the editors and is considered less important than Washington news, which is more often put on the front page. Their stories poorly played, local government reporters have another reason for becoming discouraged—a lack of ego satisfaction. And news that is buried in the back of the paper is less likely to be read by most people.

OLD OBJECTIVITY AND
THE NEW INTERPRETIVE REPORTING

Bound by outmoded traditions and rules, reporters each day descend on the community, performing a historically important mission that is as little understood by the public as the activities of the government itself. They pry into people's lives, wonder about the most personal secrets of strangers, and badger officials with questions. And to what purpose?

In reporting political and government activities, the press' job is to serve as a record of daily events, explain in a simple and interesting way the processes of government and expose corruption.

In the last decade or so, the style of government and political reporting has changed. A new type of journalism has come into being since the appearance of Theodore White's *The Making of the President 1960.*

The older syle of "objective" reporting consisted of accounts of what was happening on the surface, the vote counts, the meetings, the speeches, the endless press conferences, all the things that fail to tell the public of the forces actually shaping cities, counties and states. Who were the political campaign contributors and why did they give? Who were the advertising men who designed political campaigns and how did they do it? How did polls and computers measure public opinion, enabling candidates to appeal to a public's innermost hopes and fears? All these were unanswered questions.

To answer such questions, the press has had to learn new

techniques. It has had to forget its previous techniques of merely objectively recording what a political leader said, and begin to interpret what he said—placing today's statements in context with last week's, pointing out changes in position, noting failures to take a position, considering the influence of campaign contributors, party leaders and friends.

At one time the old objectivity had been a welcome addition to American journalism. It first appeared on the wires of the Associated Press in the mid-nineteenth century. Before that newspapers had generally been slanted, often libelous, party presses, and their reporters and editors reflected their biases. As a cooperative organization of many newspapers, the Associated Press had to distribute stories acceptable to all, and adopted a terse, calm style, recording what happened, without comment. As the Civil War approached, Lawrence A. Gobright, the AP's Washington correspondent, summed up his organization's philosophy:

"My business is to communicate facts; my instructions do not allow me to make any comment upon the facts which I communicate. My dispatches are sent to papers of all manner of politics, and the editors say they are able to make their own comments upon the facts which are sent them. I therefore confine myself to what I consider legitimate news. I do not act as a politician belonging to any school, but try to be truthful and impartial. My dispatches are merely dry matters of fact and detail."

For many years, this stood as the governing precept of good journalism. But it was a limited precept, as the press learned in the early 1950s when it covered the speeches of Senator Joseph McCarthy, printing his false charges of Communism as if they were fact. At the end of the McCarthy era, journalists began assessing what they had done, and discovered that their stenographic objectivity had permitted charlatans, thieves and demagogues to operate without fear of exposure. Louis Lyons, for twenty-five years curator of the Neiman Fellowships for newspapermen at Harvard University, wrote that "McCarthy exploited the news convention that what a public man says is news, and the reporter doesn't go in back of the quotation to test its truth. But McCarthy forced the press out of this. It had to come to 'interpretive reporting' to look beneath the surface of the demagogue's claim as to the facts. Slowly it moved into the arena of reporting in more depth, in order to explore and explain the meaning of an event."

Such reporting often puts the press directly in opposition to those running the government, for the reporter must quote a politician and then contradict him with the facts. One of the first local government stories I covered was the 1970 selection of the Los Angeles County district attorney. The previous prosecuting attorney had been elected attorney general of the state, and the law required the five county supervisors to choose his successor. A leading candidate for the appointment was W. Matt Byrne, Jr., who had been U.S. attorney in Los Angeles. (Later Byrne became a federal judge and presided at the Pentagon Papers trial of Daniel Ellsberg and Anthony Russo.) One of the supervisors refused to vote for Byrne because Byrne, while U.S. attorney, had successfully prosecuted a friend of the supervisor for cheating at gin rummy at the Friar's Club, a Los Angeles hangout for show business people. The debate raged among the supervisors, but only in private. None would offer their views at a public supervisors' meeting. The reason for the debate was the importance of the job of district attorney. The district attorney prosecutes business and government crime, as well as other kinds of felonies. Byrne, as U.S. attorney, had shown an interest in prosecuting political and business corruption, and had prosecuted fraud connected with a large land development, a case that county law enforcement officials had been reluctant to tackle. Pro-business supervisors did not want such a man serving as chief law enforcement officer of the county.

It was possible, from private conversations with a dissenting supervisor and from another candidate for the job who was acquainted with the supervisors' discussions, for me to find out what was happening behind the scenes. Publicly, the supervisors said there was no dispute. Privately, they voted, and Byrne could not get a majority. A second choice, a federal judge, was approached. He turned down the job. Finally, a compromise choice was picked in a closed meeting. When his name was brought up publicly, the vote for him was unanimous, and he was introduced as the first and unanimous choice of the board. The judge who had turned down the job, however, willingly told me how he had been approached, who had approached him and the reaction when he rejected the proffered appointment. His statement, plus the statements of others, showed that the supervisors' public deliberations had little relation to what they actually did in private.

Such a glimpse of how government works is rare. It happened only because the city editor was suspicious and was willing to give a reporter enough time and freedom to poke about the county administration building. But suspicion was not enough. Luck was also involved—the luck to find a county supervisor who was feuding with his colleagues and was willing to supply details of secret meetings. His motive was the satisfaction of seeing his colleagues embarrassed by the disclosures and of shedding light on secret practices he felt should be made public.

Investigative stories based on informers and government records are only one way to report what is happening in government.There are public reports and budgets to be read and events, meetings and speeches to be covered. Often it is not easy to make them into interesting news stories, even when the news is important. Morrie Landsberg, who was the bureau chief for the Associated Press capital bureau in Sacramento, California, for almost fifteen years, explained to newcomers on his staff that what happened in the legislature and the state departments was not interesting to those who lived miles away from the capital. He instructed his reporters to stimulate interest by giving their stories excitement, emphasizing the conflict of an event, explaining its meaning to the reader, and putting it in historical perspective. Reporters were to assume their readers knew nothing about the subject and that complicated government jargon had to be explained in a simple manner.

That resulted in a style of journalism reflecting the capital's controversies and pinpointing the heroes and villains. It was not popular with the subjects of the stories, who often disagreed with the reporter's perspective. But Landsberg's attitude was that a news story without excitement and clarity was worthless in explaining the complex workings of government.

Covering the Candidate for
State and Local Office

This type of coverage also caused conflicts with political candidates, who were or wanted to be elected officials. On most papers, political campaigns and government activities are covered separately and by different reporters. By the 1960s, politics were changing as much as styles of journalism. Political managers had new tools, of a sophistication beyond the comprehension of most reporters. At the heart of the technology was a well-known device, the public opinion poll. Computers and behavioral scientists made the poll a formidable weapon.

In the late 1960s, for example, a California firm specializing in managing political campaigns, Spencer-Roberts, was able to prepare an analysis of specific precincts, listing the population, voter registration, average income and education, crime rate, racial mix and the like. The information was obtainable from a variety of sources, ranging from lodge membership lists to the U.S. Census. Then pollsters would be sent into the precincts to ask many questions of a subjective nature, such as "What bothers you most about the United States?" Other questions would be more specific, such as "What is your impression of Candidate X?"

From this, Spencer-Roberts would prepare a profile of an area. Reading this profile, the candidate would get an indication of the type of voters living there, and what they were concerned about. When studies in the late sixties showed voters were worried about crime, student dissent, and racial troubles, candidates managed by Spencer-Roberts all talked about "law and order" and promised to be tough disciplinarians.

Such polls had been used years before, but their use was limited because an analysis was slow and difficult. Once facts were gathered, there was no quick way to put them together meaningfully. But by the 1960s, political managers had begun to use computers to digest the facts; with these machines, they could analyze all the information and produce a precinct profile. By 1970, Spencer-Roberts had improved its technique enough to run a daily poll of carefully selected areas of California, and Spencer-Roberts' candidates, Governor Ronald Reagan and Senator George Murphy, could modify their positions when the polls showed voters' changes of heart.

By 1972, the technology was so sophisticated that different letters could be prepared, appealing to the sentiments of specific groups of voters. The computer could quickly decide which people would get a particular letter. A member of the Knights of Columbus, for example, would get an anti-abortion statement; a voter with a Jewish last name would get one on aid to Israel. Important state and local candidates with big campaign treasuries began to use these tools. In the 1973 Los Angeles mayor's race, both Tom Bradley, the winner, and Mayor Sam Yorty, the loser, sent out a number of these mailings. Computer analyses were also given to filmmakers who used them to prepare persuasive commercials.

The new techniques were no guarantee of victory. Nevertheless, they came to dominate practical political thinking. Political managers, placed in charge of incredibly expensive campaigns, moved toward a philosophy of anything to win. They operated in secrecy, afraid the opposition would learn of the next trick. To insure secrecy, they had to lie to the press and mislead reporters.

It took the press years to catch up with the new technology and the campaigners' new attitudes. In the past, political managers, their candidates and reporters had operated, for the most part, in mutual trust and even friendship. There was a camaraderie about a political campaign—the managers and the press eating and drinking together, traveling on a campaign bus or plane that became a world of its own, with mutual jokes, confidences, memories of campaigns gone by. But the new political campaign showed political reporters what Watergate later taught the rest of the nation— that political managers, candidates and elected officials were to be observed, at best, suspiciously. The Watergate break-in—and all it implied—was nothing more than the new political manager's craft carried to its most perverted extreme.

Political managers and their candidates held public statements in such contempt that they frequently changed them when the computer showed a change of public sentiment. Seeing that was the case, the conscientious political writer decided that it was more important to inform the public about the computer than the public statement. And if it were true that a television commercial would influence voters, it was more important to write about the commercial than a luncheon speech made to three hundred Kiwanians. Candidates complained about this type of coverage. What they wanted to see in the paper was a stenographic account of a speech they had made or the enthusiastic listing of endorsements by influential people. They preferred the old journalism, for the new style was destructive to their new brand of politics. If a news story told the public that a commercial was designed to appeal to their secret hopes and fears, that appeal was made ineffective.

The new methods of journalism permitted the press to tell more about the backroom side of politics and government. But the press cannot accomplish reform by itself. The citizens must take advantage of the new journalism. And if the press of their city is part of the backroom gang, they must learn how to pressure it.

"BANGING THE PRESS"

What the public must do is learn to influence the media to improve its performance and take advantage of the capabilities of responsible newspapers and broadcast stations. One method is a letter to the editor. But even though they are often printed, these letters are often as ineffective as those sent to the President of the United States. They are a safety valve for the paper, a way to allow readers to let off steam.

A better method for citizens to use is "banging the press," a colorful term used by David Garth, a professional political campaign strategist and maker of television campaign commercials. Garth, when he is unhappy with news coverage, calls up the responsible reporter and curses at him. Garth's theory is that if he shouts long and often enough, the reporter will begin to listen, become afraid of having been unfair and give the Garth candidate a better break. But such methods backfire as much as they work and those who too crudely "bang the press" may find that reporters will no longer talk to them.

What is needed is a more subtle method of banging the press. People who want to expose government or spotlight an abuse must first understand the internal workings of their community's newspapers and broadcast stations—who the reporters and editors are, what reporters specialize in government, politics, the environment and the rest. Generally, the press is governed by the same sort of hierarchy throughout the country. But the citizen trying to influence it must understand a simple, but unusual, rule: Often, the most valuable contact is low in the pecking order.

At the top is the newspaper publisher or the station owner or general manager. This person's decisions set broad policy. The publisher often approves editorials and, at best, limits influence to the editorial page. At worst, the publisher meddles in the writing of news stories, dictating their content to suit his political or economic needs. But even the worst dictators lack absolute control, something many people fail to realize. Community activists like to boast of their friendship with a publisher, believing it gives them some special influence in the paper. What they do not understand is that the publisher usually takes no part in the hundreds of smaller decisions that actually shape the content of a paper.

It is more important to know the editor, who is the publisher's agent. On a broadcast station, he might be an executive in charge of news. Often given considerable discretion, the editor shapes the paper on a day-to-day basis. He directly supervises the city editor, who is in charge of daily news, including the coverage of local government agencies. But not even the editor will have much to say about whether a meeting is covered.

The city editor is in charge of daily coverage of local news. He decides if a meeting will be covered. Once it has been covered, he will decide if the story is important. If he feels it is, he will recommend it to the managing editor or the editor for good display. Citizens trying to influence a newspaper should make it a point to visit the city editor so that he becomes acquainted with them and their group. In that way, when they send the newspaper a notice of a meeting for publication or suggest that a potential scandal might be investigated, the city editor will know them and, quite possibly, trust them. On a television or radio station, the news director or assignment editor performs the function of a city editor.

The person at the bottom, the reporter, is often the most important contact for a citizen activist, particularly if the newspaper or broadcast station permits independent news coverage without interference from the publisher or advertisers. On such newspapers, reporters are encouraged to initiate stories. Investigative reporters welcome tips and are pleased to develop them into stories.

Once the public understands how the press works, they can bring information to the attention of papers and stations, not as rumors or gossip, but as research products. Responsible, well-edited newspapers are always in search of a good story. But even the best are limited by time, staff, and space. Ralph Nader's effectiveness stems from his own well-documented investigations and his use of the print and electronic press to promote his exposés. Community groups fighting city hall would do well to emulate his methods. In every community, there are men and women who can search records, interview sources, and build a dossier of corruption, indifference, or neglect. As the next chapter will show, officials' conflicts of interest can be tracked down through campaign contribution lists and government contracts. Once information is located, checked and written down, the citizen group can approach a reporter or editor who is responsible for that type of news. That is why it is important to know the reporters who cover specific areas, to know the city editor, to have a knowledge of how the community paper or station works.

In Los Angeles, residents of a community near the beach used the press effectively in fighting a plan by the Occidental Petroleum Corporation to test drill for oil on the beach near Santa Monica Bay. They organized into a group called No Oil and mustered the neighborhood's resources—housewives, attorneys, whoever could help. They used the courts and engaged in political campaigns. But one of No Oil's most effective weapons was to mobilize the press. The group did it by investigating hidden ties between the petroleum company, Mayor Sam Yorty, the city council, and the planning commission. Tirelessly sifting through city records, volunteers documented many questionable aspects of how the city granted permission to drill. They compiled a convincing dossier, researched by people who were not journalists but possessed the time, intelligence, and common sense required to go through public documents. At times, these citizens were ignored by the press, but they persisted, always on the lookout for reporters who would be interested in such stories. They found them at the *Times,* on smaller papers in surrounding communities, and on major television stations. On their own time, the reporters would not have been able to do the basic research. When the research was given to them, they could build on the citizens' investigations. It was the same sort of role played by the Better Government Association in Chicago.

Not every newspaper is receptive to public pressure. In some cities, the paper is as much a part of the backroom structure as any land developer. And while the Federal Communications Commission imposes minimum standards for public service on television, there is no way to force an irresponsible monopoly newspaper to serve its community as it should. But often the press is willing to listen. Shortcomings the public think are deliberate are more often the result of a lack of time, space, or staff. In such cases, it is possible for well-organized citizen groups to become allies of the press and focus attention on the activities of government.

12

A Few Who Have Succeeded

How to organize politically is a major subject of this book. As we explored the political system at the lower levels of government, we found instances when citizens succeeded in making officials responsive. In this chapter, we will describe the tactics they used. Sometimes they were able to beat more powerful influence groups at their own sophisticated political games, using less money. In other cases, they were effective when they used the rude tactic of confronting a politician with the responsibility for a decision—the reasons behind it as well as its consequences.

More citizen reformers are needed. In our look at state and local government, we traveled from California to the District of Columbia. Wherever we went, we could see the need to return the control of community government to those it was intended to serve. People were angry at the decline in the quality of life in metropolitan America, a decline that had continued through Democratic and Republican administrations in Washington. Despite his immense power, the President—no matter who he was— could do little to save things in the neighborhoods around the country. He could deal, to an extent, with the issues of war and peace. He could promote domestic policies that could influence the economy or the environment. But the countless problems of everyday life—of garbage, sewers, police protection, transportation, zoning, air pollution—were beyond his control.

Across the country, there is evidence that some citizens are beginning to realize the power of the level of government closest to them. They are placing the blame for the destruction of their way of life where it belongs—on the officials who make countless seemingly unimportant local decisions. As a result, people are beginning to seek a role in the obscure process of home rule. It could be seen in the suburban governments miles from the scandal-stricken federal buildings at the nation's capital. Middle-level bureaucrats returned home from dead Washington offices to spend their evenings working on county political campaigns. Citizen reformers were taking over offices formerly held by land developers and their friends.

And in Los Angeles, later that summer, we saw another kind of beginning. We drove along the scenic highway at the crest of the Santa Monica Mountains to view a canyon where local government is planning one of the sanitary landfills described in Chapter Seven. It was discouraging to think of what this meant to the people living here. They had saved their money to move out of the crowding, dirt, crime, and noise of the city—only to end up watching garbage trucks every day.

We viewed the proposed garbage dump site and were returning to our car when we noticed a woman watching us from her front yard. We spoke with her and learned that Dolores Wolfe was a walking encyclopedia of that dump. She had been fighting it for years, alone some of the time and now with the help of her neighbors. The information spilled out, torrents of it, sad stories of useless trips to city hall and lost battles with arrogant officials. Later in the year, as our research drew to a close, she and her neighbors had organized for the fight, hiring a lawyer. They had located another group of homeowners—miles away in another area—with an identical problem. In close communication, they made sure bureaucrats didn't succeed in pitting one part of the community against the other, as had been done in the past. They were preparing for the legal battle that was their last hope of saving their neighborhoods.

In the awakening of people like Ms. Wolfe, we found that democracy is alive in America, much to the discomfort of state and local officials who have had things their way too long. Democracy is alive in the growing number of citizen groups who sit over coffee or drinks after work and plot their respectable revolution, their takeover of city hall or the county administration building.

Our purpose in writing this book was to help prepare for the fight by describing the system and illustrating how it works—and, more important, by showing that it's not impossible to beat it. The following are some of the ways it has been done:

FIGHTING THE POLITICAL CLIQUE WITH YOUR OWN ORGANIZATION

Around the country, most citizen groups who have forced politicians to listen to them have one thing in common. It is organization—permanent organization. The failures also have something in common. They are temporary and fall apart once the immediate crisis is over. But when professionals are hired by big business and big labor, they persist until the fight is won. They are there long after citizen volunteers have disbanded in the false belief that their victory is something more than temporary.

The need for leadership, permanence, and long- and short-range goals is illustrated by the story of two strongly motivated citizen groups. One failed, the other succeeded.

As inflation became worse in the spring of 1973 and meat prices soared, two housewives in the San Fernando Valley of Los Angeles proposed citizen action in the form of a meat boycott. The goal was to pressure government into doing something about inflation. They announced their plan to local television, radio stations and newspapers, and it caught on. Network television and national wire services picked up the idea. To a nation fuming over the cost of living, the one week boycott was a perfect form of protest—unlike picketing or passing petitions, it was uncontroversial and easy to do. The boycott was a success, with widespread participation, focusing attention on the problem and actually lowering meat prices in some areas.

But when the week ended, the movement died. It failed because the group had no long-range strategy, other than the boycott; and it failed to use the week's enthusiasm to create an organization that would force the government to change its policies of inflation control. The meat boycott group could have united with others critical of the administration's economic policies, such as the AFL-CIO. A coalition of organizations could have presented a strong lobbying front. But boycott leaders lacked know-how, persistence, a workable long-range strategy, permanent organization and most important, a goal they could achieve. Inflation is too complex to be cured by such a crusade.

In contrast to the failure of the meat price protesters is the work of a tightly organized grassroots group in Chicago, the Citizens Action Program or CAP. Chicago, unique in so many ways, originated a way for citizens to force government to improve life around them. CAP uses this formula, which is a simple, but effective one. The technique developed west of the Chicago stockyards, in the late 1930s, when the late Saul Alinsky taught the divided Slovaks, Poles, Lithuanians, and Bohemians who worked in the yards that they could obtain higher wages and better conditions if they worked together. Led by Alinsky, workers confronted bosses, embarrassed city officials with noisy protests, and engaged in boycotts.

CAP's techniques of using facts to expose government and business misbehavior and confronting officials with them will be discussed later. What is important here is that these tactics are carried out by CAP's well-structured organization.

It draws its membership from the white, working-class neighborhoods in Chicago, and is one of several such activist groups in the city. CAP has a few paid staff workers, a nucleus of community organizers trained at Alinsky's Industrial Areas Foundation Training Institute. They are assisted by a handful of part-time student workers. Among other duties, this group of CAP leaders trains volunteers recruited from the neighborhood in confrontation techniques. The task of raising money goes to the volunteers, who hold fund-raising events to finance the organization's $70,000 a year budget. All of the money comes from the neighborhoods that benefit from CAP's crusades.

One example of the group's effectiveness can be seen in the Anti-Crosstown Coalition, which CAP put together. It grew in reaction to Mayor Daley's desire to build another freeway to go with the ones he had already given to the city: the Dan Ryan, named after an old Chicago politician; the Adlai Stevenson; and the John F. Kennedy. This one would be the last in the network of expressways Richard Daley wanted for Chicago. The cost was estimated as high as $2.2 billion, and the destruction to old, solid residential neighborhoods would be awesome—3,470 homes and other residential units; 10,400 people forced to search for new lodgings; razing of buildings in which 6,500 people worked; destruction of parks, schools and churches. Although the city would pay those displaced the market price of those homes, it was doubtful they could find comparable values in the city of Chicago. Stable, middle-class neighborhoods are in short supply in big cities.

"A great thing for our city and our people," said the mayor. A great thing for business, too. The city, for example, was studying whether to finance, through the sale of revenue bonds, the development of an industrial park on six hundred acres just east of the expressway. Industries would be interested in this land once it was provided with the new transportation artery.

Since the mayor was at the top of Chicago government and in control of all the layers below him, it was difficult to foresee why the crosstown expressway would not be built, just as the others were before it. Since the American freeway has had an inevitability about it—from the first request by the chamber of commerce, to the eager agreement of the engineers, to the ribbon-cutting and the first traffic jam—opposition usually has come only from those unfortunates living in its path. These victims saw the coming freeway in the light of their own predicament—the destruction of a family home, the loss of a neighborhood park, the tearing down of the parish church. Although they were angry, there were never enough of them for effective political action.

But in 1973, several years after the freeway had been announced, it still had not been built. Under CAP's leadership, the neighborhoods had rebelled, and while Mayor Daley might win in the end, the people had on their side the governor of Illinois and were getting help from the state's two United States Senators.

CAP had organized the separate neighborhoods by locating other community groups opposed to the crosstown; communication was carried on mostly through Catholic churches. These groups joined with CAP in the Anti-Crosstown Coalition. In the

1972 election, the coalition supported Daniel Walker for governor, over the incumbent, Richard Ogilvie. Walker opposed the freeway; Ogilvie's administration wanted to build it. Walker won, and so did another opponent of the freeway, Senator Charles Percy.

Both Percy and Walker would have won without the support of CAP's coalition. But in the politicians' account books, support like that provided by the coalition is listed as a debt, and it is helpful to be a creditor to a politician. When he took office, Governor Walker blocked the freeway, and when Mayor Daley went to Congress for help, Senator Percy spoke up for the neighborhoods, as did the other U.S. Senator from Illinois, Adlai Stevensen III. The unbeatable Daley machine had met a new, home-grown political force that knew how to make itself heard.

How do you organize to beat the system? Every community situation takes a different kind of strategy. It has to fit the talents of its leaders, the capacity of volunteers, the resources available. But, like CAP, most successful, permanent community organizations are a blend of paid staff employees and hard-working volunteers. The staff does not have to be large. A group trying to affect local government's policies could hold fund-raising events so it could pay one or two of its members—housewives, students, or others with available daytime hours for essential jobs that will be described more fully later in the chapter: appearing at government meetings and hearings or researching government records that, as a rule, are only available during regular weekday office hours.

Why are paid staff employees needed?

The opposition—special interests who control the invisible layers of government—is on the job every day, with paid lobbyists, researchers and attorneys. It is difficult for even the most highly motivated volunteer to match that sustained effort. As anyone who has ever done volunteer work knows, giving such time costs money—gasoline, parking, postage, office supplies, baby-sitters, restaurant lunches. In addition, those regularly donating their time begin to realize that for a little more effort they could be earning money. Another discouragement is that time given free is frequently not valued by those who make use of volunteers. More often than not, their work is wasted on useless activities. All of these disadvantages cause a high dropout rate among unpaid volunteers.

Another requirement for a successful group is talented leadership—a rare commodity. CAP gets its paid community workers from the Alinsky institute. These professionals are trained by the institute to go out and use Alinsky's techniques in community and labor groups all over the country. What they possess is an understanding of issues, a talent for enlisting and motivating volunteers, an understanding of the complexities of a political campaign.

Aside from permanent organization and the right leader, there must be an issue of importance to many people. Everyone has a grievance against the government. Sometimes it is so small that it is important only to a family, or one member of that family. A disagreement with the Internal Revenue Service about whether a trip to Miami was an allowable business expense is of interest to the traveler and the federal government, but not to others. A successful citizens movement must be founded on an issue of general interest—the need for more parks; a desire to check the runaway power of a government agency; a plan to make a legislature repeal a giveaway to big business. Short-range goals can be included, too: upgrading a neglected school, getting a traffic light for a dangerous intersection. Part of CAP's success in motivating volunteers is that it focuses on issues that are close to the community and that can be won. Each short-term victory sustains the group and gives it the energy to continue.

Once an issue is chosen and an organization is set up, one or a combination of the following tactics can be used to hassle state and local officials.

THE POLITICS OF THE BALLOT BOX

One effective way to make an elected official respond to your demands is to offer proof that you and your group are a threat to him on election day. Obviously, appearing at the polls and voting against him every four years won't accomplish this—especially if you are one of an unorganized minority. But with a well-organized group, the odds are changed. Aside from your own organization, you need persuasive evidence of enough votes at the grass-roots level to represent a real threat. You can, as CAP did in challenging the crosstown expressway, use a coalition of organizations to gain sufficient vote strength. Even an official who is heavily influenced by special interests will react to the fear of losing his office, as the following story shows.

California state Senator Hugh Burns was an old man who had been in the legislature more than thirty years, and only those he had known a long time were trusted enough to share his liquor and confidences in his office—four or five senators, three or four lobbyists. Among them was Danny Creedon of the breweries and loan companies and Al Shults of the oil companies. Another was a bear-like man whose face was as cynical and battered by time and excess as that of Burns himself. His name was James Garibaldi, although people called him Judge because he once served on the bench. He abandoned the judiciary for a more profitable calling, representing the liquor companies and the racetracks as their lobbyist.

Not a large group. But in the late sixties it was enough to run the Senate in the most populous state in the nation. The lobbyists controlled Burns, a few senators close to him, and enough of the others to prevent the passage of any legislation that would hurt their clients. No matter how many people signed petitions or wrote letters to their legislators, the decision was made in Burns' office by the men who regularly sat around on the comfortable couches and chairs.

Senator Richard Dolwig was one of the group. He was an attorney from San Mateo County, a suburb south of San Francisco, along the shore of the bay. That shoreline was mostly mud flats and shallows. It was not beautiful, but it was a rare sanctuary for wildfowl and bird lovers. The companies that owned the land wanted to fill it in and build houses, hotels and industrial plants. Senator Dolwig supported them and, as is often the custom in the legislature, profited from his beliefs. A few years before, Dolwig had introduced a bill creating a government district, which made it easier for developers to fill in a part of the shoreline for a residential development. With the subdivision built, attorney Dolwig was now its counsel.

With his connnections, Senator Dolwig was assumed to be able to kill any bill he did not like by mentioning his preference in Senator Burns' office. In 1969, the bill he wanted to defeat was one supported by those trying to save the San Francisco Bay shoreline. It would impose controls on filling of the bay and on construction along its shore. In the past, conservationists had never won, and Dolwig was not worried about beating them this time. Judge Garibaldi was working with him on this one. He had been retained by the Leslie Salt Company, one of the largest owners of shoreline land.

But this time Burns' friends lost. Neither the Judge nor anyone else could help Dolwig resist the political attack of a group of well-organized citizen activists in his district. They presented him with something a senator listens to—persuasive evidence that they had a political organization strong enough to beat him in an election. Instead of the futile task of writing letters, this group had offered Senator Dolwig a proposition as old as politics: vote our way or you lose. These citizens made their demand in a full-page ad in a local paper. Dolwig and his pals had to listen. They knew the reputation of the group—and feared it. They were the same volunteers who had organized support at the grassroots level—much of it from housewives—in a doorbell-pushing campaign that elected Pete McClosky to Congress over the better-financed Shirley Temple. His upset victory and the role of the volunteers had attracted widespread publicity, and a book, *The Sinking of the Lollipop*, was written about the campaign and the strategies used by the large corps of enthusiastic precinct workers. They harnessed the membership of established organizations, marched precincts, telephoned voters, and, most important, made good use of the lowest level of volunteer campaign workers.

That is why, one surprising afternoon, Senator Dolwig called reporters together in the Capitol and announced he had a new proposal. It was a complete turnabout. He was supporting legislation for strong controls to prevent bay filling. By the end of the legislative session, the control bill was signed by Governor Reagan.

FIGHTING SECRECY WITH INFORMATION

Facts are essential ammunition in the battle for influence in government decisions. Evidence of corruption or neglect is often hidden in government records, but it takes time and determination to dig out the information. This is another reason that it is necessary to have a paid staff for research. Regular employees will provide continuity and follow through in researching government records.

Without facts, a protester can easily be dismissed as a nut. Confronted with incontrovertible facts, a public official is forced to answer. This can be seen in the skilled and thorough research that is one of the tools of Chicago's CAP organization. Bookshelves along a wall in its small basement office are filled with the results of its work.

CAP workers, for example, suspected that the Cook County assessor, P. J. Cullerton, was not levying high enough property tax assessments on politically well-connected businesses. If this were true, it would mean that other government services were being deprived of needed tax support. Citizens often suspect their local assessor of favoring business. Proving it is difficult, but CAP's paid staff of researchers dug through public records until it had the facts. They obtained records of how much five racetracks were being assessed. Then, searching documents on file at the Illinois Racing Board, they calculated the market value of the tracks' facilities. Applying the assessor's publicly announced standard, the CAP researchers learned how much the tracks should have been assessed. It released this information to the press in a detailed presentation full of indisputable facts.

CAP's exposé said, "With schools and other public services strapped for funds, Cullerton's underassessments of Hawthorne and Sportsman's Park racetracks is directly responsible for cheating the people of Stickney and Cicero out of needed public services. The Berwyn-Cicero-Stickney High School District alone lost $109,471 in 1970 alone—enough to hire an extra eleven teachers. Cullerton's favoritism allowed $106,117 to go into the pockets of wealthy racetrack owners (including prominent politicians) that would have gone to the Cicero Elementary School District." This information—obtained by computing how many tax dollars the two school districts would have received if Cullerton followed his promised formula—made the presentation a news story. Vague allegations would have been useless. The irrefutable figures and resulting publicity forced Cullerton to make the racetracks' tax assessments more equitable.

Public records are a citizen reformer's greatest ally. But few people know how to use them. Any well-informed person can dig up useful information from public records, if willing to put up with uncooperative clerks, hard-to-find offices, and complex and disorganized records. Sometimes public officials try to discourage the use of such records. For example, until recently in Los Angeles County, when someone wanted to examine campaign contribution lists of the county supervisors, he was required to give his name, address, the agency he represented and reason for examining the records. The inference was that an unaffiliated citizen without an official reason had no right to the lists. The names of those looking at the campaign records were sent to the head of the supervisors' board each week, so that he would know who was digging into their past. It was a not-very-subtle form of intimidation.

A researcher must know he has the right to examine public records, and he must understand what kinds of documents are available. They vary from city to city and from state to state. But in general documents that are available and useful to citizens include:

> The files of planning commissions. The planning commission usually makes the first decision on how land will be used—whether houses, apartments, parks, service stations, factories or stores will occupy a piece of property. The planning commission's decision is usually ratified by the governing board of a city or county. In the planning file are kept all zoning information, zoning variance requests, inspection records, permits and other written reports pertaining to use of the property. The file can provide a wealth of information on a controversial project.

> Reports of campaign contributions. These important documents can be found in the offices of the secretary of state, county clerk and other elections officers, and they provide evidence of the influences on elected officials. But unless a state or county law is particularly

specific, these reports give only the names of donors, and only sometimes the amounts of the contributions. Usually they do not list an essential fact—the nature of the donor's business. This must be obtained from other sources, generally by making inquiries around the community, following up addresses or other clues that might be included on the contribution lists. How to use this information will be discussed later.

Records of corporate ownership. These, kept usually by the state agency regulating corporations, provide evidence of business affiliations of campaign contributors. If a contributor is an officer of a firm doing business with a government agency or is regulated by it, these documents can back up charges of impropriety.

Votes of government bodies. These may be difficult to obtain because many such bodies, like legislative committees, do not record votes. If they are to be found, they will be in minutes of meetings of city councils or county supervisors, in journals of state legislatures, or in newspaper accounts.

Reports of grand juries. In California and some other states, grand juries investigate local government for impropriety and waste. Generally, their reports are available for the asking from the county grand jury office.

Government budgets and financial reports. These are usually available from the agency involved.

Records of loans and mortgages. If a public official is suspected of corruption, look at the records of his loans and home mortgage. This information is usually available in the hall of records or other county offices. If a public official suddenly pays off a mortgage or buys an expensive house, it might be worthwhile to investigate his background further.

Property tax assessment. If businesses or individuals are suspected of getting tax breaks, it's a good idea to look up their property tax assessment. This would be available at the county assessor's office. To find the information, you must know the address of the property you're investigating.

Newspapers. These provide background information and are valuable records of officials' public statements. Most newspapers' clipping libraries are closed to the public. But public libraries keep newspapers and microfilms of back copies on file. Except for *The New York Times,* few are indexed, and it is a tedious job to dig through back copies for specific information. But in the one or two months before an election, the papers generally contain full statements by candidates on the issues. Rather than reading all the newspapers during an official's term, start by reading the paper for the two months prior to his last election. Weekly neighborhood or ethnic newspapers should also be checked, for often a candidate will say one thing to one paper and something else to another. The organization's staff should also keep its own clipping file, another reason for paid help. Clipping is a tedious job requiring more commitment and consistent follow-up than most volunteers can give.

Reports of state legislative investigations. These might be on file at a public library. Or the main branch may have a listing of what legislative investigation reports are available, and often they can be obtained through inter-library loan from the state library. They can also be requested by mail from the committee that performed the investigation.

Most of the groups described in the rest of this chapter used some or all of these research materials as background for their techniques, whether they involved defeating someone in an election, lobbying, or confronting and embarrassing an official.

THE POLITICS OF
CONFRONTATION AND EMBARRASSMENT

Often, influencing government decisions can be unpleasant work. The masters of confrontation are groups like CAP, using Alinsky's method of marching on the official's office, backed up by a hundred or so mean-looking fellow volunteers. One or two CAP leaders do all of the talking at such a demonstration. The others are well-disciplined CAP members who are instructed to say nothing. The organization feels that too many spokesmen confuse the issue.

A typical example of this was their treatment of a corporate official whose factory was smoking up the neighborhood. As the army of silent CAP volunteers crowded into the office, one of the spokesmen inspected the executive's tailoring. "That's a nice suit," the CAP leader said. "You must make a lot of money." He also commented on the expensive office carpets and furnishings. With those preliminary remarks, he went on to ask why such a wealthy company couldn't afford filters on its smokestack. Whether or not the incident would get the desired results had to be seen, but the factory official was visibly nervous and intimidated. CAP often uses the same methods on local government officials. But one of the organization's community workers told us that not everyone has the stomach for CAP's methods and that they have no room for "liberals" who, he felt, tend to be squeamish about confrontation techniques.

Is such militancy productive? It is in Chicago for CAP. And there is reason to think it would work in other places. We talked to a young county official in California who had been disillusioned with the democratic process as it works at the local level. He had seen neighborhood groups lose repeatedly when they tried to fight decisions of county supervisors. In the end, he concluded, citizens had to revise their tactics, and the only way to win was by "the politics of embarrassment."

"Inexperienced people come in and they think that by speaking to the issues, that's how to present their point of view," he said. "They don't realize they have to probe, question and embarrass officials. You have to put them on the spot." It is necessary to confront them armed with facts from the public records, as discussed in the previous section. He described one woman who, in dealing with a planning commissioner at a public meeting, pointed her finger at him and said, "I think it's in the public interest for the public to know where your holdings are in the valley." Before she confronted the official, she had investigated his land holdings in the area where he was making planning decisions.

"That takes a certain toughness that comes only when you've been through this time and time again," he said. "The point is, when the stakes are small, people can win by being nice. When they're big, people have to get organized to the point where they are willing to make themselves obnoxious and even willing to take risks of libeling somebody. Because only by—and I hate to say this—this isn't the way our system is supposed to work—but only by using political means can they sensitize these guys and make their presence really known and counted because they're up against all kinds of money." This can be hard to sustain. The woman who confronted the official with his land holdings was gaveled into silence by the presiding officer. But it forced officials to face facts they would otherwise have ignored. And it attracted public attention to the cause.

REVERSING THE INFLUENCE OF CAMPAIGN CONTRIBUTIONS

Elected officials tend to be skittish about revealing who their campaign contributors are. This is because they would prefer that voters not understand that there is a relationship between government decisions and the people who pay money to keep a politician in office. We talked to one neighborhood leader who was battling a decision of her city council. When it was suggested that she look up campaign contributors to the council members who had cast the offending votes, she was surprised. She mentioned the names of several council members and said she knew they were honest men who couldn't be bought. That may have been true. But what she failed to realize was that political donations buy access and a sympathetic ear to big business lobbyists' arguments. Such contributions are not illegal. But, as we saw in Chapter Five, politicians would like to keep the identity of their contributors quiet. They prefer that constituents not know that the people who pay for political campaigns often get direct benefits from the investment. When this relationship is exposed, politicians are afraid it will appear that they have been bought.

We could find few cases where citizens had used campaign finance information to their own advantage. But when a populist TV newsman, Baxter Ward, was elected to the Los Angeles County Board of Supervisors in 1972, he attempted to spotlight the relationship between the other supervisors' political donors and the board's decisions. Ward himself had accepted no donation over $45 to his own campaign.

There is no reason why an individual—armed with the kind of research information gathered from the sources described earlier in the chapter—could not use Ward's system. His staff color-coded index filing cards for the other four supervisors. On the cards, they put the name of contributors who had given in each official's most recent election. Further research, in most cases, uncovered the identity of the firms they worked for and what they wanted from county government. It might be a county contract, a franchise for a service regulated by the county, a zoning exception or a smog control variance. Connections between individuals and the firms they represented were traced down by looking in a *Los Angeles Times* publication, "The Roster of California's Leading Companies," which lists their officers. Brochures put out by publicly held corporations also listed people who represented the companies. In the case of lobbyists or lawyers representing clients, inquiries around the community revealed the connection.

Jeanie Kasindorf described Ward's system in *Los Angeles Magazine:* "As the cards were typed and alphabetically filed, a pattern developed. The cards showed that often one company blanketed the County's elected officials with a $500 or $1000 contribution to each man's campaign. From January through April Baxter [Ward] read off contributions [at supervisors meetings] from architects, appraisers and health center owners as they got County contracts." Ward admitted the confrontations were unpleasant.

"Once you did it you knew how rough it was going to be. But you just gritted your teeth, looked down at the card, and read. It was very awkward."

In public, the supervisors tried to discount the idea that the contributions had bought anything. They claimed that a campaign manager had handled the money and that they, as candidates, had been ignorant of who their supporters were. But sometimes they were so embarrassed that they reconsidered their votes. In one case, an unincorporated area was about to vote on becoming a city. The residents' motivation was that their neighborhoods were becoming overdeveloped under the planning policies of the county supervisors. By incorporating, they would gain control over their own city planning. A few days before the incorporation election, the supervisor from their district pushed through an emergency ordinance—taking effect immediately—that would have permitted a cluster of condominiums in the area. It was the very thing the homeowners were trying to stop. Ward revealed publicly that the condominium developer's attorney had contributed $5,000 to the supervisor's campaign. The story ran on the front page of the *Los Angeles Times* for two days. The publicity forced the supervisor who had introduced the emergency ordinance to abstain from voting on it. It failed to pass, allowing local residents to decide the fate of the condominiums.

Citizens who suspect elected officials of consistently voting against their constituents' interests will find contribution lists a gold mine of information. But, lacking time and manpower, individuals might dispense with Ward's file card system and simply look up contributors who benefit from a few decisions or a single one. Armed with facts, they can appear at public meetings and ask to be heard. Or they can publicize the information through the press.

USING THE PRESS

Losing out to those with more influence in the competition for government's favors, citizen groups have to find extraordinary methods of forcing elected officials to be more responsive. One method is to use the press to publicize a group's position and the information it has obtained by research.

Dealing with the media is a puzzling experience for those unfamiliar with it. Few people understand why a newspaper or broadcast station covers a particular story or how the story is printed in the paper or sent out on the air. The process—described in Chapter Eleven—is not complicated. What is harder to figure out is how to interest an editor or reporter in a story. Hardest of all is sustaining that interest. A single story is a morale booster to volunteers—it may even embarrass a local official. But consistent follow-up and daily news headlines spotlighting government activities are weapons that are hard to equal. They are also hard to get.

Those who are able to use the media regularly have usually spent years building up credibility with news executives and reporters. In Southern California, a woman with little previous experience in hassling government undertook the role with a masterful use of the media. The results were outstanding. Ellen Stern Harris of Beverly Hills, like most citizen reformers, started with an issue of interest only to her immediate neighborhood, battling city government when it refused to trim the trees on her street. Moving into broader issues, she formed her own conservation group, keeping interested people informed about the activities of government through her monthly newsletter.

When Ms. Harris began her lonely conservation battles, not many people knew her. But she worked hard to meet reporters who were becoming involved in the newly developed specialty of environmental writing. She got to know editors of newspapers. She called reporters on the telephone. Her name became known. Most important, she supplied the reporters with accurate tips for stories and leads to sources of more information that often produced good stories. Her tone was always unimposing, and if a reporter didn't think her idea merited a story, she took it in good grace.

After a few years of this work, she found herself in a unique position for a citizen activist. She was appointed to the regional water quality board by Governor Brown. As a member of a policy-making board, she thought she would be able to put her ideas into action. But she found her power was limited. She had expected to be serving on the board with people who were interested in cleaning up Southern California's water, especially the badly polluted Los Angeles Harbor. "Instead I found a Board set up by law to protect the interests of polluters. Conflict-of-interest was mandated right into its very structure, to insure that there would always be a five to two majority to protect the interests of present and prospective polluters and to preserve a deplorable status quo."

Her one vote failed to influence board policies. As a result, Ms. Harris resorted to another tactic. Using the personal contacts she had built up with the press, she devoted her energy to publicizing the issue. She alerted reporters to meetings that would give them stories. She got experts to testify that the harbor was badly polluted and that it could be corrected. She set up a weekend symposium on water quality "to lay the case before the public." She set up a coalition of interested organizations, and she encouraged gadflies to attend the water board's meetings, which she managed to change to evening sessions so the public could come. Most important, she made sure the press knew what was happening and covered it.

Because of the publicity, big industry's representatives on the water board were pressured into cracking down on pollution. Regulations were tightened up and enforced. As a result of Ms. Harris' work, Los Angeles Harbor was cleaned up, and the wildlife that had been killed off began to return.

Ms. Harris' skill in using the media makes her a special case. More typical is the experience of Leonard Levine, the smog fighter in Chapter Ten. He found that as an unknown citizen it was nearly impossible to get stories in the paper. At best he felt that a story in the paper might focus attention on his cause for one day, but could give little help in his long-range battle. "But," he said, "what the media will do is unite you with somebody out there who hopefully can help you. Just reading about something doesn't do anything. You have to convert to action."

If he called the paper or sent in material, sometimes it was used for a story. But, more often than not, he was ignored. He found his access was limited because reporters and editors didn't know his name. He concluded, "The media is used to getting information from people in government agencies who normally make press releases—creditable sources of information. So they will respond and take information from them. I've called up local newspapers and I've tried to give them information. Now, I'm a completely unknown individual. You don't have any credentials, so you have to represent an organization—a reputable one. [If you don't] you have to either make a splash, where you have a demonstration and get the media down, or you create controversy and draw attention to yourself."

If the local press is responsive, and a citizens group decides it's worth the effort, it can designate a member of the group as its press representative, a job best held by a paid staff employee, who will be more likely to be available than a volunteer. There are several methods for communicating with the news media, but if they are to succeed, they must be preceded by the same sort of careful cultivation engaged in by Ms. Harris. It helps to meet the reporters who cover your organization's cause or the level of government involved, and it helps to know the editors they report to.

The most commonly used method of giving out news is the news release, or "a handout." But such printed material sent out by mail is probably the least effective way to disseminate a story. Dozens of these releases come across newspapermen's desks each day, and a handout is likely to be ignored, unless editors have been alerted that it is coming, know the organization sending it, and are convinced of the news release's significance. The release takes the form of a typed sheet, written like a news story; it is a summary of what the group wants to say. It should be on letterhead stationery with the name, address and telephone number of the person who prepared it, in case the reporter has questions.

Another method of contacting the media is to call a press conference, inviting reporters from television and radio stations and the newspapers. But this, too, is likely to be ignored unless the editors and reporters know and trust the group calling the press conference. A person setting one up should be aware of newspaper and television news show deadlines. The event must be planned well before these deadlines to allow time for reporters to prepare a story. It should be held in a place accessible to the media, in a centrally located hotel or office. There should be no more than one or two spokesmen for the group. To satisfy egos, those in charge of press relations often find themselves forced to put five or six leaders of the group at the head table, giving each of them a chance to speak. That irritates reporters, who are usually in a hurry to get back and write their stories. And, as a practical matter, newscasts and news stories have neither time nor space to quote a long list of speakers.

What is most important in sending out a press release or calling a news conference is having something to say—some new information dug out by the group's research and investigative workers. A citizens group interested in maintaining credibility will call a press conference to announce an important plan of action or make disclosures of new facts, not to make a rhetorical attack that lacks substance.

Chicago's Better Government Association—described in Chapters Two and Eleven—uses the press in a unique manner. Over the years, it has become respected by newsmen, and has its investigators work in teams with reporters on exposés of government misconduct. Wrote Roy Fisher, former editor of the *Chicago Daily News,* "It speaks well for the integrity of the BGA that it can conduct such intricate relations with four competing papers and yet maintain the respect of each."

While few community organizations could match the size and skill of the BGA, it could serve as a model for citizen groups around the country. In addition to executive director J. Terrence Brunner, the association has a chief investigator, a research coordinator and four other investigators, including one in the state capital of Illinois, Springfield. The association also has someone in charge of bringing in members—an experienced fund-raiser. In 1972, the BGA had a budget of about $180,000, all raised from individuals, businesses and private groups in the community. It is an impressive amount, considering that most PTAs raise only a few hundred dollars a year. But for a community-wide organization producing such results, the cost is small. The association is also helped by twenty interns from nearby colleges and universities, who work with association investigators and newspaper reporters, in exchange for class credit.

The BGA tries to rotate stories among the Chicago papers, providing information to reporters the staff knows are interested in the subject. Speaking of the association staff's relationship with reporters, Director Brunner said, "We've built up a certain relationship. We go to each other's houses. We start thinking alike." No single Chicago newspaper can match the manpower of the BGA, with its investigators and college interns who can search public records. Without the BGA, the newspapers could not engage in such complex investigations. But without the newspapers, the BGA's investigations would go unnoticed.

The BGA has been in existence for decades; it has been involved in investigations, working with the press on them, for about thirteen years. But for a citizens group just getting started, it's not realistic to expect the kind of cooperation that the press gives the BGA.

TAKING A MODEST PLACE AMONG THE LOBBYISTS

In a citizen action group, one important function of a paid staff is attending the meetings of government bodies. It is impossible for the news media to cover the huge volume of business transacted by a legislative body, whether it be a city council, a county board of supervisors, a state legislature or the Congress of the United States. That is why a group interested in a specific category of legislation must do its own reporting. The League of Women Voters often sends a representative to observe government meetings, and this is a valuable way to keep public meetings public.

But for a group with specific goals, government decisions and actions must be understood in terms of their significance to the cause. A sheaf of uninterpreted minutes is meaningless if it doesn't tell what effect a government decision will have on a neighborhood.

Much of the work of lobbyists for businesses and organized labor consists of this type of reporting. And, while it is true that lobbyists buy plenty of lunches and dinners for public officials and oversee the distribution of campaign contributions, they also spend many hours reading legislation and passing information on to their clients in the form of reports. They read bills and sit through long, boring meetings. If something occurs that threatens a client's interest, a lobbyist is expected to be on hand to find out about it, and try to stop it.

Most often, citizen lobbying groups must be content with the modest goal of keeping track of what is happening in government meetings. Competing to influence lawmakers with professional lobbyists, who have power and money behind them, is hard. Citizen lobbyists will have no campaign contributions to offer nor expense accounts for entertaining. All they have is the power of persuasion—and organizing their membership for combat, as Ms. Adams did when she led housewives and other volunteers to victory on bay fill controls, discussed earlier in the chapter.

Janet Adams is one of the most effective citizen lobbyists in California. The wife of an engineer, she began battling officialdom in the 1950s when she headed a group who wanted to create a scenic parkway. Through years of political work, she has gained enough recognition and respect to give her access to the offices of legislators. For an unknown citizen, representing an unestablished organization, it might be impossible to get past a secretary. For those fortunate enough to get an appointment with an elected official, there are a few rules that Ms. Adams is willing to share.

When she calls on a politician, she makes sure he understands what her organization is—its size, its purpose, its history. After this preliminary, she advocates a direct approach. If you want legislation introduced, she said, "The oldest thing and the best thing, really, is to just come forward with it; tell what you want; tell them what you have. See if they'll handle it, and if not, get somebody else." Ms. Adams does not advocate bringing large delegations to an official's office when asking for his help. Nor does she advocate going alone. "I don't think you should ever bring eighty people to his office. But I've always made it a point—for one very good reason, there's less misunderstanding—if you bring along some other people." That provides a witness to the conversation, someone to back you up if the official changes his mind. She also tries to bring a lawyer "because when you're dealing with legislation, there are always questions beyond which even a knowledgeable person can't go." Ms. Adams' technique of bringing one or two witnesses is just one way to do it. Other groups, such as Chicago's CAP, use the opposite strategy—making use of large numbers of disciplined citizens, crowding into an official's office as a means of intimidating him and dramatizing their point.

Ms. Adams is what is known as a "good guy" lobbyist. Common Cause is another one. The League of Women Voters has been in the good guy lobbying business for years, as has the American Association of University Women. Often these groups are slow to act on legislative issues because they traditionally make detailed studies before taking a stand. This can take several years. Also, they tend to shy away from controversial subjects and partisan issues. And what such organizations need—but often lack—are specific lobbying goals. The lobbyist for an organization of retailers, for example, does not lobby for "private enterprise" but for specific legislation that will help retail business and against specific proposals that will hurt it. Common Cause's effectiveness improved greatly when it centered its attention on campaign contribution reform.

There is some debate about how effective the good-guy lobby can be. Gladys Meade, a former member of the California Air Resources Board, worked for years as a citizen lobbyist for the League of Women Voters. She saw a basic weakness in the lobbying efforts of such groups, especially when they don't realize their own limitations. They are eclipsed by powerful special interest groups with more persuasive tools at their disposal. Ms. Meade explained, "I've been in the League for fifteen years, and it's given me a lot of training and help and assistance in what I'm doing. But it doesn't have the clout that a lobbying group has. Neither does Common Cause, neither does AAUW—or the Friends Committee on Legislation. There's a good-guy lobby in Sacramento, but it is not as effective as it thinks it is or needs to be. I think they should give up illusion; they are not in there battling it out with lobbyists because they can't compete on that basis. Better to go back to the high principle idea and just shout it out on the rooftops, Yes, we support, or no we oppose this for the following reasons. Then give the reasons; use facts and names, but don't think you're in there battling with the pros because you're not."

Often citizen groups find lobbying activity impossible because they have no access to lawmakers. Leonard Levine, who fought the local air pollution control district, found that getting in to see a county supervisor was nearly impossible. He had sent his first volume of research about smog control to a candidate for the supervisors' board. The man used the material in his campaign and managed to beat the incumbent. But afterward, Levine found his access to the new supervisor was cut off. The man was too busy to see him and had moved on to other issues. Without access, Levine realized it was impossible to lobby. Instead, he moved on to another technique, which is discussed later in the chapter.

MAKING YOUR OWN LAW: THE BALLOT INITIATIVE

One of the legacies of the Progressive Movement, early in the century, was the ballot initiative. It is the process with which citizens can overrule recalcitrant legislators and pass their own laws. The mechanism is part of the lawmaking process of about twenty states. Most of these states are west of the Mississippi. But the following initiative campaign of the California Coastal Alliance could serve as a model for any citizens group who needs to organize on a large-scale basis and sustain their political movement.

To get an initiative measure on a statewide ballot, a group must draft a proposition and then circulate it in petition form among registered voters. The number of signatures necessary is prescribed by law. If enough are obtained, the measure goes before the voters of the state, to be decided in an election.

Getting signatures and votes for an initiative measure takes a tremendous amount of effort, teamwork and professional know-how. Through the years, many have become disillusioned with the process because, as we will see, well-heeled special interests have used it to their own advantage, winning votes with trickery, misleading slogans and expensive advertising.

But there are times when citizens groups can—with the right combination—put together a winning formula. One such group was

the Coastal Alliance, which passed the California Coastal Initiative
in 1972. They had a well-thought-out plan, long-range goals and a
framework of permanent organization. Meeting defeat with the
technique of lobbying, they turned to the initiative process. In the
end, they achieved their purpose, reformed irresponsive government and beat big business interests at their own game. Here is
their story:

In 1971 Janet Adams and some of the conservationists who had
persuaded the legislature to impose controls on filling San Francisco Bay were in the state capital again. This time, they wanted
passage of a bill creating a public-minded commission to control
development along the entire California coastline. Ms. Adams was
joined by some other highly skilled volunteers, including professional planners, a conservation lobbyist, a veterinarian who had led
a fight for public beach access in Northern California, and a
Republican conservation activist from Orange County. They put
together the Coastal Alliance—a coalition of over a hundred groups
from all over the state. To do it, said Ms. Adams, "every lead to an
interest individual or interest group, every list, every available
sports and ecology club to civic and professional organization was
contacted."

But they faced many more obstacles than in the San Francisco
Bay fight. It was a bigger issue, involving the whole state. The
building trades unions, fearing a loss of construction jobs, joined
with lobbyists for land developers, property owners and local
levels of government, who opposed state interference with their
prodevelopment policies. State regulation of development, local
officials said, would reduce property tax revenue. And, instead of
facing one powerful senator, the conservationists had several
legislative opponents, from the entire state.

The Coastal Alliance started talking to legislators, trying to
persuade them to vote for the bill. But instead of sending a small,
well-directed lobbying force to the capital, they had a large and
unmanageable army. They were enthusiastic, but misdirected.
They talked to some legislators they knew, but ignored others.
They reached an agreement with one official, then forgot when
talking to another. They could not agree on a single plan. "They
were simply running in circles up there," said Ms. Adams. "No-

body was doing anything except working at cross purposes, and it really was a debacle." As a result of their misdirected efforts and the powerful opponents of the bill, it failed to pass.

But even before the debacle, those against coastline development were preparing an alternative. The Coastal Alliance had been getting ready to put the same law before the people as a ballot initiative. Running the campaign would be Ms. Adams and E. Lewis Reid, a lawyer with experience in political campaigns. As a believer in the cause, Reid donated his time. As soon as the legislation was defeated, they took charge of obtaining the signatures needed to put the measure on the 1972 ballot. This remarkably successful campaign illustrates each phase of a well-planned volunteer effort.

The opposition was the same as it had been in the legislature, the coalition of labor, business and bureaucracy—with the professional help of a campaign management firm, Whitaker and Baxter. Governor Ronald Reagan also opposed the coastline controls. Winning out over these well-financed forces was almost unheard of.

One of the unforeseen side effects of the initiative process has been the growth of an industry that feeds off political campaigns for and against the ballot measures. Political campaign management firms were actually born in California because of these profitable campaigns. Whitaker and Baxter was the first of them, founded in 1933 when the Pacific Gas and Electric Company obtained enough signatures to place on the ballot a measure to repeal a state law authorizing a federal Central Valley water and power project, which would compete with private power companies. Irrigation districts, wanting the federal water, hired a young newspaperman, Clem Whitaker, to run the campaign against PG & E, and he won. But, in a manner not imagined by the Progressives, the initiative process had now become another way for special interests to put laws on the books or repeal laws they opposed, rather than giving citizens a role in the lawmaking process. Hundreds of thousands of dollars were spent on campaigns in which advertising men used incredibly simple slogans to convince voters to approve blatant giveaway bills. A ballot proposal to give a property-tax break to private golf courses was advertised on billboards with the slogan, "Keep California Green." Whitaker and his wife, Leone Baxter, managed many of the initiative campaigns, as well as political campaigns for individuals. So rich was the market that other firms entered. Around the country, political specialists began their own management firms, following the Whitaker and Baxter example.

Part of the new industry were companies that specialized in obtaining signatures to place these measures on the ballot. Several such companies approached the Coastal Alliance and offered to gather the signatures for them. But the fee would run between $160,000 and $200,000, a sum Ms. Adams knew they could never raise. They needed the signatures of about 225,000 registered voters, and it is tedious, complicated work to obtain them. Each signature must be that of a currently registered voter. That means each one must be checked in voter registration books. Then it must be matched with the voter's precinct as proof of registration. "It's a hideous task," said Ms. Adams. Yet, without professional help, the Coastal Alliance collected enough signatures in a month, entirely because of the efforts of volunteers.

Where did the alliance find the volunteers? First, appeals were made to conservationist groups, such as the Sierra Club, and "good government" organizations, among them the League of Women Voters and the American Association of University Women. The people who responded were not used to the unpleasant job of standing in front of a shopping center for several hours, asking passersby to sign petitions. The fact that they did it was an indication of deep citizen interest in the preservation of the coastline—another essential element in the campaign's success. "People who supported the legislation are essentially establishment people," said Ms. Adams. "It was very alien to any of their natures to go out and collect signatures. And it took some real feeling of desperation to go out and do it."

Another job was fund-raising, and here the alliance was not as successful. "They outspent us 5-1" said Ms. Adams of her opponents' campaign. The alliance had only $300,000 to spend, compared to $1.5 million for the opponents. But the alliance made do. They had thousands of volunteers by now. And in many communities around the state, they were led by talented people who were devoting most of their free time to the campaign. In San Diego it was run full-time by a retired man; in Los Angeles, a couple on leave from doctoral programs in marine biology; in Marin County, a biology teacher and a chemist. Other cities had groups run by college students, professors, members of the League of Women Voters, surfers, and professional planners.

Together, the volunteers inundated voters with information, mostly by telephone. In Orange County, for example, which was thought to be anticonservation, every voter was called twice. Precinct workers walked door-to-door handing out literature. Legislators who supported the measure announced their support and made public appearances to generate publicity. Meanwhile, the alliance made use of volunteers to keep track of how it was going. Ms. Adams, who had once worked in advertising, knew how to take public opinion polls. She instructed other workers.

A paid employee—a legislative aide on leave—took charge of press relations, working with television and radio stations and newspapers. The opposition had put its money to work in an advertising campaign in the best, or worst, tradition of California political campaigning. The theme of the billboards and television and radio advertising was that passage of the proposal would close the beaches to the public. "Keep our beaches free" was the theme of the message heard daily on radio and television. But the alliance knew how to use the press to its own advantage, in much the same ways described earlier in the chapter. Press conferences were held in front of opposition billboards, so the alliance could visually point out that the ads were misleading. Another device was a bike ride along the California coast, led by Senate President Pro Tem James Mills. Mills bicycled from San Diego to San Francisco, followed along the way by an average of one hundred riders. Groups on the route gave barbecues, breakfasts and wine tastings. Senator Mills, the bicyclists and the beachside parties got widespread press coverage.

Another boost came from a court ruling, discussed later in the chapter, allowing the alliance to get some free radio and television time to balance the $1 million in air time purchased by the opponents of the initiative. "As it was, we won by about a million votes," said Ms. Adams.

The initiative got about 55 percent of the vote. That placed regulation of anything built on the coastline in the hands of one statewide and six regional commissions. In August of 1973, Philip Fradkin, environmental reporter for the *Los Angeles Times,* was able to write, "In the first six months of their existence, the coastline commissions have emerged as the most powerful regulatory agencies in the state."

USING THE LEGAL PROCESS

Leonard Levine, who was unsuccessful in using the press and lobbying, turned to a different citizen strategy.

Failing to get responsive action and information from his local smog district, he studied the state laws governing smog enforcement. He discovered that the state Air Resources Board could, on request, hold hearings on the conduct of the local district board. Levine set the mechanism in motion. When the hearings failed to produce all of the information he wanted, he prepared to go to court to force the county smog district to be less secretive.

Levine sees effective citizen strategy in using the law to deal with government misbehavior, under existing statutes. "The first thing a citizen does is he educates himself about what the problem is and gathers the basic facts. The second thing he has to do is gain support of other individuals who are in the same situation. . . . Then you try administrative and political remedies. You talk to the politicians who are responsible. You try to use the media because these people do come up for reelection. If [these measures] don't work, then you have to seek redress through the courts. You get legal help, and you test the issue in the courts."

For Levine, getting legal help was not a financial burden. He found a lawyer through the Beverly Hills Bar Association's environmental committee, who was willing to donate his time. Levine was also able to raise a small amount from other groups to handle court costs. There are a number of law firms dedicated to handling citizens' environmental cases. (Usually, there is no charge for legal services, although a client might be asked to pay nominal amounts for out-of-pocket expenses.) One is the Center for Law in the Public Interest, in Los Angeles. It is run by young lawyers who get their funding from private sources, including the Ford Foundation. Some others are the Natural Resources Defense Council, in Washington and New York; the Environmental Defense Foundation, in Berkeley; and the Sierra Club Legal Defense. Nearly every major city has similar public interest law firms.

The Coastal Alliance used the legal process in its campaign for the Coastal Initiative. When opponents of the measure were buying over $1 million in TV and radio time, the alliance's lawyer took the matter before the Federal Communications Commission. The FCC has a rule that stipulates air time must be given to candidates whose opponents are allowed on the air. Because of the alliance's appeal, the fairness doctrine was extended to cover ballot initiatives. While it did not give equal free time to the Coastal Initiative supporters, it did give them some free time, a lift in morale, and a ruling that would benefit other underfinanced initiative campaigns.

In other instances, the courts have not ruled favorably for citizen groups. When some environmentalists opposed the New Jersey Hackensack Meadowlands stadium, for example, the courts turned them down. The case was based on the contention that the traffic around the new sports facility would increase smog in the area. But the courts didn't agree that this would be grounds to stop the project.

There are drawbacks to taking your cause to the courts. One is the expense of lawyers, unless you can find some who will handle the work for free. Also, there is the knowledge that if you lose in court and in subsequent appeals, it will be fatal to your cause.

RUNNING YOUR OWN CANDIDATE

Another strategy is for a group to use the election process to defeat incumbent officeholders. This is a tremendous job—one that most citizen groups, interested only in one or two issues, are unwilling to undertake. But one recent volunteer campaign is interesting because of the manner in which the inexperienced grassroots workers were taught the practical details of modern politics as a means of bringing about change.

In 1973, the California Teachers Association realized that its

150,000 members had little influence with local school boards who run public education in California. The board members tended to ignore teachers' pleas for more money and better working conditions, including smaller sized classes. The teachers were dismissed as impractical, unworldly people who let themselves get pushed around. The image was firmly ingrained, and teachers realized their lobbying efforts were consistently ignored when they took their complaints to elected representatives in Sacramento. As a result, the association's number one legislative goal, a bill giving teachers the right to bargain collectively for better pay and working conditions, had no hope of passing.

The association decided that the only way to succeed was to demonstrate teacher political power, and the best method was to defeat recalcitrant officeholders at the polls. It would have required too many volunteers and too much money to defeat legislators, who spend $75,000 or more in a campaign, but local school board elections were perfectly suited for the teachers association, which was composed of community-based chapters around the state. In each chapter, there generally was a cadre of enthusiastic and hard-working members—too few to make a difference in a large race, but enough for a school board election. For such elections, often less than 10 percent of the voters turn out, and winners have been elected with as little as 5 percent of the eligible voters casting ballots for them. In a district of 60,000 voters, someone can get elected to the school board with slightly more than 1,500 votes. With a low voter turnout, well-directed volunteers can win an election.

The association assessed its members for campaign funds for the candidates it was going to back. But more important than the fund-raising was the practical assistance offered volunteers in a manual written by professional campaign managers Charles Winner and Kris Pueschel, who were hired by the CTA for the purpose. The manual—unique in its specific, practical approach to grass-roots politics—instructed the teachers how to take polls, raise money, write advertisements, enlist volunteers and influence the press.

The manual, given to CTA members working on that election,

outlined a campaign from beginning (choosing a candidate) to the end (paying off all debts).

The teachers were told how to conduct three types of polls—door to door, in shopping centers, and by telephone. "The first thing you want to find out is whether your candidate should, in fact, be a candidate at all," the manual said. "Can his potential opponents be beaten? Are there major issues which will spark your campaign? Taking an early public opinion poll will help you in obtaining this information."

Among the hints:

Gather information. Research material on issues and potential opponents' views, and on the voters themselves. This is done by obtaining lists of registered voters from county officials, from political party committees. Conduct polls to find out how voters feel about the issues, and about the candidates. Shape the campaign around these issues.

Establish good press relations by having the candidate meet with local editors, publishers, and reporters, by sending out press releases and by holding press conferences when the news warrants it.

Using polling and past election results, determine the neighborhoods the candidate is most likely to carry and concentrate on them. If, for example, your candidate is black, liberal and dedicated to integrating the local school system, waste no time in conservative, anti-integration neighborhoods.

Set up telephone committees to contact voters. Later, polling will tell how the candidate is perceived by the voters and if he is failing to make headway in his best precincts. Neighborhood volunteer organizations can help supply this information from polling and talking to people.

If money permits, groups can advertise on radio and
television or on billboards and posters.

When the school board elections were over, the CTA had won
205 of its races and lost only 98.

Lobbying, passing a ballot initiative, researching facts for an
exposé or a public confrontation, appealing through the legal
process, demonstrating political power on election day—all of
these techniques have special meaning in America today. To stop
the destruction of metropolitan communities it is crucial that state
and local governments open their processes to scrutiny and debate.
They must be forced to let the public in. Only persistent, well-
organized citizen activist groups can make them do it, by using the
techniques outlined here or by using other methods gathered from
successful grassroots leaders.

The need for such campaigns is immediate and critical. U.S.
Senator Henry Jackson explained why when he introduced federal
legislation on the use of land: "Between now and the year 2000,
we must build again all that we have built before. We must build as
many homes, schools and hospitals in the next three decades as we
built in the previous three centuries. In the past, many land-use
decisions were in the province of those whose interests were
selfish, short-term and private. In the future—in the face of
immense pressures on our limited land resource—these land-use
decisions must be long-term and public." That same need would
apply to any government decision that has an impact on Americans in their daily living, from street signs and transportation to
schools and medical care.

As Westerners watching the destruction of the frontier, we were
prompted to write this book. We knew what the pioneers had
brought with them—a mixture of greed and generosity, a need to
build and continually expand the boundaries of their cities. What
earlier generations had failed to bring was a system of government
strong enough to control the greed and to direct creative energy
into building cities and suburbs to match the magnificence of the
land.

Reform is difficult to achieve because of the arrogance of those who inhabit city halls and statehouses and because of the flawed political structure bequeathed us by our forefathers. The levels of government closest to the people are set up to encourage more and more growth, more and more buildings. The result, at least in metropolitan areas, is that we are running out of space. Now, in the 1970s, people are beginning to notice—to want to preserve what is left. The fact that a few citizen groups are beginning to make the system work for them is evidence that reform is not dead.

Bibliography

Most of the information in this book was gleaned from original research, including personal interviews, government and citizens' groups' meetings, reports and records. Other valuable sources were private files kept by citizen activists. A few staff workers in government agencies also provided information.

Newspaper accounts were helpful, too, particularly stories from the *Los Angeles Times,* the *Washington Post,* the *Chicago Daily News,* the *Riverside Press Enterprise,* the *New York Times,* the *Wall Street Journal,* the *San Francisco Chronicle,* the *San Francisco Bay Guardian,* the *Oakland Tribune.*

While we used few books in our research, the following titles may be helpful to the interested reader:

General Political Background

Banfield, Edward C., and James Q. Wilson. *City Politics.* Cambridge, Mass.: Harvard University Press and M.I.T. Press, 1963.

Cannon, Lou. *Ronnie & Jesse.* New York: Doubleday, 1969.

Hill, Gladwin. *Dancing Bear.* Cleveland, Ohio: World, 1968.

Peirce, Neal R. *The Megastates of America: People, Politics, and Power in the Ten Great States.* New York: Norton, 1972.

Peirce, Neal R. *The Pacific States of America: People, Politics and Power in the Five Pacific Basin States.* New York: Norton, 1972.

Royko, Mike. *Boss: Richard J. Daley of Chicago.* New York: Dutton, 1971.

Samish, Arthur H., and Bob Thomas. *The Secret Boss of California: The Life and High Times of Art Samish.* New York: Crown Publishers, 1971.

Specific Problems

Buel, Ronald. *Dead End: The Automobile in Mass Transportation.* Englewood Cliffs, N.J.: Prentice-Hall, 1972.

Burby, John. *The Great American Motion Sickness.* Boston: Little, Brown, 1971.

Small, William E. *The Third Pollution.* New York: Praeger, 1971.

The Press

Bagdikian, Ben H. *The Effete Conspiracy and Other Crimes by the Press.* New York: Harper and Row, 1972.

Crouse, Timothy. *The Boys on the Bus.* New York: Random House, 1972.

Epstein, Edward Jay. *News from Nowhere.* New York: Random House, 1973.

Lyons, Louis M. (ed.). *Reporting the News: Selections from Nieman Reports.* Cambridge, Mass.: Belknap Press of Harvard University, 1965.

Steffens, Lincoln. *The Autobiography of Lincoln Steffens.* New York: Harcourt, Brace, 1931.

Community Action Techniques

Brugmann, Bruce B., Greggar Sletteland, and the *Bay Guardian* Staff. *The Ultimate Highrise.* San Francisco: San Francisco Bay Guardian Books, 1971.

Alinsky, Saul D. *Rules for Radicals: A Pragmatic Primer for Realistic Radicals.* New York: Random House, 1971.

Huenefeld, John. *The Community Activists' Handbook: A Guide to Organizing, Financing and Publicizing Community Campaigns.* Boston: Beacon Press, 1970.

Minott, Rodney G. *The Sinking of the Lollipop: Shirley Temple Vs. Pete McCloskey.* San Francisco: Diablo Press, 1968.

Ross, Donald K. *A Public Citizen's Action Manual.* New York: Grossman Publishers, 1973. (Introduction by Ralph Nader.)

Index

Adams, Janet, 309-310, 312-315
AFL-CIO, 84, 102, 292
Agnew, Vice-President Spiro, 2, 121
Air pollution control districts, 229,
    233, 236, 251-253; of Los Angeles
    County, 234-237, 240-249; of
    Riverside County, 229, 234, 238
Air Resources Board, 232-233, 235-
    236, 242, 244-247, 316
Alabama legislature, 123
Alinsky, Saul, 290, 300
Alioto, Mayor Joseph, 4, 32-35, 37,
    39, 43-45, 220; campaign con-
    tributors of, 33
Allen, Sidney, 197
Allied Chemical Company, 241-249
Alquist, Al, 120
Alton, Joseph, 121
American Association of University
    Women, 310, 314
American Football League, 186, 202
American Medical Association, 129
American Motors, 225-226
Architectural Record, 41
Arnebergh, Roger, 89, 92
Associated Press, 258, 275-276,
    278-280
Atkisson, Dr. Arthur, 246
Atlanta (Ga.), 205, 224, 226
Atlanta Constitution, 261
Atlanta Journal, 261
Auto Manufacturers Association, 225

Bagdikian, Ben, 255, 260
Ballot initiatives, 16, 42, 311-316
Baltimore (Md.), 205, 229
Bay Area Rapid Transit District, 201,
    211, 218-224, 226
Bechtel Corporation, 194, 220, 223
Bechtel, Stephen, 223
Bergholz, Richard, 262

Berthelson, John, 147
Better Government Association of
    Chicago, 17, 23, 268-271, 307-308
Beverly Hills Law Review, 242
Biaggini, B. F., 114
Biddle, State Senator Craig, 103,
    108-110, 112-113; campaign con-
    tributors of, 109
Birmingham (Ala.), 229
Black Panther Party, 192-193
Bonelli, Supervisor Frank, 52-53, 55,
    57-70; campaign contributors of,
    52-53, 50-60, 62-63
Boss, 24
Boston Globe, 261-264
The Boys on the Bus, 260
Bradley, Tom, 239, 282
Brian, Dr. Earl, 130-132, 135, 144,
    146-147
Briggs, John, 143
Brissette, Ralph, 82
Brooklyn (N.Y.), 178, 186
Brown, Governor Edmund G., 83,
    218, 221, 262, 304
Brown, California Secretary of State
    Edmund G., Jr., 106, 124, 141
Bruckner, Don, 26
Brunner, J. Terrence, 269-271, 307-
    308
Bureaucrats, 15-16
Burns, State Senator Hugh, 104,
    294-295
Business, as a special interest, 16, 19-
    20, 28-29, 43-44, 47-48, 52, 57,
    59, 72, 84, 96-97; campaign con-
    tributions from, 33, 38, 98, 103,
    221
Byrne, Dennis, 30
Byrne, W. Matt, Jr., 279

Cahill, Governor William, 181-183

California Chamber of Commerce, 102, 114, 212-213
California Coastal Alliance, 311-317
California Coastal Initiative, 312-317
California Council for Health Plan Alternatives, 138, 147
California Highway Users Conference, 213
California Manufacturers Association, 100, 102, 113, 252
California Railroad Association, 109, 114, 120
California Teachers Association, 111, 119, 317-320
Call, Asa, 212-213
Campaign contributions, 38-39, 60, 62, 73, 84, 96, 98-99, 103, 115, 119-125, 174, 231, 244; reports of, 299-303; *see also individual officeholder's name*
Canter, Donald, 44
Center for Law in the Public Interest, 316
Chace, Supervisor Burton, 156-158, 160, 169, 171; campaign contributors of, 156, 169
Chandler, Norman, 262
Chandler, Otis, 262
Chicago (Ill.), 4, 18, 20-32, 205, 229; city council, 22, 25; city hall, 29-31; downtown, 25-31; mobsters, 28-29; neighborhoods, 25; patronage, 23-34
Chicago Central Area Committee, 30
Chicago Daily News, 24, 30, 112, 265-267, 269-270, 307
Chicago Journalism Review, 270-271
Chicago Sun Times, 26, 265-267, 269-271
Chicago Today, 265, 267
Chicago Tribune, 265, 267, 270-271
Christian Science Monitor, 256
Citizens Action Program, 290-293, 296, 300
City government, 18-47; power of, 18-19; services of, 20, 32
Clean Air Act, 1970, 239
Coliseum, Inc., 197-200, 202
Collier, State Senator Randolph, 148, 222
Colliers (magazine), 117
Columbia Journalism Review, 260
Common Cause, 123, 310
Community organization, 289-293
Conflict of interest clause (in Medi-

Cal Reform Bill), 147-149
Consolidated Medical Systems, 136-137
Cooke, Jack Kent, 203
Cosell, Howard, 185
Cowles, John, 261
Crouse, Timothy, 260
Cullerton, Assessor P. J., 296

Daley, Mayor Richard, 4, 21-32, 290-292
Dallas Cowboys, 178
Democratic Party, 14, 23-24, 26, 28-29, 84
Denver (Colo.), 225, 229
Department of Health Care Services, 130, 139, 141, 149
De Paulo, Dr. Vincent, 126-128, 139-140
Despres, Leon, 26
Diamond Bar, 60-70
Di Julio, David, 250
District of Columbia. *See* Washington, D.C.
Dodger Stadium, 186
Dodgers (baseball team), 178, 186
Dolwig, Senator Richard, 194-195
Dorfman, Ron, 270
Duffy, Assemblyman Gordon, 131, 145, 147-148
DuPont Company, 260
Dymally, State Senator Merv, 142-143, 146

Edwards, Paul, 121
Environmental Defense Foundation, 317

Fairbanks, Robert, 136, 139
Fairfax County (Va.), 51, 172-177, 273; special interests in, 173-174
Farr, William, 95
Fenton, Assemblyman Jack, 102-103, 108, 110-113, 115; campaign contributors of, 111-112
Field Enterprises, 261, 265
Field, Mervyn, 213
Fisher, Roy, 307
Foran, Assemblyman John Francis, 85-87
Fortune (magazine), 188
Fradkin, Philip, 316
Freeways, 5, 16, 20, 25, 41, 50, 204-205, 207-208, 212-214, 221, 228, 290-291

Garbage, disposal of, 19, 152-153, 163-167
Garibaldi, James (judge), 294-295
Garth, David, 283
Gasoline tax, 211-214, 225
General Motors, 208, 225-226
Gobright, Lawrence A., 278
Gonzales, Assemblyman Raymond, 118-119
Great America park, 7-12, 17
Greenberg, Carl, 262-263
Group Health Cooperative of Puget Sound, 133

Haagen-Smit, A. J., 236
Hackensack Meadows (N.J.), 178-185, 202
Hahn, Councilman Gilbert, 250
Hahn, Supervisor Kenneth, 252
Harris, Ellen Stern, 304-305
Hayes, Supervisor James, 234, 253; campaign contributors of, 234
Health Maintenance Organization Act, 129
Health maintenance organizations. *See* Prepaid Health Plans
Highrises, 5, 16, 25, 40-43
Highway lobby, 107, 124, 207-208, 210, 212-215, 218, 222, 230, 232
HMO International, 136-137
Hoffman Estates (Ill.), 51
Hosie, Ron, 234
Houston (Tex.), 229
Houston Astrodome, 202-203
Humphrey, Vice-President Hubert, 99
Hunter's Point, 44

Industrial Areas Foundation Training Institute, 290
Industrial safety laws, 72, 83, 85-87, 98, 100-115
Investigative reporting, 266-271, 285

Jackson (Miss.), 260
Jackson, Senator Henry, 320
Jackson Clarion Ledger, 260
Jackson Daily News, 260
Johnson, Hiram, 194
Johnson, Jack, 90, 92
Johnson, President Lyndon, 129
Jones, Bill, 267
Jones, H. Bradley, 137, 140-141

Kaiser, Edgar, 194, 196, 199
Kaiser, Henry, 132, 194

Kaiser Industries, 132-133, 194, 196, 200, 216, 220
Kansas City Star, 261
Kansas City Times, 261
Karabian, Assemblyman Wally, 143, 146
Kasindorf, Jeanie, 302
Kean, Assemblyman Thomas, 185
Keane, Alderman Thomas, 21, 22, 269-270
Kelly, Dr. Donald, 136-137
Kennedy, President John, 99, 129
Knowland, Joseph, 194
Knowland, Senator Williams, 193-196, 199, 219

Labor, as a special interest, 14-15, 19, 28-29, 43-44, 47-48, 73, 77, 84, 87, 96, 97; campaign contributions from, 33, 38, 98, 107, 234
Labor unions, 80, 84, 86, 87
Land development, 8, 52, 55, 57, 62, 157, 161-162, 173, 208, 212, 230
Landsberg, Morrie, 280
Law suits, public interest, 16, 316
League of California Cities, 211
League of Women Voters, 173, 308, 310, 314-315
Legg, Supervisor Herbert, 58, 60
Lembke, Daryl, 34
Levine, Leonard, 240-249, 305, 311, 316
Lewis, Owen, 64, 66-67
Lindsay, Mayor John, 4, 185-187
Lobbyists, 84, 97-125, 231, 292, 294, 308-312, 318
Lockheed Shipbuilding and Construction Co., 71-72, 75-78, 80-81, 83, 88-96, 215
Longshoremen's union, 133
Look (magazine), 33-34
The Loop, 25-28, 32
Los Angeles (Calif.), 4, 165, 208-218
Los Angeles Chamber of Commerce, 214-215
Los Angeles County government, 49-70; board of supervisors, 52-57, 210, 234, 236, 248, 251-253
Los Angeles County Medical Society, 127, 138
Los Angeles Department of Water and Power, 74
Los Angeles Herald Examiner, 262-264

Los Angeles Magazine, 302
Los Angeles Times, 27, 34, 95, 118, 136, 139, 261-265, 274, 286, 303, 316
Louisiana Superbowl, 188
Louisville Courier-Journal, 261
Lyons, Louis, 278

Machine, Cook County political, 21-29, 31, 122, 269, 292
Mafia, 33
The Making of the President—1960, 277
The Making of the President—1972, 261
Malibu (Calif.), 154-163, 177
Manassas Battlefield, 6-7, 9-10, 12, 17
Mara, Wellington, 183
Marriott Corporation, 7-12, 17
Marvin Health Systems, 139
McCarthy, Senator Joseph, 278
McClosky, Senator Pete, 295
McCrane, Joseph, 181-182
McFettridge, Jerry, 90
McWilliams, Carey, 97
Meade, Gladys, 233, 242, 310
Medicaid, 129-130
Medi-Cal, 126, 151; limits on benefits, 130-131; partisan views on, 131-132, 142, 144; special interests' influence on, 128
Megastates of America, 23
Merrill Lynch, Pierce, Fenner and Smith, 182
Metropolitan Washington Council of Governments, 249-250
Metropolitan Water District, 74-77, 81, 170
Metro transit system, 47, 208, 226
Miami Herald, 264
Mikvah, Abner, 27-28, 31-32
Minneapolis Star, 261
Minneapolis Tribune, 261
Mission Canyon, 167-171
Moore, Supervisor Audrey, 172-176
Moore, Tom, 138, 147
Moretti, Assemblyman Bob, 34, 90, 110-111, 146-147
Mt. Trashmore, 163-164
Muckrakers, 13-14, 36, 257, 267
Mulholland, William, 73-74
Municipal bonds, 69, 181-185, 220; general obligation, 181-182;

revenue, 181-182, 197-198, 214, 291; interest on, 181-182, 198

Nader, Ralph, 285
National Football League, 186, 189
National Health Law Foundation, 144-145
Natural Resources Defense Council, 317
Nation (magazine), 97
Nelson, Bryce, 27
New Jersey, 180, 229; State legislature, 180, 182
New Jersey Sports and Exposition Authority, 181, 183-185
New Jersey sports complex, 181-185, 317
New Orleans (La.), 188, 202, 229
Newsday, 261
Newspapers. *See* Press coverage
News release, 306
Newton, Huey, 192
New York (city), 178, 185-188, 205, 229; city council, 187
New York (state), 4, 130, 182, 184
New York Giants, 178, 181-183, 185, 188
New York Jets, 186
New York Mets, 186
New York Times, 188, 256, 261, 263
New York Yankees, 185-187
Nicodemus, Charles, 270-271
Nixon, President Richard, 2, 4, 34, 76, 99, 101, 123, 129, 212, 262-263

Oakland (Calif.), 189-203; city council, 196; problems of, 191-193, 200-201
Oakland As, 189
Oakland-Alameda County Coliseum Complex, 189-203; cost of, 200
Oakland Chamber of Commerce, 194, 196-197, 199, 201
Oakland Raiders, 189
Oakland Tribune, 193-195, 198-199, 219, 262, 274
Occupational Safety and Health Act, 101
O'Malley, Walter, 186

Packard, Supervisor Jean, 173-176, 273
Pacoima Memorial Lutheran

Hospital, 138
Parkhurst, John, 161, 166
Parsons, Brinckerhoff, Quade and
    Douglas, 220, 223
Pasadena (Calif.), 214, 217
Pastore, Senator John, 99
Pedigo, Eugene, 74-80, 92-95
Peirce, Neal, 23, 28
Pitts, Dr. James, 238, 253
Planning commissions, 4-5, 54, 63-
    67, 161, 297
Playboy Club accident, 83, 85-87
Political campaigns, 38-39, 317-320;
    cost of, 99; public financing of,
    123
Post, A. Alan, 135, 150, 222-223
Prepaid Health Plans, 127-151;
    audits on, 149-150; history of,
    132-133; operation of, 127, 133-
    134; profits, 135-137; public
    hearings on, 139-140; significance
    of, 132, 150-151
Press coverage, 5, 51, 70, 123, 125,
    139, 148, 195, 210, 255-286, 299;
    history of, 256-257; in Chicago,
    265-271; in Fairfax County, Va.,
    273; in Los Angeles, 261-265; of
    political campaigns, 281-283;
    using, 303-308, 319
Press conference, 306-307
Prince William County (Va.), 6, 8-12;
    board of supervisors, 6-8, 11-12
Progressive Era, 36, 101, 311
Property tax, 53, 54, 221, 299
Public officials, mistrust of, 5, 12-13
Public opinion polls, 281, 315, 319
Public records, 297-299, 301

Racial problems, 180, 191-193, 195,
    209
Reagan, Governor Ronald, 39, 59-60,
    90, 93, 130-134, 141-143, 145-
    146, 192, 233, 237, 251-253, 282,
    295
Rechtenwald, William, 267
Reck, Al, 274-275
Ree, Otha G. (Bob), 72, 91-95
Reich, Kenneth, 118
Republican Party, 14, 29, 212
Riverside (Calif.), 108, 228-230, 234,
    238
Riverside Press Enterprise, 234
Rohr Corporation, 224-226
Romeo, Robin, 78-80

Roosevelt, President Theodore, 257
Royko, Mike, 24, 27, 122-123, 265-
    267
Rubin, Dr. Edward, 143
Rubin, Dr. Morris, 149-150
Ruppert, Col. Jacob, 186
Ruth, Babe, 185-186

Saar, John, 249
Sacramento Bee, 85, 143, 147
St. Louis Post-Dispatch, 261
Sales tax, 217, 220
Samish, Art, 117-118
San Diego (Calif.), 202
San Fernando Tunnel explosion, 72-
    73, 75-83, 87, 89, 95-96, 98, 100,
    102, 110, 113
San Fernando Valley, 204, 214-215,
    217
San Francisco (Calif.), 18, 20, 32-46,
    218-224, 226; board of super-
    visors, 37-38, 45; city hall, 35, 37;
    city employees, 35-37; downtown,
    35, 38; highrises, 40-43; lack of
    machine, patronage, 35-37; urban
    redevelopment, 44-46
San Francisco Bay Guardian, 42-43,
    268
San Francisco Chamber of
    Commerce, 220
San Francisco Chronicle, 197, 262,
    268
San Francisco Examiner, 32, 44, 205,
    268
San Gabriel Valley, 49-50, 54-55,
    59-70, 214, 217
Sanitation districts, 153-154, 160,
    163-164, 166, 171; election, 154,
    157-158
Sanitary landfills, 163-171, 180, 288
San Joaquin Foundation for Medical
    Care, 133
Santa Monica Mountains, 165-171,
    288
Savage, Loren, 72, 77-78, 80-81, 91-
    95
Schabarum, Supervisor Pete, 60
Schools, 16, 64-65, 296
Seale, Bobby, 192-193
Seattle (Wash.), 133, 188, 202
The Secret Boss of California, 117
Sewers, 9-10, 12, 19, 152-163, 172-
    177
Sewer bond elections, 157-160; cam-

paign contributors of, 159
Shell Oil Co., 104, 234
Short, Senator Alan, 103-108, 112-
115; campaign contributors of,·
105-107
Sierra Club, 245, 314, 317
Smog, 49, 54, 56, 70, 208, 228;
alert, 229-230, 247, 249; auto
caused, 231-233, 235-236; health
effects of, 229-230, 239-240; industry caused, 231, 233-235, 248;
solutions for, 231-233, 235-236
Song, State Senator Al, 143-144, 146,
148
Southern California Automobile Club,
212-214
Southern California Rapid Transit
District, 206, 210-218, 235;
board of, 207, 210-211
Southern Pacific Railroad, 36, 52,
114, 120, 194
Special interest groups, 3, 5, 6, 19-
20, 39, 86, 128, 164-165, 173-
174, 183, 207, 292; see also
Business, Labor
Stadiums, 178-203; vote on, 181,
188; financing, 181-185
Standard Oil Corp., 104, 109, 234,
241-249
Statewide Air Pollution Control
Center, 229, 238
Steffens, Lincoln, 13, 257, 271
Stein, Gertrude, 190
Stevenson, Senator Adlai III, 292
Stokes, Bill, 219
Super Bowl, 202
Swig, Ben, 33, 39-40

Teamsters Union, 138
Television news coverage, 6, 257-259,
265
Temple, Shirley, 295
The Trade, 84-87
Trammell, Judge George, 93-95
Transamerica building, 40-43
Transamerica Corp., 40-42, 60-66,
68, 215
Transit bond election campaigns, 215-
216, 220-221; campaign con-
tributors of, 215-216, 220
Transit lobby, 207-208, 227
Transit, public, 5, 15, 18-20, 26, 30,
47, 56, 70, 124; rapid, 205-227
Troy, Councilman Matthew, 187

Unemployment, 180, 192-193, 201

Unincorporated land, 54, 60, 162,
203
Unions. See Labor
United Press International, 258
Unruh, Jess, 84, 194-205
U.S. Environmental Protection
Agency, 164, 167, 211, 237-239,
245, 250

Velie, Lester, 117
Vapotester, 79, 81, 91-92
Virginia Beach (Va.), 163-164
Virginia Freedom of Information
Act, 11-12

Wagoner County (Okla.), 52
Walker, Governor Dan, 122-123, 292
Wall Street Journal, 256
Ward, Supervisor Baxter, 302-303
Warren, Chief Justice Earl, 117, 194
Washington, D.C., 8, 46-48, 205,
226, 229, 249-250; downtown,
46-48, 172
Washington, Mayor Walter, 47
Washington Post, 9, 11, 121, 226-227,
249, 261, 263, 273
Watts, 142, 209
Waxman, Assemblyman Henry, 134,
145, 149-150
Werblin, David (Sonny), 183
Western Addition, 44-45
Whitaker and Baxter, 313-314
White, Theodore, 261, 276
Williams, Edwin, 260
Wilmington Evening Journal, 260
Wilmington Morning News, 260
Winfield, County Supervisor C. Scott,
6-9, 11-13
Winner, Charles, 318
Woodbridge, Virginia, 9
Woodlawn, 27
World Series, 289, 202

Yankee Stadium, 4, 178, 183, 186-
187
Yerba Buena Center, 45-46
Yorty, Mayor Sam, 109, 211, 282,
285
Younger, Attorney General Evelle,
247

Zafman, Norman, 242-247
Zavaterro, Wallace, 80-82, 91-92
Zoning, 19, 55, 61-67, 70, 161-162,
173-174, 268, 297